Communications
in Computer and Information Science 1855

T0172219

Rationale
The CCIS series is devoted to the publication of proceedings of computer science conferences. Its aim is to efficiently disseminate original research results in informatics in printed and electronic form. While the focus is on publication of peer-reviewed full papers presenting mature work, inclusion of reviewed short papers reporting on work in progress is welcome, too. Besides globally relevant meetings with internationally representative program committees guaranteeing a strict peer-reviewing and paper selection process, conferences run by societies or of high regional or national relevance are also considered for publication.

Topics
The topical scope of CCIS spans the entire spectrum of informatics ranging from foundational topics in the theory of computing to information and communications science and technology and a broad variety of interdisciplinary application fields.

Information for Volume Editors and Authors
Publication in CCIS is free of charge. No royalties are paid, however, we offer registered conference participants temporary free access to the online version of the conference proceedings on SpringerLink (http://link.springer.com) by means of an http referrer from the conference website and/or a number of complimentary printed copies, as specified in the official acceptance email of the event.

CCIS proceedings can be published in time for distribution at conferences or as post-proceedings, and delivered in the form of printed books and/or electronically as USBs and/or e-content licenses for accessing proceedings at SpringerLink. Furthermore, CCIS proceedings are included in the CCIS electronic book series hosted in the SpringerLink digital library at http://link.springer.com/bookseries/7899. Conferences publishing in CCIS are allowed to use Online Conference Service (OCS) for managing the whole proceedings lifecycle (from submission and reviewing to preparing for publication) free of charge.

Publication process
The language of publication is exclusively English. Authors publishing in CCIS have to sign the Springer CCIS copyright transfer form, however, they are free to use their material published in CCIS for substantially changed, more elaborate subsequent publications elsewhere. For the preparation of the camera-ready papers/files, authors have to strictly adhere to the Springer CCIS Authors' Instructions and are strongly encouraged to use the CCIS LaTeX style files or templates.

Abstracting/Indexing
CCIS is abstracted/indexed in DBLP, Google Scholar, EI-Compendex, Mathematical Reviews, SCImago, Scopus. CCIS volumes are also submitted for the inclusion in ISI Proceedings.

How to start
To start the evaluation of your proposal for inclusion in the CCIS series, please send an e-mail to ccis@springer.com.

Alexander Smirnov · Hervé Panetto ·
Kurosh Madani

Editors

Innovative Intelligent Industrial Production and Logistics

First International Conference, IN4PL 2020
Virtual Event, November 2–4, 2020, and Second International
Conference, IN4PL 2021, Virtual Event, October 25–27, 2021
Revised Selected Papers

 Springer

Editors
Alexander Smirnov
Russian Academy of Sciences
St. Petersburg, Russia

Hervé Panetto
University of Lorraine
Nancy, France

Kurosh Madani
University of Paris-EST Créteil
Créteil, France

ISSN 1865-0929   ISSN 1865-0937 (electronic)
Communications in Computer and Information Science
ISBN 978-3-031-37227-8   ISBN 978-3-031-37228-5 (eBook)
https://doi.org/10.1007/978-3-031-37228-5

This Springer imprint is published by the registered company Springer Nature Switzerland AG
The registered company address is: Gewerbestrasse 11, 6330 Cham, Switzerland

Preface

The present book includes extended and revised versions of a set of selected papers from the International Conference on Innovative Intelligent Industrial Production and Logistics IN4PL 2020 and 2021, which were exceptionally held as online events due to COVID-19.

IN4PL 2020 received 18 paper submissions from 12 countries, of which 17% were included in this book. IN4PL 2021 received 26 paper submissions from 17 countries, of which 23% were included in this book.

The papers were selected by the event chairs and their selection is based on a number of criteria that include the classifications and comments provided by the program committee members, the session chairs' assessment and also the program chairs' global view of all papers included in the technical program. The authors of selected papers were then invited to submit a revised and extended version of their papers having at least 30% innovative material.

This conference focuses on research and development involving innovative methods, software and hardware, whereby intelligent systems are applied to industrial production and logistics. This is currently related to the concept of Industry 4.0 - an expression reflecting the trend towards automation and data exchange in manufacturing technologies and processes which include cyber-physical systems, the industrial internet of things, industrial robotics, cloud computing, cognitive computing and artificial intelligence. These technologies can be applied to industrial manufacturing and management as well as to supply-chain or logistic problems, involving for example transportation management or the optimization of operations.

The papers selected to be included in this book contribute to the understanding of relevant trends of current research on Innovative Intelligent Industrial Production and Logistics, including: Informatics Applications, Safety, Security and Risk Management, Quality Control and Management, Big Data and Logistics, Smart Manufacturing Systems & Networks, Operations Optimization, Enterprise Resource Planning, Systems Modeling and Simulation, Data Analytics, AI-Enhanced Cyber-Physical Systems, Knowledge Management in Industry, Interoperability in the Context of Internet of Things, Interoperability in a Big-Data Society and Internet of Things and Services.

We would like to thank all the authors for their contributions and also the reviewers who have helped to ensure the quality of this publication.

October 2021

Alexander Smirnov
Hervé Panetto
Kurosh Madani

Organization

Conference Chair

2020

Alexander Smirnov   SPC RAS, Russian Federation

2021

Kurosh Madani   University of Paris-Est Créteil, France

Program Co-chairs

2020

Kurosh Madani   University of Paris-Est Créteil, France

2021

Marco Macchi   Politecnico di Milano, Italy

2020 and 2021

Hervé Panetto   University of Lorraine, France

Program Committee

Served in 2020

Abderrezak Rachedi   Université Gustave Eiffel, France
Anuj Kumar   CSIR-CBRI, India
Berna Dengiz   Baskent University, Turkey
Deana McDonagh   University of Illinois at Urbana-Champaign, USA
Farshad Khorrami   New York University, USA

Served in 2020 and 2021

Ahmad Rasdan Ismail	Universiti Malaysia Kelantan, Malaysia
Andrea Matta	Politecnico di Milano, Italy
Arturo Molina	Tecnológico de Monterrey, Mexico
Benoît Iung	University of Lorraine, France
Bernard Kamsu-Foguem	National School of Engineering of Tarbes, France
Bruno Vallespir	University of Bordeaux, France
Burak Eksioglu	University of Arkansas, USA
Carlos Alberto Kamienski	Universidade Federal do ABC, Brazil
Cathal Heavey	University of Limerick, Ireland
David Romero	Tecnológico de Monterrey, Mexico
Dongping Song	University of Liverpool, UK
Fabio Nonino	University of Rome La Sapienza, Italy
François Vernadat	University of Lorraine, France
Hing Kai, Chan	University of Nottingham Ningbo China, China
Juan Carlos Mendez	AdN Procesos Empresariales, SC, Mexico
Martin Zelm	INTEROP-VLab, Germany
Mauro Dell'Amico	University of Modena and Reggio Emilia, Italy
Michela Robba	University of Genoa, Italy
Morteza Yazdani	Universidad Autónoma de Madrid, Spain
Neeraj Kumar Singh	National School of Electrical Engineering, Electronics, Computer Science, Hydraulics and Telecommunications, France
Nico Adams	Swinburne University, Australia
Norbert Gronau	University of Potsdam, Germany
Nursel Öztürk	Bursa Uludag University, Turkey
Ramon Vilanova	Universitat Autònoma de Barcelona, Spain
Seokcheon Lee	Purdue University, USA
Sergio Martin	UNED - Spanish University for Distance Education, Spain
Simone Zanoni	University of Brescia, Italy
Stefano Rinaldi	University of Brescia, Italy
Udo Kannengiesser	Johannes Kepler University Linz, Austria
Vincent Chapurlat	IMT Mines Alès, France
Virginie Goepp	Institut National des Sciences Appliquées de Strasbourg, France
Wei Wang	Xi'an Jiaotong-Liverpool University, China
Yongjian Li	Nankai University, China
Zbigniew Banaszak	Koszalin University of Technology, Poland

Invited Speakers

2020

Andreas Oroszi	Festo AG & Co. KG, Germany
László Monostori	MTA SZTAKI, Hungary

2021

Joseph Sarkis	Worcester Polytechnic Institute, USA
Fei Tao	Beihang University, China

Contents

On Kernel Search Based Gaussian Process Anomaly Detection

Jan David Hüwel[1](✉)(iD), Andreas Besginow[2](iD), Fabian Berns[1](iD),
Markus Lange-Hegermann[2](iD), and Christian Beecks[1]

[1] Department of Computer Science, University of Münster, Münster, Germany
{jan.huewel,fabian.berns,christian.beecks}@uni-muenster.de
[2] Department of Electrical Engineering and Computer Science, OWL University of Applied
Sciences and Arts, Lemgo, Germany
{andreas.besginow,markus.lange-hegermann}@th-owl.de

Abstract. Anomaly detection becomes more important with increasing automation. Especially for time series data, prevalent in industry, there are numerous methods that have been well researched. In this work we provide a proof of concept for a novel approach using the interpretability of Gaussian processes. To detect an abnormal section, the data is split into equally sized segments which are then interpreted individually using separate kernel searches. The resulting kernels can then be compared and clustered by one of multiple presented methods. The segments that contain an anomaly end up in their own cluster.

To test all possible configurations of our proposed approach, we applied them to a subset of the SIGKDD 2021 anomaly dataset mutliple times and evaluated the results. Almost all configurations were able to succeed, although not yet reliably reproducible. The results of our performance evaluation indicate that kernel searches are in principle applicable to anomaly detection in univariate time series data.

Keywords: Anomaly detection · Gaussian process · Kernel search · Machine learning · Data mining · Knowledge discovery

1 Introduction

This work is an extended version of the paper "Towards gaussian processes for automatic and interpretable anomaly detection in industry 4.0" [6].

With the rise of the internet of things and an ever growing information basis, the fourth industrial revolution is taking place. It focuses on data driven automation and optimization of processes up to the point where products can be individually developed in the sense of lot-size one. The most prominent example of the fourth industrial revolution are the so-called smart factories, which integrate interconnected devices and

This research was supported by the research training group "Dataninja" (Trustworthy AI for Seamless Problem Solving: Next Generation Intelligence Joins Robust Data Analysis) funded by the German federal state of North Rhine-Westphalia.
J. D. Hüwel and A. Besginow—Equal contribution to this work.

A. Smirnov et al. (Eds.): IN4PL 2020/IN4PL 2021, CCIS 1855, pp. 1–23, 2023.
https://doi.org/10.1007/978-3-031-37228-5_1

sensors that provide their state and sensor value to many other machines (and often a central database) to allow quick reaction to production spikes and unusual system behaviours.

Such unusual behaviours are called anomalies. They need to be detected and remedied as fast as possible, since the increased production speed and demands on the machine uptime cause system failures to be a costly issue for companies. Methods to predict, and thus prevent, such failures are therefore of special interest to the industrial sector and have received a lot of attention in research [1–3,9,11,12,15,16,20,26,33,43, 51,58,59,61,68,70,71]. Due to the growing availability of data, more advanced data-driven approaches are developed to predict system failures and find anomalies which, among others, use Deep Learning (DL) based models [1,11,23,27,37,58,70,71]. A major issue in regard to the data is the availability of labels, which usually has to be added manually and cost-intensively by domain experts. This causes most algorithms to run in an unsupervised way and using labels only to verify the model performance during development [67].

In this work, we focus on methods based on Gaussian Processes (GPs) [54] and present a proof of concept implementation of our approach, which makes use of kernel selection methods [18] to find anomalies in univariate time series data, based on the interpretability of the found covariance functions. Due to their Bayesian nature, GPs excel in environments with little data, compared to Neural Networks (NNs) which still struggle with overfitting to small datasets. In particular, GPs are more resistant to noise and can more easily be applied in many real life applications automatically and without intervention of a data scientist. Additionally GPs have inherent interpretability due to their covariance functions (or kernel) and the trained hyperparameters of the covariance function, which is typically built from common base covariance functions, that represent specific trends in the data. For example many covariance functions allow to estimate the rate of change over the X values (e.g. time) through its lengthscale hyperparameter.

Our anomaly detection approach is based on multiple GPs that are independently trained on disjoint segments of data. For each segment the covariance function is selected using the Compositional Kernel Search (CKS) [18] algorithm, including the hyperparameter optimization for best likelihood. We then compare the covariance function for each segment using a selection of distance or similarity metrics [54], and finally cluster [44,49] the segments based on the employed metric. In practice, these clusters describe different modi of production, and while large clusters correlate to regular, and therefore normal, activity, small clusters indicate anomalies. In this work, we thus assume the smallest cluster to be an anomaly. This approach is possible due to the mentioned inherent interpretability of the covariance functions. They will represent characteristics of the segments in their covariance structure as well as in the corresponding hyperparameter values.

We evaluate our method on a subset of the anomaly dataset provided in the KDD time series challenge [34]. These experiments serve as a proof of concept for a range of simple anomaly detection methods that directly use GP kernel search. We show that methods of this kind can work and are worth investigating further in future work.

This paper is structured as follows: We begin with the required theoretical background on GPs in Sect. 2 before discussing the state of the art in anomaly detection in Sect. 2.2. We follow with a description of our method in Sect. 3, present the used dataset and the results of our evaluation in Sect. 4 before closing with our conclusion and future working directions in Sect. 5.

2 Background

Before introducing our anomaly detection method, we begin by giving a background on GP basics and an overview over the related research literature on anomaly detection.

2.1 Gaussian Processes

A Gaussian Processes (GP) [54] is a stochastic process over random variables $\{f(x) \mid x \in \mathcal{X}\}$, indexed by a set $\mathcal{X}$, where every finite subset of random variables follows a multivariate normal distribution. The distribution of a GP is the joint distribution of all of these random variables and it is thus a probability distribution over the space of functions $\{f : \mathcal{X} \to \mathbb{R}\}$. A GP is formalized as

$$f(\cdot) \sim GP\big(m(\cdot), k(\cdot, \cdot)\big), \tag{1}$$

where the mean function $m : \mathcal{X} \to \mathbb{R}$ and the covariance function (also called kernel function or simply kernel) $k : \mathcal{X} \times \mathcal{X} \to \mathbb{R}$ are defined via

$$m(x) = \mathbb{E}\left[f(x)\right] \tag{2}$$
$$k(x, x') = \mathbb{E}\left[(f(x) - m(x)) \cdot (f(x') - m(x'))\right] \tag{3}$$

A kernel k applied to two vectors $x \in \mathbb{R}^n$ and $x' \in \mathbb{R}^m$ results in a matrix $K \in \mathbb{R}^{n \times m}$ with $K_{ij} = k(x_i, x'_j)$. This matrix K is called the covariance matrix between x and x' [54].

The most common kernel functions include the (SE),

$$k_{SE}(\mathbf{x}, \mathbf{x}') = \sigma^2 \exp\left(\frac{-(\mathbf{x} - \mathbf{x}')^2}{2l^2}\right) \tag{4}$$

Matern

$$k_{mat32}(\mathbf{x}, \mathbf{x}') = \sigma^2 \left(1 + \frac{\sqrt{3}\mathbf{x} - \mathbf{x}'}{l}\right) \exp\left(-\frac{\sqrt{3}(\mathbf{x} - \mathbf{x}')}{l}\right) \tag{5}$$

$$k_{mat52}(\mathbf{x}, \mathbf{x}') = \sigma^2 \left(1 + \frac{\sqrt{5}\mathbf{x} - \mathbf{x}'}{l}\right) \exp\left(-\frac{\sqrt{5}\mathbf{x} - \mathbf{x}'}{l}\right) \tag{6}$$

and periodic kernels

$$k_{PER} = \sigma^2 \exp\left(\frac{-2\sin^2\frac{(x - x')}{2}}{l^2}\right) \tag{7}$$

Note

where the common hyperparameters l and σ denote the characteristic lengthscale and the output variance used to weight covariance functions [17,54]. Additionally we also use the linear kernel, defined as

$$k_{lin}(\mathbf{x}, \mathbf{x}') = \sigma^2(x - c)(x' - c) \tag{8}$$

with σ the same output variance as above and c a learnable x intercept [17].

We assume a constant zero mean function, since we normalize the date and the modeling capabilities of a GP through its covariance function are flexible enough.

By training hyperparameters of the mean and covariance functions the model is fitted to the data using the negative log-likelihood given by

$$\mathcal{L} = -\frac{n}{2}\log 2\pi - \frac{1}{2}\log|K + \sigma_n^2 I| - \frac{1}{2}\mathbf{y}^T(K + \sigma_n^2 I)^{-1}\mathbf{y} \tag{9}$$

with σ_n being the signal noise, K the covariance matrix and $\mathbf{y}$ the data's y-values. By calculating the derivatives of the negative log-likelihood in the direction of the covariance functions' hyperparameters they can be optimized using gradient based methods like Stochastic Gradient Descent (SGD) [72] or ADAM [36].

With their Bayesian approach to regression GPs are a suitable choice to train reasonable models in environments where only little data exists, in contrast to NNs, which require more training data to reach high levels of accuracy. An additional advantage of GPs is their inherent interpretability through the covariance function. The selection of the covariance function strongly impacts the function samples that are generated by a GP, e.g. a periodic kernel causes the GP to always generate functions with repeating patterns. Beside the covariance function the value of its hyperparameters also gives insight on the GPs' behaviour. For example the lengthscale l of the SE kernel determines the rate of change that is allowed, a large lengthscale causing smoother functions while a lengthscale close to 0 causes more rapid changes in the samples. In cases where a single kernel isn't able to model the structure of the data, GPs can be given a combination of covariance functions through e.g. addition ($k(x_1, x_2) = k_1(x_1, x_2) + k_2(x_1, x_2)$) and multiplication ($k(x_1, x_2) = k_1(x_1, x_2) \cdot k_2(x_1, x_2)$) [54, p. 95]. These operations allow to construct more complex kernels and model non-trivial behaviour while using a finite set of base kernels. Applying addition of covariance functions is equivalent to adding the samples of two independent GPs as

$$f_1 \sim \mathcal{GP}(0, k_1)$$
$$f_2 \sim \mathcal{GP}(0, k_2)$$
$$f_1 + f_2 \sim \mathcal{GP}(0, k_1 + k_2)$$

and thus creates a sum of the function spaces to increase the size of potential functions to be drawn from the GP, which (in most cases) can't be modeled with only one covariance function. Similarly, multiplying covariance functions correlates with taking the tensor product of the two spaces. These properties expand the function space efficiently, which leads to better fitting approximation.

With this we can model behaviour which consists of a combination of trends like the CO_2 concentration in the atmosphere which has a seasonal aspect, but also has a smooth component which shows the increase from year to year [54, p. 119]. Note that kernels exist for specific applications, e.g. [39,40].

Thanks to the characteristic of GPs to work well with little data they are also popular in anomaly detection tasks [13,25,38,42,50,55], either to model the data and define deviations from the model expectation as anomalies or by modelling post processed data [13,25].

The main problem of GPs has been their runtime of $O(n^3)$ due to the Cholesky decomposition of the covariance matrix but thanks to developments in sparse approximation methods for GPs, they are now able to handle large datasets in roughly $O(nm^2)$ time with m the number of selected inducing locations and $m \ll n$ [28,53,63]. Our proof of concept implementation confines itself to exact GP regression to allow a more focused evaluation without approximations.

2.2 Related Work

Anomaly detection is subdivided in general methods and GP supported methods. The GP supported methods methods usually use a GP to model the data directly and look at outliers, either directly or after various preprocessing steps.

Anomaly Detection. An anomaly is generally understood as a deviation from expected behaviour which, in case of industrial applications, can e.g. mean that a machine sensor either suddenly stops working or is returning unusual values.

In the era of Industry 4.0, anomaly detection has become an essential field. Throughout the recent years, many classical anomaly detection algorithms have been proposed, such as Z-Score [16], Mahalanobis Distance-Based, Empirical Covariance Estimation [12,51], Robust Covariance Estimation [12,57], Subspace-based PCA Anomaly Detector [12], One-Class SVM [12,20,51,59], Isolation Forest (I-Forest) [45,51], Gaussian Mixture Model [12,51,52], Deep Auto-Encoder [10,22], Local Outlier Factor [2,9,12,51], Self-Organizing Maps [65], Least Squares Anomaly Detector [62], GADPL [24], Automata [64], and k-Nearest Neighbor [2,20,21]. Current approaches [1,3,11,15,26,33,43,58,61,68,70,71] frequently use generative models for anomaly detection, e.g. Variational Autoencoders [37], Generative Adversarial Networks [23], GP Latent Variable Models [14], or Normalizing Flows [56], in particular for sequence data [8]. These models can be trained automatically for the usage of anomaly detection [48].

While all these algorithms are possible approaches for anomaly detection, as shown in different surveys [12,21,52], they are not directly suited for describing the inherent structure of anomalies, which is one advantage of our proposed method. We choose GPs [54] for anomaly description due to their capability to not only gather statistical indicators, but deliver the very characteristics of specific anomalous behavior from the data.

For automatically describing the underlying data characteristics, [46] have proposed the Automatic Bayesian Covariance Discovery System that adapts the Compositional Kernel Search Algorithm [19] by adding intuitive natural language descriptions of the function classes described by their models. The paper [32] further expand on those concepts by expanding these models to discover kernel structures which are able to explain multiple time series at once. Recently, the 3CS [7], LARGe [4] and LGI [5] algorithms have shown to outperform the aforementioned approaches in terms of efficiency.

Wu et al. [69] highlight flaws in multiple popular time series anomaly detection datasets, including Yahoo [41] and NASA [31] and show that all these datasets can be evaluated using a single standard line of MATLAB code, which is their definition of a "trivial" dataset. They further introduce their own dataset which, they state, is free of the flaws they discuss. It is to be published at [69].

In [27] unsupervised and supervised anomaly detection is combined through the use of sparse anomaly labels, which are included as learned parameters in the Variational Autoencoder (VAE). In such an approach, hyperparameters can be automatically trained using Bayesian optimization [48].

GP Supported Anomaly Detection. A large number of works in anomaly detection use GPs at their core, commonly by modelling the data using GP regression [13,25, 38,50] in combination with a fitting metric [25] or by predicting the next points and checking whether they are outliers compared to the GP posterior [38,50]. Other works are expanding the theoretical background by introducing kernels [55] or modifying the approximative GP regression calculation [42] to detect and correct deviations in the data or do classification.

In [25] Gu et al. use a sliding window to train a sparse GP regression and calculate the likelihood as well as a threshold ϵ_p, in addition to a likelihood threshold ϵ_l. Both the likelihood thresholds are compared against the output of an approximated Q-function at the current timestep. To calculate the Q-function's output, normal distributions over the past W errors and likelihoods are generated as well as a normal distribution over a shorter interval W'. The difference over the means, normalized by the variance is inserted into the Q-functions and if one of the values fell below the thresholds, the current new datapoint is considered an anomaly.

Pang et al. also train GPs based on a sliding window approach on windows of size m and predict the mean μ_{m+1} and variance σ_{m+1} for position $m + 1$ [50]. It is then checked whether the observation of position $m+1$ lies in the 95% confidence interval. If that is the case, the point is considered normal and is added to the training data (sliding window). Otherwise it is an abnormal point and only added to the training data if it lies below a threshold.

In [38] two GPs are trained to predict the position of maritime vessels by inferring their Cartesian coordinates. Kowalska et al. run an "active learning"-scheme which adds or leaves points out based on the resulting model performance. The observations are then scored using anomaly scores (squared residual and predictive log-likelihood) to decide whether they are abnormal or not.

Cheng et al. [13] detect local and global anomalies in image sequences. First Cheng et al. pre-process video data to extract spatio-temporal interest points (STIPs) and then use k-Neirest Neighbour and a user defined threshold for their low-level anomaly detection. And use GPs to learned the translation of the three dimensional STIP information to predict the k-NN distance. The nearest neighbouring GPs neg. log likelihood is then added to the local anomaly score to form a weighted sum for the total anomaly position.

3 Method

Our overall goal is to find an arbitrary anomaly in a given univariate time series. Since an anomaly can be any aberration from the normal behaviour of the data, we need a way to determine that normal behaviour first. GPs can be used to model time series data, by finding a kernel function that approximates high level descriptions in said data. Although such a kernel search can be applied to the entire dataset, the resulting kernel expression might consider the anomaly as a normal part of the time series, e.g. by increasing the noise hyperparameter to increase the model fit. To solve this problem, we first separate the series into disjoint segments and conduct a GP kernel search on every segment individually. A segment with normal data should be similar to other segments, while a segment containing an anomaly should stick out. The results of the kernel search are then used to quantify difference or similarity between all pairings of segments through affinity and difference metrics. The resulting affinity or distance matrix can then be normalized and used to group the segments into clusters. An anomaly, if present, is defined to lie in the smallest individual cluster.

As depicted in Fig. 1, every step in this process has multiple methods that can be used. In our experiments, we compare different combinations of these methods to determine if any one combination outperforms the rest, a standard run of the algorithm is depicted in Fig. 2. To properly present all possibilities, we will now describe every step in more detail.

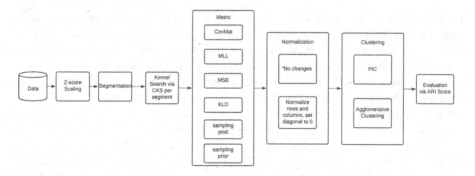

Fig. 1. The flow of our method. In every block, only one of the processes is used. The data is normalized and then segmented. We perform a kernel search on ever segment. The results are then used by one of six metrics to build an affinity and a distance matrix. Those matrices are either normalized or not and the results are then used in two possible clustering algorithms. The resulting clustering is compared to a known ground truth to evaluate its performance.

3.1 Kernel Search

To conduct the kernel search, we first normalize the data by applying Z-score scaling to both input and output data, setting the data mean to 0 and standard deviation to 1. Afterwards, the data is divided into segments of equal size. Currently, the length of the segments needs to be determined beforehand, ideas to develop a potential strategy to automatically determine the segment size are discussed in Sect. 5. We test segment

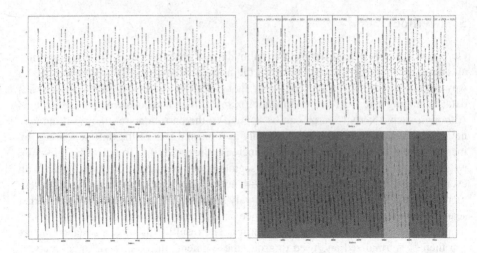

Fig. 2. An example of a usual run of the algorithm. Based on the re-scaled dataset (top left) the kernels are selected using CKS (top right) and based on a distance/affinity metric (bottom left) the clusters are selected (bottom right). As a representative for all distance metrics we show the posterior mean used in the MSE score (see Algorithm 3) from the first kernel applied on all other segments.

lengths mainly based on the size of the anomalies and the overall length of the time series. Shorter segments improve the runtime of the kernel search, which is the bottleneck of this process since we need to run n/n_{seg} kernel searches, with n the length of the timeseries and n_{seg} the segment length. They can also locate the anomaly more accurately, since segments that get marked as abnormal will include less real datapoints and therefore have to fit anomalous data instead of actual data. Longer segments on the other hand provide more stable results, as the kernel search can analyze longer patterns. They also require less space to store intermediate results.

Once the segments are determined, we can apply a kernel search algorithm. We chose CKS [18], because of its simplicity, accuracy compared to Scalable Kernel Composition (SKC) [35] and relatively short runtime compared to Automatic Bayesian Covariance Discovery (ABCD) [46] and 3CS [7]. CKS looks for the optimal combination of a number of base kernels to approximate the given data. The base kernels can be combined via addition or multiplication, as discussed in Sect. 2. In the first step, we determine optimal hyperparameters for every base kernel individually by using Variational Stochastic Gradient Descent [47]. Every step after that takes the best fitting kernel expression from the last step and combines it with every base kernel using both addition and multiplication to construct all candidates for the next optimal kernel expression. We limit the depth of our kernel combinations to three kernels and use the linear (Eq. (8)), the periodic (Eq. (7)) and the squared exponential kernel (Eq. (4)) as base kernels. These kernels are very commonly used and can be combined to approximate most realistic time series.

While a local kernel search algorithm like 3CS [7] would combine the segmentation and kernel search and could therefore be used as well, a change point detection and corresponding segmentation is counter productive to our approach since it can lead to large segments and therefore longer runtimes and less exact detection results.

3.2 Comparison of Segments

Given the optimal kernel and corresponding hyperparameters for each segment, our next goal is to measure similarity between every possible two segment pairs. There are six approaches that we use. For every approach we define ways to measure the affinity a and the distance d between two given segments. Both of these can then later be used for clustering.

The first approach compares the covariance matrices that result from the obtained kernels. To compare two segments S, S' with respective input data X, X' and output data Y, Y' and kernels k, k', we apply k to the combined dataset $X \cup X'$ to get covariance matrix K. Similarly, we get matrix K' from the kernel k'. The distance between the segments is then defined as $d = \|K - K'\|_F$ with $\|\cdot\|_F$ being the Frobenius norm, defined as $\|M\|_F := \sqrt{\sum_{i=1}^m \sum_{j=1}^n |M_{ij}|^2}$. The affinity between the segments is defined as $a = \frac{1}{\|K - K'\|_F + 1}$.

Algorithm 1. Cov.

Input: Segments $S = (X, Y)$, $S' = (X', Y')$ and corresponding kernels k, k'
Output: Affinity a, distance d

$K \leftarrow k(X \cup X', X \cup X')$
$K' \leftarrow k'(X \cup X', X \cup X')$
$a \leftarrow 1/(\|K - K'\|_F + 1)$
$d \leftarrow \|K - K'\|_F$

The second approach uses the log-marginal-likelihood (9) to compare the segments. The log-marginal-likelihood is a very important measure in GP analysis and is used to optimize the results during the kernel search. This makes it a very convenient measure of comparison. To calculate the relation between the segments S and S', we build the covariance matrices K and K' by applying the corresponding kernel to the input data in each segment respectively. Then we calculate the log-marginal-likelihood of covariance matrix K on the data of segment S' and the other way around. Those two results can then be summed up to receive a distance between the segments, or the sum can be inversed for an affinity measure. It is important to note, that in this case "distance" is a loose term, since the result for a segment compared to itself will not be zero.

An interpretation of this approach is the test, whether or not the optimal kernel for one segment also seems probable for another. If a segment includes an anomaly, it is possibly fundamentally different from other segments, which would lead to lower values of the log-marginal-likelihoods.

The third approach measures the capabilities of a segment's kernel to predict another segments data [54]. The prediction is based on the trained GP of one segment and by including the X data of the other segment we calculate the posterior mean for it.

Algorithm 2. Likelihood.

Input: Segments $S = (X, Y)$, $S' = (X', Y')$ and corresponding kernels k, k'
Output: Affinity a, distance d

$K \leftarrow k(X, X)$
$K' \leftarrow k'(X', X')$
$L_1 \leftarrow loglike(K, Y')$
$L_2 \leftarrow loglike(K', Y)$
$a \leftarrow L_1 + L_2$
$d \leftarrow 1/(L_1 + L_2)$

To measure these errors, we first determine the covariance matrices K and K' like in the previous approach. Then we determine adjusted covariance matrices $\hat{K}$ and $\hat{K}'$ by applying the kernel of one segment to the corresponding input data in one dimension, and to the input data of the other segment in the other dimension. More precisely, we define $\hat{K} = k(X', X)$ and $\hat{K}' = k'(X, X')$. To predict the data in one segment, we can now multiply the known data in the other segment with the inverse of the corresponding covariance matrix and then with the fitting mixed covariance matrix: $\hat{K}' K'^{-1} Y'$. The mean squared error over all datapoints in a segment summarizes the difference between the segments. To assure symmetry, we add up the results of symmetrical application of the method.

Algorithm 3. Mean Squared Error.

Input: Segments $S = (X, Y)$, $S' = (X', Y')$ and corresponding kernels k, k'
Output: Affinity a, distance d

$K \leftarrow k(X, X)$
$K' \leftarrow k'(X', X')$
$\hat{K} \leftarrow k(X', X)$
$\hat{K}' \leftarrow k'(X, X')$
$Error \leftarrow \frac{1}{|Y|} \sum_{i=1}^{|Y|} \left(Y - \hat{K}' K'^{-1} Y' \right)_i^2$
$Error' \leftarrow \frac{1}{|Y'|} \sum_{i=1}^{|Y'|} \left(Y' - \hat{K} K^{-1} Y \right)_i^2$
$a = 1/(Error + Error')$
$d = Error + Error'$

The fourth approach calculates the Kullback-Leibler (KL) divergence between two segments using their respective covariance matrices. As in Algorithm 4, we first calculate the covariance matrices K and K'. Next, we apply the KL divergence to the multivariate normal distributions with zero mean and covariance matrices K and K'. We guarantee symmetry by summing up two symmetric applications. The result is a measure of distance, which can be inverted to gain a measure of affinity.

This approach is very comparable to the first one, with the KL divergence induced metric replacing the Frobenius norm induced metric.

Algorithm 4. Kullback-Leibler Divergence.

Input: Segments $S = (X, Y)$, $S' = (X', Y')$ and corresponding kernels k, k'
Output: Affinity a, distance d

$K \leftarrow k(X, X)$
$K' \leftarrow k'(X', X')$
$a \leftarrow 1/(D_{KL}(\mathcal{N}(0, K)\|\mathcal{N}(0, K')) + D_{KL}(\mathcal{N}(0, K')\|\mathcal{N}(0, K)) + 1)$
$d \leftarrow D_{KL}(\mathcal{N}(0, K)\|\mathcal{N}(0, K')) + D_{KL}(\mathcal{N}(0, K')\|\mathcal{N}(0, K))$

The fifth approach compares two segments by drawing samples from their respective posterior Gaussian processes and calculating the maximal difference between them. Each sample is drawn at a number of uniformly distributed points, so we get the maximal difference between two such samples by calculating the distance at each point and then determining the maximum. The process of obtaining the posterior Gaussian process is well-known from GP Regression and is fundamental to GP analysis. It uses input and output data that is already known to draw possible output values for specified input points. In this application, we use prior knowledge from both segments to draw sample functions on a wide interval, exceeding the length of the original time series. This way, even small differences in the kernels can lead to large average differences over the sample functions.

Algorithm 5. Posterior Sampling.

Input: Segments $S = (X, Y)$, $S' = (X', Y')$ and corresponding GPs GP and GP'
Output: Affinity a, distance d

Get posterior Gaussian processes GP_{post} and GP'_{post} from data $X \cup X'$
Draw 100 samples $\{f_1, ..., f_{100}\}$ from GP_{post}
Draw 100 samples $\{f'_1, ..., f'_{100}\}$ from GP'_{post}
for all $i = 1...100$ **do**
　　$dist_i \leftarrow max|f_i - f'_i|$
end for
$a \leftarrow 100/\Sigma_{i=1}^{100} dist_i$
$d \leftarrow \Sigma_{i=1}^{100} dist_i/100$

The sixth and last approach is parallel to the fifth one. However, this time the samples are not drawn from posterior GPs, but rather from their priors. This makes the process more robust against, for example, minor differences in detection of periodic patterns or other kernel functions that can lead to major discrepancies between the samples.

3.3　Clustering

Given the results of any of the previously described metrics, the last step is to sort the segments into clusters based on their similarities or differences. To do so, we used two algorithms in particular: agglomerative clustering and Power Iteration Clustering (PIC)

Algorithm 6. Prior Sampling.

Input: Segments $S = (X, Y)$, $S' = (X', Y')$ and corresponding GPs GP and GP'
Output: Affinity a, distance d

Draw 100 samples $\{f_1, ..., f_{100}\}$ from GP
Draw 100 samples $\{f'_1, ..., f'_{100}\}$ from GP'
for all $i = 1...100$ **do**
    $dist_i \leftarrow \max |f_i - f'_i|$
end for
$a \leftarrow 100/\Sigma_{i=1}^{100} dist_i$
$d \leftarrow \Sigma_{i=1}^{100} dist_i/100$

---

[44]. The former requires a distance matrix describing the segments while the latter works with an affinity matrix. PIC is depicted in Algorithm 7. It requires the affinity matrix to be symmetrical and the work of Shi and Malik [60] suggests that the diagonal entries should be zero [44]. Symmetry is guaranteed by our selection of metrics and we add an additional normalization step before the algorithm by first dividing each row of the matrix by the square root of its diagonal entry and then dividing each column by its remaining diagonal entry. Afterwards all diagonal entries are 1, so we set them specifically to zero. With this normalization we can limit the magnitude of the matrix's eigenvalues.

Agglomerative clustering is a form of hierarchical clustering with a "bottom-up" approach. Initially every segment is considered as its own cluster. Then the closest segments are gradually combined into clusters based on the corresponding entries in the given distance matrix until the desired amount of clusters is reached. In our experiments we use complete-linkage clustering, which means that the distance of two clusters C_1 and C_2 is defined as $dist(C_1, C_2) = max(\{dist(s1, s2) : s1 \in C_1, s2 \in C_2\})$.

For completeness, we include both clustering algorithms with and without prior normalization in our experiments.

Algorithm 7. Power Iteration Clustering [44].

Input: Affinity matrix A, threshold ϵ, number of clusters k
Output: Cluster labels l

Calculate diagonal matrix D with $D_{ii} = \sum_j A_{ij}$
Get normalized affinity matrix $W = D^{-1}A$
Pick initial vector v^0
repeat
    $v^{t+1} \leftarrow \frac{Wv^t}{\|Wv^t\|_1}$
    $\delta \leftarrow |v^{t+1} - v^t|$
    $t \leftarrow t+1$
until $\delta < \epsilon$
$l \leftarrow$ k-MEANS(v^t)

---

4   Evaluation

In this section, we will briefly introduce the data we used for our experiments, before presenting the results and their implications.

To evaluate our findings we use the Adjusted Rand Index (ARI) [30,66]. It is a general measure to compare a clustering of a set of elements to a known ground truth. The ARI gives values in $[-1, 1]$, with higher scores corresponding to higher similarity between the two clusterings.

4.1   Data

To test our approach we are using the SIGKDD 2021 anomaly dataset provided in [34], of which we used a subset of 6 files for our experiments. This dataset is a collection from a large variety of domains, including medicine, sports, entomology, industry, space science, robotics, and others, which Wu et al. have collected from various scientists [69]. Almost all of the files are univariate time series, therefore showing a single channel per file (see Fig. 3), with a single anomaly somewhere after a provided test-training split. Nine of the file are multivariate. Thanks to the wide range of domains these datasets come from, the behaviour and span of the datasets is very different, ranging from 6684 datapoints to 900000 datapoints and showing behaviours from high periodicity and regularity (cf. Fig. 4 bottom right) to very noisy and rapidly changing values (cf. Fig. 4 bottom left). Furthermore the anomalies take very different shapes like increased noise or missing out periods, in Fig. 4 we can see examples for these anomalies. For example the file for Fig. 4 repeats a large peak directly followed by a small peak and the anomalous region switched the order of the peaks. Due to the timing of the challenge [34] the dataset has no labels, so we hand-labeled the data. As soon as the labels are published, we will update our results and publish them together with the code[1] (Table 1).

Table 1. This table shows some basic statistics about 241 of the 250 data files, we are excluding the 9 multivariate files for this calculation.

	whole dataset (241 files)	our subset
Maximum timeseries length	900000	12000
Minimum timeseries length	6684	7501
Average timeseries length	75612	9061.7
Maximum y-value	32306.48	32306.48
Minimum y-value	−14535.311	−14535.311
Average y-value	450	1516.2
Largest y-value span	46841.791	46841.791
Smallest y-value span	0.104071	0.118
Max ratio of anomaly to training data	76%	48%
Min ratio of anomaly to training data	2%	22%
Avg ratio of anomaly to training data	30.3%	38.3%

---

[1] Everything will be found under the repository https://github.com/JanHuewel/KernelSearch AnomalyDetection.

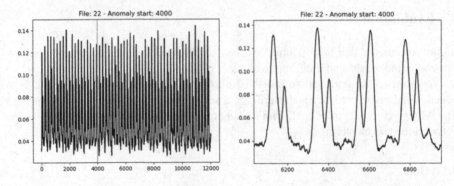

Fig. 3. Left: A plot of a data file provided in [34]. The earliest starting point for the anomaly is given by the red line. **Right:** a zoom of the anomalous area. The anomaly can be seen in the x region between 6500 and 6700 in the order of the peaks. Throughout the whole file it is large peak followed by small peak, in the anomalous region it is flipped.

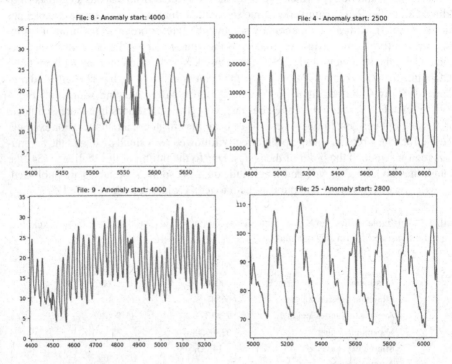

Fig. 4. Different types of anomalies in the files we selected for evaluation. They range from increased noise (top left) to missing out periods (top right, bottom left) and switching the order of peaks (bottom right).

4.2 Results

Our experiments were conducted on six separate time series, every time with two different lengths of segments, six different metrics, two possible normalizations and two

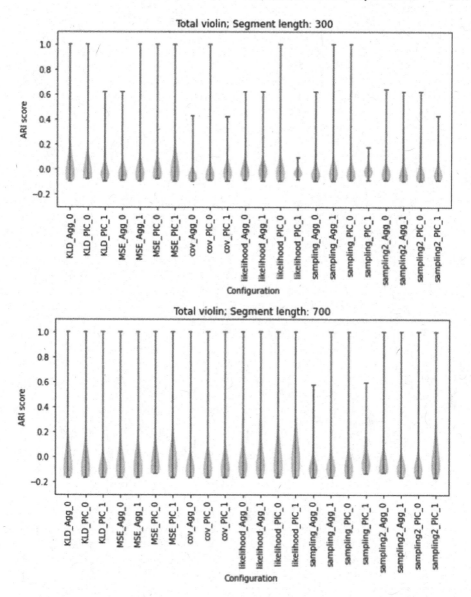

Fig. 5. Results for the individual configurations over all datasets and all 22 cycles with segment lengths 300 (top) and 700 (bottom). Configurations are listed as metric_segment length_clustering method_normalization. For normalization a 0 means 'no normalization' and 1 means 'normalization'. For the metric 'sampling' refers to the posterior sampling in Algorithm 5 and 'sampling2' refers to the prior sampling in Algorithm 6.

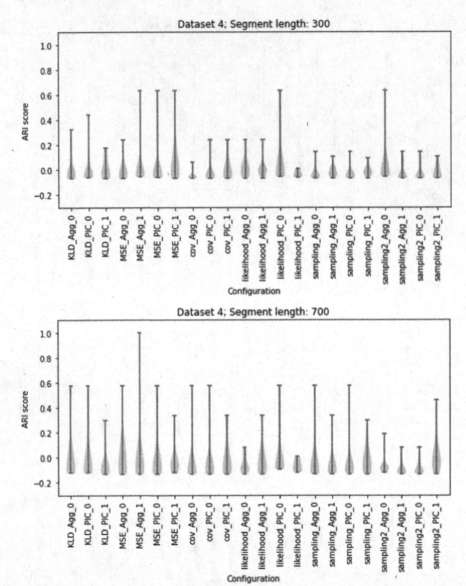

Fig. 6. Results for the individual configurations over dataset 4 across all 22 cycles with segment lengths 300 (top) and 700 (bottom). Configurations are listed as metric_segment length_clustering method_normalization. For normalization a 0 means 'no normalization' and 1 means 'normalization'. For the metric 'sampling' refers to the posterior sampling in Algorithm 5 and 'sampling2' refers to the prior sampling in Algorithm 6.

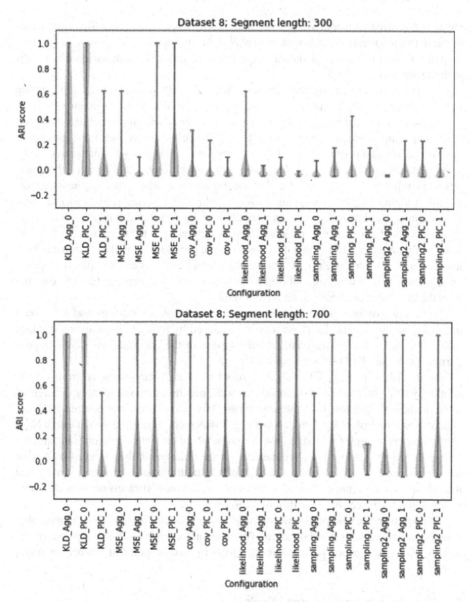

Fig. 7. Results for the individual configurations over dataset 8 across all 22 cycles with segment lengths 300 (top) and 700 (bottom). Configurations are listed as metric_segment length_clustering method_normalization. For normalization a 0 means 'no normalization' and 1 means 'normalization'. For the metric 'sampling' refers to the posterior sampling in Algorithm 5 and 'sampling2' refers to the prior sampling in Algorithm 6.

clustering methods. Overall we get 48 configurations per time series. Since some elements in the previously described method of analysis depend on random sampling or random initializations, we repeated every experiment 22 times and summarized the results in the violin plots in Fig. 5.

The results of our experiments indicate that this method can be used as a starting point for future research while also having potential for further improvement.

Figure 5 shows that most configurations can correctly identify the cluster that contains the anomaly, which results in an ARI of 1. However, on average, most runs result in lower scores that is roughly around 0. A score of 0 can roughly be interpreted as the score between two independent clusterings [66], which shows that none of the methods work reliably. It is also notable that the experiments with larger segments appear to have a higher chance of working perfectly, while also having slightly worse minimum scores. The low scores can be attributed to the fact that the anomaly cluster in the ground truth consists of a single segment, which restricts the range of possible ARI scores. Any found clustering that deviates from the ground truth will have considerably lower scores, resulting in the distributions we see in Fig. 5. As an example, if there are 36 segments, two of which are labeled as anomalies, and we correctly identify one, but miss the other we are already at an ARI of 0.63.

Some few configurations did not result in any usable clusterings and have been omitted from the results. These errors can be caused by trying to normalize a distance matrix that has 0 on its diagonal, which happens in the combinations Cov + Agg + normalization and KLD + Agg + normalization.

As described in Sect. 4.1, the examined time series vary strongly from one to another, which can be seen in our results as well, because it caused notably differences in methods' effectiveness over the time series. Most clearly this can be seen in Fig. 6, which shows the results for dataset 4 and Fig. 7 which does the same for dataset 8. Most configurations struggled with dataset 4 to a point where only one configuration was able to find the correct clustering. On dataset 8, on the other hand, they worked well, with some configurations getting the correct clustering multiple times or even in more than half of the cycles. Figure 4 shows that the anomalies in those datasets are very different, which could be the cause of the different results.

The, on average, best performing configuration uses the likelihood with larger segments and PIC without normalization. This does not comply with the expectation set in (PIC)'s original paper [44] and is therefore a potential point of interest in future research.

5   Conclusion and Future Work

In this work we described an approach that can be run with multiple distance and affinity metrics to perform anomaly detection based on the results of a GP kernel search algorithm. To detect abnormal sections in a given time series, we divide the data into equally sized segments and perform an independent kernel search on each segment via CKS. The resulting list of kernels and corresponding hyperparameters can then be used by any of the six presented metrics to construct either an affinity matrix for PIC or a distance matrix for agglomerative clustering. The clustering methods' results will then consist of two clusters, the anomaly cluster and the normal cluster.

To test all possible configurations of this method, we applied them to a subset of the SIGKDD 2021 anomaly dataset in 22 cycles and evaluated the results with the ARI. Almost all configurations were able to succeed, although those successes were not reliably reproducible. The on average best method was a likelihood-based metric with PIC without pre-clustering normalization.

Overall we have been able to show that a GP kernel search can be used for anomaly detection by using the interpretability of the GP kernels.

However, additional research is required to make the algorithm competitive to current anomaly detection algorithms. It is currently restricted to univariate datasets, but because GPs are adaptable to multivariate time series, it can be adjusted accordingly. The algorithm also currently requires the user to input a segment length. Future research could involve providing an optimized default value, either based on length and periodicity of the data or determined iteratively e.g. by applying 'divide and conquer' approaches known from quicksort [29] to automatically find the anomalies boundaries. Furthermore, more complicated kernels, tailor-made to time series in production, should be investigated, e.g. those from [39]. We have currently forgone more complicated kernels, since we observed that the selection of the kernels is unstable and hence envision a better model selection criterion. Having a bigger choice of kernels also necessitates faster algorithms.

Additionally, the presented metrics need to be examined further. To develop a reliable algorithm, one could for example combine multiple metrics to an ensemble, include additional information in the metrics or evaluate a confidence score together with the clustering to automatically estimate their success.

Lastly, further experiments could examine if this approach can be combined with state-of-the-art anomaly detection methods in order to improve them. As soon as a refined version of the algorithm exists additional work can be done on the interpretability through the covariance functions in an explicit manner. Instead of just using them to detect anomalies, the results can then be used to describe specifics of the anomalies to users and learn from the algorithms' results.

References

1. An, J., Cho, S.: Variational autoencoder based anomaly detection using reconstruction probability. Spec. Lect. IE **2**(1), 1–18 (2015)
2. Auslander, B., Gupta, K.M., Aha, D.W.: A comparative evaluation of anomaly detection algorithms for maritime video surveillance. In: Carapezza, E.M. (ed.) Proceedings of the SPIE 8019, Sensors, and Command, Control, Communications, and Intelligence (C3I) Technologies for Homeland Security and Homeland Defense X, p. 801907. SPIE Proceedings, SPIE (2011). https://doi.org/10.1117/12.883535
3. Berkhahn, F., Keys, R., Ouertani, W., Shetty, N., Geißler, D.: Augmenting variational autoencoders with sparse labels: a unified framework for unsupervised, semi-(un) supervised, and supervised learning. arXiv preprint arXiv:1908.03015 (2019)
4. Berns, F., Beecks, C.: Automatic Gaussian process model retrieval for big data. In: CIKM. ACM (2020)
5. Berns, F., Beecks, C.: Complexity-adaptive Gaussian process model inference for large-scale data. SIAM (2021). https://doi.org/10.1137/1.9781611976700.41

6. Berns, F., Lange-Hegermann, M., Beecks, C.: Towards Gaussian processes for automatic and interpretable anomaly detection in industry 4.0. In: IN4PL, pp. 87–92 (2020)
7. Berns, F., Schmidt, K., Bracht, I., Beecks, C.: 3CS algorithm for efficient Gaussian process model retrieval. In: 25th International Conference on Pattern Recognition, ICPR 2020, Virtual Event/Milan, Italy, 10–15 January 2021, pp. 1773–1780. IEEE (2020). https://doi.org/10.1109/ICPR48806.2021.9412805
8. Bowman, S.R., Vilnis, L., Vinyals, O., Dai, A.M., Józefowicz, R., Bengio, S.: Generating sentences from a continuous space. In: CoNLL, pp. 10–21. ACL (2016)
9. Breunig, M., Kriegel, H.P., Ng, R.T., Sander, J.: LOF: identifying density-based local outliers. In: Proceedings of the 2000 ACM SIGMOD International Conference on Management of Data, pp. 93–104. ACM (2000)
10. Candel, A., LeDell, E., Parmar, V., Arora, A.: Deep learning with H2O, December 2018. https://www.h2o.ai/wp-content/themes/h2o2016/images/resources/DeepLearningBooklet.pdf. Accessed 28 Sept 2020
11. Chalapathy, R., Chawla, S.: Deep learning for anomaly detection: a survey. CoRR abs/1901.03407 (2019)
12. Chandola, V., Banerjee, A., Kumar, V.: Anomaly detection: a survey. ACM Comput. Surv. (CSUR) **41**(3), 1–58 (2009)
13. Cheng, K.W., Chen, Y.T., Fang, W.H.: Video anomaly detection and localization using hierarchical feature representation and Gaussian process regression. In: Proceedings of the IEEE Conference on Computer Vision and Pattern Recognition, pp. 2909–2917 (2015)
14. Damianou, A.C., Titsias, M.K., Lawrence, N.D.: Variational inference for latent variables and uncertain inputs in Gaussian processes. J. Mach. Learn. Res. **17**(42), 1–62 (2016)
15. Dias, M.L.D., Mattos, C.L.C., da Silva, T.L.C., de Macêdo, J.A.F., Silva, W.C.P.: Anomaly detection in trajectory data with normalizing flows. CoRR abs/2004.05958 (2020)
16. Domingues, R., Buonora, F., Senesi, R., Thonnard, O.: An application of unsupervised fraud detection to passenger name records. In: 2016 46th Annual IEEE/IFIP International Conference on Dependable Systems and Networks Workshop (DSN-W), pp. 54–59, June 2016. https://doi.org/10.1109/DSN-W.2016.21
17. Duvenaud, D.: Automatic model construction with Gaussian processes. Ph.D. thesis, University of Cambridge (2014)
18. Duvenaud, D., Lloyd, J.R., Grosse, R.B., Tenenbaum, J.B., Ghahramani, Z.: Structure discovery in nonparametric regression through compositional kernel search. In: Proceedings of the 30th International Conference on Machine Learning, ICML 2013, Atlanta, GA, USA, 16–21 June 2013, vol. 28, pp. 1166–1174. JMLR Workshop and Conference Proceedings (JMLR.org) (2013). http://proceedings.mlr.press/v28/duvenaud13.html
19. Duvenaud, D., Lloyd, J.R., Grosse, R.B., Tenenbaum, J.B., Ghahramani, Z.: Structure discovery in nonparametric regression through compositional kernel search. In: ICML, vol. 28, no. 3, pp. 1166–1174. JMLR Workshop and Conference Proceedings (JMLR.org) (2013)
20. Eskin, E., Arnold, A., Prerau, M., Portnoy, L., Stolfo, S.: A geometric framework for unsupervised anomaly detection. In: Barbará, D., Jajodia, S. (eds.) Applications of Data Mining in Computer Security. Advances in Information Security, vol. 6, pp. 77–101. Springer, Boston (2002). Series ISSN 1568-2633. https://doi.org/10.1007/978-1-4615-0953-0_4
21. Goldstein, M., Uchida, S.: A comparative evaluation of unsupervised anomaly detection algorithms for multivariate data. PLoS ONE **11**(4), 152–173 (2016). https://doi.org/10.1371/journal.pone.0152173
22. Gong, D., et al.: Memorizing normality to detect anomaly: memory-augmented deep autoencoder for unsupervised anomaly detection. In: Proceedings of the IEEE International Conference on Computer Vision, pp. 1705–1714 (2019)
23. Goodfellow, I., et al.: Generative Adversarial Nets. In: NeurIPS (2014)

24. Graß, A., Beecks, C., Soto, J.A.C.: Unsupervised anomaly detection in production lines. In: Machine Learning for Cyber Physical Systems. TA, vol. 9, pp. 18–25. Springer, Heidelberg (2019). https://doi.org/10.1007/978-3-662-58485-9_3
25. Gu, M., Fei, J., Sun, S.: Online anomaly detection with sparse Gaussian processes. Neurocomputing **403**, 383–399 (2020)
26. Guo, Y., Liao, W., Wang, Q., Yu, L., Ji, T., Li, P.: Multidimensional time series anomaly detection: a GRU-based Gaussian mixture variational autoencoder approach. In: Asian Conference on Machine Learning, pp. 97–112 (2018)
27. Hammerbacher, T., Lange-Hegermann, M., Platz, G.: Including sparse production knowledge into variational autoencoders to increase anomaly detection reliability (2021)
28. Hensman, J., Matthews, A., Ghahramani, Z.: Scalable variational Gaussian process classification. In: Artificial Intelligence and Statistics, pp. 351–360. PMLR (2015)
29. Hoare, C.A.: Quicksort. Comput. J. **5**(1), 10–16 (1962)
30. Hubert, L., Arabie, P.: Comparing partitions. J. Classif. **2**(1), 193–218 (1985)
31. Hundman, K., Constantinou, V., Laporte, C., Colwell, I., Soderstrom, T.: Detecting spacecraft anomalies using LSTMs and nonparametric dynamic thresholding. In: Proceedings of the 24th ACM SIGKDD International Conference on Knowledge Discovery & Data Mining, pp. 387–395 (2018)
32. Hwang, Y., Tong, A., Choi, J.: Automatic construction of nonparametric relational regression models for multiple time series. In: Balcan, M.F., Weinberger, K.Q. (eds.) Proceedings of the 33rd International Conference on Machine Learning, ICML 2016, vol. 48, pp. 3030–3039. Proceedings of Machine Learning Research. PLMR (2016)
33. Kawachi, Y., Koizumi, Y., Harada, N.: Complementary set variational autoencoder for supervised anomaly detection. In: 2018 IEEE International Conference on Acoustics, Speech and Signal Processing (ICASSP), pp. 2366–2370. IEEE (2018)
34. Keogh, E., Dutta, R.T., Naik, U., Agrawal, A.: Multi-dataset time-series anomaly detection competition. In: SIGKDD 2021 (2021). https://compete.hexagon-ml.com/practice/competition/39/
35. Kim, H., Teh, Y.W.: Scaling up the automatic statistician: scalable structure discovery using Gaussian processes. In: Proceedings of the 21st International Conference on Artificial Intelligence and Statistics, vol. 84 (2018)
36. Kingma, D.P., Ba, J.: Adam: a method for stochastic optimization. In: Bengio, Y., LeCun, Y. (eds.) 3rd International Conference on Learning Representations, ICLR 2015, San Diego, CA, USA, 7–9 May 2015, Conference Track Proceedings (2015). http://arxiv.org/abs/1412.6980
37. Kingma, D.P., Welling, M.: Auto-Encoding Variational Bayes. In: ICLR (2014)
38. Kowalska, K., Peel, L.: Maritime anomaly detection using Gaussian process active learning. In: 2012 15th International Conference on Information Fusion, pp. 1164–1171. IEEE (2012)
39. Lange-Hegermann, M.: Algorithmic linearly constrained Gaussian processes. In: NeurIPS, pp. 2141–2152 (2018)
40. Lange-Hegermann, M.: Linearly constrained Gaussian processes with boundary conditions. In: International Conference on Artificial Intelligence and Statistics, pp. 1090–1098. PMLR (2021)
41. Laptev, N., Amizadeh, S., Billwala, Y.: S5 - a labeled anomaly detection dataset, version 1.0(16m). https://webscope.sandbox.yahoo.com/catalog.php?datatype=s&did=70
42. Lemercier, M., Salvi, C., Cass, T., Bonilla, E.V., Damoulas, T., Lyons, T.: SigGPDE: scaling sparse Gaussian processes on sequential data (2021)
43. Li, D., Chen, D., Jin, B., Shi, L., Goh, J., Ng, S.-K.: MAD-GAN: multivariate anomaly detection for time series data with generative adversarial networks. In: Tetko, I.V., Kůrková, V., Karpov, P., Theis, F. (eds.) ICANN 2019. LNCS, vol. 11730, pp. 703–716. Springer, Cham (2019). https://doi.org/10.1007/978-3-030-30490-4_56

44. Lin, F., Cohen, W.W.: Power iteration clustering. In: Fürnkranz, J., Joachims, T. (eds.) Proceedings of the 27th International Conference on Machine Learning, ICML 2010, 21–24 June 2010, Haifa, Israel, pp. 655–662. Omnipress (2010). https://icml.cc/Conferences/2010/papers/387.pdf

45. Liu, F.T., Ting, K.M., Zhou, Z.H.: Isolation forest. In: Giannotti, F. (ed.) 2008 8th IEEE International Conference on Data Mining, pp. 413–422. IEEE, Piscataway (2008). https://doi.org/10.1109/ICDM.2008.17

46. Lloyd, J.R., Duvenaud, D., Grosse, R.B., Tenenbaum, J.B., Ghahramani, Z.: Automatic construction and natural-language description of nonparametric regression models. In: AAAI, pp. 1242–1250. AAAI Press (2014)

47. Mandt, S., Hoffman, M.D., Blei, D.M.: Stochastic gradient descent as approximate Bayesian inference (2018)

48. Müller, A., Lange-Hegermann, M., von Birgelen, A.: Automatisches training eines variational autoencoder für anomalieerkennung in zeitreihen. In: VDI Kongress Automation 2020, vol. VDI-Berichte 2375, pp. 687–698. VDI Wissensforum GmbH, VDI Verlag GmbH, Baden-Baden (2020)

49. Müllner, D.: Modern hierarchical, agglomerative clustering algorithms. CoRR abs/1109.2378 (2011). http://arxiv.org/abs/1109.2378

50. Pang, J., Liu, D., Liao, H., Peng, Y., Peng, X.: Anomaly detection based on data stream monitoring and prediction with improved Gaussian process regression algorithm. In: 2014 International Conference on Prognostics and Health Management, pp. 1–7. IEEE (2014)

51. Pedregosa, F., et al.: Scikit-learn: machine learning in Python. J. Mach. Learn. Res. **12**, 2825–2830 (2011). http://dl.acm.org/citation.cfm?id=1953048.2078195

52. Phua, C., Lee, V.C.S., Smith-Miles, K., Gayler, R.W.: A comprehensive survey of data mining-based fraud detection research. CoRR abs/1009.6119 (2010). http://arxiv.org/abs/1009.6119

53. Quinonero-Candela, J., Rasmussen, C.E.: A unifying view of sparse approximate Gaussian process regression. J. Mach. Learn. Res. **6**, 1939–1959 (2005)

54. Rasmussen, C.E., Williams, C.K.I.: Gaussian Processes for Machine Learning. MIT Press (2006)

55. Reece, S., Garnett, R., Osborne, M., Roberts, S.: Anomaly detection and removal using nonstationary Gaussian processes. arXiv preprint arXiv:1507.00566 (2015)

56. Rezende, D.J., Mohamed, S.: Variational inference with normalizing flows. In: ICML, vol. 37, pp. 1530–1538. JMLR Workshop and Conference Proceedings (JMLR.org) (2015)

57. Rousseeuw, P.J.: Least median of squares regression. J. Am. Stat. Assoc. **79**(388), 871–880 (1984)

58. Sabokrou, M., Khalooei, M., Fathy, M., Adeli, E.: Adversarially learned one-class classifier for novelty detection. In: Proceedings of the IEEE Conference on Computer Vision and Pattern Recognition, pp. 3379–3388 (2018)

59. Schölkopf, B., Platt, J.C., Shawe-Taylor, J.C., Smola, A.J., Williamson, R.C.: Estimating the support of a high-dimensional distribution. Neural Comput. **13**(7), 1443–1471 (2001). https://doi.org/10.1162/089976601750264965

60. Shi, J., Malik, J.: Normalized cuts and image segmentation. IEEE Trans. Pattern Anal. Mach. Intell. **22**(8), 888–905 (2000). https://doi.org/10.1109/34.868688

61. Suh, S., Chae, D.H., Kang, H.G., Choi, S.: Echo-state conditional variational autoencoder for anomaly detection. In: 2016 International Joint Conference on Neural Networks (IJCNN), pp. 1015–1022. IEEE (2016)

62. Tavallaee, M., Stakhanova, N., Ghorbani, A.A.: Toward credible evaluation of anomaly-based intrusion-detection methods. IEEE Trans. Syst. Man Cybern. Part C (Appl. Rev.) **40**(5), 516–524 (2010). https://doi.org/10.1109/TSMCC.2010.2048428

63. Titsias, M.: Variational learning of inducing variables in sparse Gaussian processes. In: Artificial Intelligence and Statistics, pp. 567–574. PMLR (2009)
64. Vodenčarević, A., Büning, H.K., Niggemann, O., Maier, A.: Using behavior models for anomaly detection in hybrid systems. In: 2011 XXIII International Symposium on Information, Communication and Automation Technologies, pp. 1–8. IEEE (2011)
65. Von Birgelen, A., Buratti, D., Mager, J., Niggemann, O.: Self-organizing maps for anomaly localization and predictive maintenance in cyber-physical production systems. Procedia CIRP **72**, 480–485 (2018)
66. Wagner, S., Wagner, D.: Comparing clusterings: an overview. Universität Karlsruhe, Fakultät für Informatik Karlsruhe (2007)
67. Wang, J., Ma, Y., Zhang, L., Gao, R.X., Wu, D.: Deep learning for smart manufacturing: methods and applications. J. Manuf. Syst. **48**, 144–156 (2018)
68. Wang, X., Du, Y., Lin, S., Cui, P., Yang, Y.: Self-adversarial variational autoencoder with Gaussian anomaly prior distribution for anomaly detection. CoRR, abs/1903.00904 (2019)
69. Wu, R., Keogh, E.J.: Current time series anomaly detection benchmarks are flawed and are creating the illusion of progress (2020). https://wu.renjie.im/research/anomaly-benchmarks-are-flawed/arxiv/
70. Zenati, H., Romain, M., Foo, C.S., Lecouat, B., Chandrasekhar, V.: Adversarially learned anomaly detection. In: 2018 IEEE International Conference on Data Mining (ICDM), pp. 727–736. IEEE (2018)
71. Zhang, C., Chen, Y.: Time series anomaly detection with variational autoencoders. CoRR abs/1907.01702 (2019). http://arxiv.org/abs/1907.01702
72. Zinkevich, M., Weimer, M., Smola, A.J., Li, L.: Parallelized stochastic gradient descent. In: Lafferty, J.D., Williams, C.K.I., Shawe-Taylor, J., Zemel, R.S., Culotta, A. (eds.) 24th Annual Conference on Neural Information Processing Systems 2010. Advances in Neural Information Processing Systems, vol. 23, 6–9 December 2010, Vancouver, British Columbia, Canada, pp. 2595–2603. Curran Associates, Inc. (2010). https://proceedings.neurips.cc/paper/2010/hash/abea47ba24142ed16b7d8fbf2c740e0d-Abstract.html

Measuring Dependencies in Cyber-Physical Systems: Overhead Cranes Case Study

Janusz Szpytko and Yorlandys Salgado-Duarte[(⊠)]

AGH University of Science and Technology, Krakow, Poland
{szpytko,salgado}@agh.edu.pl

Abstract. Complex cyber-physical systems with multifunctional duties generally degrade simultaneously due to common factors such as the designed structure, the operating environment, and the exploitation history (we refer to exploitation when we include operation and maintenance processes together). Risk-oriented modeling is a well-established methodology for degradation analysis and prediction, and one of the major challenges is the modelling features of the marginals that describe, and store information related to the degradation process. Usually, the modelling process for each component of the system is analyzed independently, but in recent years the multivariate copulas developed and implemented in formal programming languages allow us to consider both sides of the modelling process in one (independent and dependent components). In this paper, we discuss the impact through sensitivity analysis of the paradigm shift between the assumption of independence or dependencies between components. The paper measures the impact of the decision in a parameterized scenario showing significant changes.

Keywords: Copula · Risk Assessment · Marginal Degradation · Cranes

1 Introduction

Industry 4.0 is the name assigned to refer to the current trend of automation and data exchange in manufacturing technologies, i.e., industries with continuous processes as a broader definition. The trend includes concepts and practical applications such as cyber-physical systems [1], the Internet of Things [2], cloud computing [3], and cognitive computing [4]. The convergence of the concepts mentioned above constitutes what we know as a smart factory, and all the aforementioned concepts are connected in some way through the system or process analyzed and its needs.

Most of the contributions in this trend are oriented on how to automate decision-making processes. To mention just a few more, we have as examples research [5, 6], and [7], which are automations of decision making in different fields of study, and as a common convergence, all of them are based on simulation. Certainly, the needs of the process under analysis and the nature of the decision-making define the solution to be addressed; however, simulation approaches are appealing due to the modeling flexibility they offer. As we know, modelling and simulation practices allow us to analyze the systems interactions using computational tools, knowing that we usually analyze running systems and that the main duty of modelling is to find a better qualitative and/or quantitative operation state by modelling logical interactions disconnected from the real running system, with the idea in the final stage of improving decision-making when we transfer to the modeled underline process the satisfactory results achieved in the digital environment.

In this paper, we contribute to the same trend, with a practical example of simulation-based automation of a decision-making process. In our case, the proposed solution adopts the advantages of simulation approaches when the need arises to simulate some variables considered in the system under analysis, in the absence of real data or experience of the experimental variable under analysis. Also, the solution, since it models a decision-making process, takes advantage of the gradual understanding of human beings to analyze the interrelationship between systems with a holistic view and proposes the synthesis of the performance of the modeled decision-making process through a single holistic indicator, easy to infer and evaluate.

The decision-making process under analysis in this paper is composed of an overhead crane system in operation and its relationship with the production line, as well as the supporting maintenance activities associated with overhead cranes, and the simulation-based automation of the decision-making process is addressed through modelling practices (i.e., applying concepts such as Digital Twins), comprehensive experiments (i.e., searching physical and/or logical connections and interactions) and sensitivity analysis (stress analysis changing sensible variables of the modelled system).

In other words, the system analyzed is a set of overhead cranes in a steel plant that performs critical tasks in continuous processes, and the subject of the modelling is the decision-making of maintenance activities.

The model under study in this work has contributions [8, 9] as precedents. The first describes the model variables involved and the dataflows, and the second stores the risk-oriented model designed to manage maintenance scheduling in the closed online optimization loop. In risk-oriented approaches, such as the one presented in [8, 9], independent stochastic degradation processes between components in the system under analysis, is one of the most common assumptions made. For example, in our case, all the results achieved in previous work [8, 9] assume that historical failures of overhead cranes are independent. The decision made is somehow reasonable; the complexity of the system structure (referring to structures with high redundancy) and the low probability of common failures in practice, result in a low dependency between the stochastic degradation processes of the components. However, as we know, one of the contributors to the stochastic process is historical degradation, and its correct modeling ensures accurate simulations.

Specifically, the idea of this paper is to challenge the precedent work, i.e., challenge the assumption of independence by measuring the dependency between historical failures of overhead cranes. If some dependency is found, then the copula approach is used to establish the dependencies between historical failures, introducing an additional self-analysis dependency layer (SAD) into the model [8, 9]. As expected, in this work we introduce the measurement of dependencies as a modelling improvement of the maintenance activities decision making, but at the same time we automate the decisions made during the process with layers of self-analysis.

Addressing the details of the proposed improvement, we can say that the SAD layer transfers the information of the dependencies structure to the pseudo-random generator by cranes identifier (ID), and consequently, the random numbers generated to simulate the historical failures have embedded the dependencies. The rationale for looking for dependencies within historical failures in structures with high redundancy has a well-known motivation; if two overhead cranes have high dependencies together, it is a sign of poor practice in maintenance strategies and potential risky scenarios with common failures.

Knowing that the copula approach allows us to simulate failures with a dependent stochastic degradation function with a given dependence structure, a good practice before starting to search for copula structure candidates is to analyze the impact of dependencies in the model.

Specifically, in this paper, we analyze the impact of possible dependencies on historical degradation data between overhead cranes. As we know, dependencies and system structure are connected in some way, so in addition to the search for dependencies, we also present the discussion on changes in system structure, not presented in previous works.

The study is conducted by means of a sensitivity analysis with an established dependency structure, which illustrates in detail all impacts at the component and system level. Before introducing the experiment, brief observations on the main properties of the copula are discussed in the first section to lay the groundwork for the sensitivity analysis conducted.

2   Copula Approach, Impacts at Component Level: Overhead Cranes

Copula theory is a common method for addressing the multivariate dependence problem. Copulas are multivariate functions that describe dependencies between variables and provide the possibility to construct distributions that model multivariate and correlated data. The copula allows the construction of a multivariate distribution by specifying the univariate marginal distributions, in our case the random distributed historical degradation data for each overhead crane, and the dependence structure between variables, usually a positive definite correlation matrix in the case of elliptical copulas. The copula theory has been applied in recent years to degradation data and strong contributions are [10] and [11]. Both references are used in this document to support some decisions taken in the modelling process.

In the adopted Monte Carlo simulation-based model, an important process is to select the probability distributions for the random inputs, in our case, the degradation data (*TTF*: time-to-failure and *TTR*: time-to-repair). Selecting a distribution for each individual variable or marginal is straightforward (see Fig. 3). Fitting selection decision-making flow diagram in reference [8], fitting single distributions with 18 possible selections) but deciding what dependencies should exist between the degradation data may not be.

Ideally, given the fitted distributions, the simulated marginals should reflect what we know about the dependence between the actual quantities we are modelling. However, there may be little or no information on which to base any dependencies in the simulation.

Accurate pure multivariate copulas are difficult to construct in practice, even more so when the selection best-fitting options are limited (*Gaussian* and *t*) in our case.

Knowing the difficulties and limitations associated with fitting copulas, it is always good practice before starting the journey to analyze the impact of the modelling decision, as we discussed above.

Thus, for overview, an *N*-dimensional copula is a function *C* with the following properties:

Dom $C = I^N = [0; 1]^N$.

C is grounded and *N*-increasing.

C has marginals C_n that satisfy $C_n (u) = C (1; ...; 1; \underline{u}; 1; ...; 1) = u$ for all *u* in *I*.

A copula corresponds also to a function with several properties. In particular, because of the second and third properties, it follows that Im $C = I$, and therefore *C* is a uniform multivariate distribution. Furthermore, it is obvious that if $F_1; ...; F_N$ are univariate distribution functions, $C (F_1 (x_1); ...; F_n (x_n); ...; F_N (x_N))$ is a multivariate distribution function with margins $F_1; ...; F_N$ because $u_n = F_n (x_n)$ is a uniform random variable.

Copula functions or distributions are thus an adapted tool for constructing multivariate distributions, and the fundamentals are supported by Sklar's Theorem 2.

As an illustration of how the dependencies are embedded in the random numbers and how the correlation matrix guides the dependencies in the elliptical copulas, we analyze and visualize for a given parametrized copula, in this case a *Gaussian* copula, the impact of increasing the pairwise correlation between two marginals.

A typical expression of a *Gaussian* copula distribution for bivariate random variables is defined in (1).

$$c(u_1, u_2; \rho) = \Phi_\rho \left[\Phi^{-1}(u_1), \Phi^{-1}(u_2) \right] \tag{1}$$

where u_1 and u_2 are random variables or marginals defined between [0, 1], and the copula parameter ρ is a positive definite linear correlation matrix.

For comparison reasons and as a starting point in the discussion, we select two 50 tons cranes with ID 807 and ID 808, and the final fit selection is summarized in Table 1 (the final fits used are a subset of Table 2 in reference [9]), then, with the inverse cumulative distribution function fitted to historical degradation data, we generate independent random marginals (usual approach implemented in the model when dependencies are not considered). Figure 1 shows the resulting scatter plot.

Table 1. Parameters of the selected distributions.

Crane ID	Failure time distribution
807	Exponential $\mu = 743.80$
808	Weibull $a = 1796.93; b = 0.60$

Now, using the multivariate (bivariate in this analysis) inverse cumulative distribution function of $c(u_1, u_2; \rho)$ defined in (1), and setting the pairwise correlation parameter ρ (bivariate, only two marginals) to $\rho = 0.2, 0.5$ and 0.8 for testing purposes; we scatter plot the generated correlated marginals (resulting impact of the SAD layer, see Figs. 5, 6 and 7), and then given the correlated samples from the copula, we use the inverse cumulative distribution function fitted to historical degradation data to scatter plot correlated *TTF* (see Figs. 2, 3 and 4).

Figures 2, 3 and 4 are shown by steps, the scatter plot *TTF* when the correlation parameter ρ is changed to $\rho = 0.2$, 0.5 and 0.8, respectively. Visible in the generated scatter plot space is how the points (*TTF* values) are more aggregated when the pairwise correlation increases.

At this point, we can conclude that values of pairwise correlations greater than 0.2 impact somehow the model when the random numbers are generated (see scatter plots in Figs. 2, 3 and 4), and the copula approach is consistent with all overhead crane system dependencies, which means that, if no dependencies were found, the simulation will remain independent.

The visual space distribution of the random numbers and the dependence between them are shown in Figs. 5, 6 and 7. In the case of the Gaussian copula, when the correlation parameter ρ increases, the symmetric structure in the generated random values is more visible.

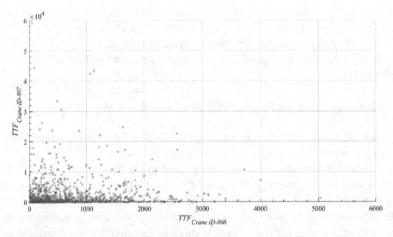

Fig. 1. Scatter plot of *TTF* with independent random samples generated.

The analysis above visualizes the impact of dependencies among two cranes, and as we know, the system presented has 33 overhead cranes. Following the same shape as previous contributions [12], analyzing impacts through sensitivity analysis and using as a starting point the results from [8, 9], we propose to analyze the impact of the dependencies structure in the model, now at the system level, considering the logical series-parallel configuration of the system. In the next section, the analysis performed is fully described.

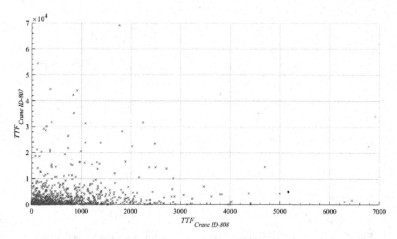

Fig. 2. Scatter plot of *TTF* with correlated ($\rho = 0.2$) random samples generated.

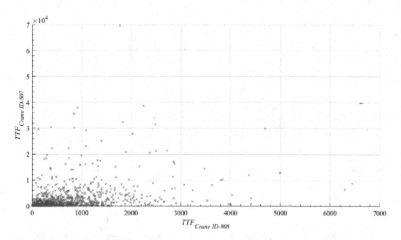

Fig. 3. Scatter plot of *TTF* with correlated ($\rho = 0.5$) random samples generated.

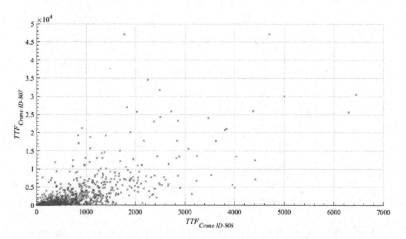

Fig. 4. Scatter plot of TTF with correlated ($\rho = 0.8$) random samples generated.

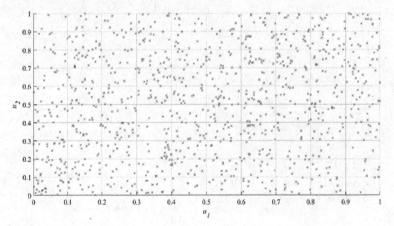

Fig. 5. Scatter plot with correlated ($\rho = 0.2$) random samples generated.

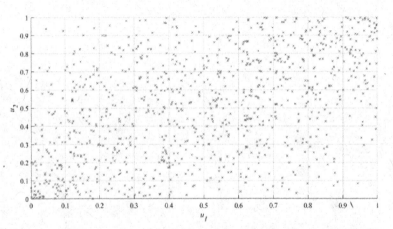

Fig. 6. Scatter plot with correlated ($\rho = 0.5$) random samples generated.

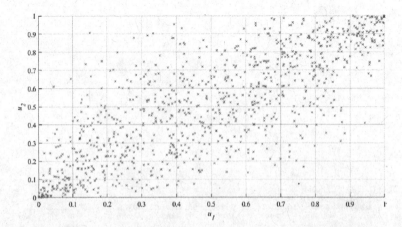

Fig. 7. Scatter plot with correlated ($\rho = 0.8$) random samples generated.

3 Copula Approach, Impacts at the System Level: Overhead Crane System

Before discussing the dependencies, we present an additional issue that has not been analyzed in previous contributions. The dependencies search relies on the series-parallel structure of each system (considered as an input for sensitivity analysis in our case), but it may be the case that the structure changes in the future and the conclusions highlighted in this paper are impacted. Therefore, we decide, before showing the impact of dependencies on the system, to visualize how the change of the series-parallel system structure from the current overhead crane system structure to full-parallel (all the overhead cranes in parallel) impacts the modelling procedure by assessing the impact on the *Loss Capacity* risk indicator as before in [12].

Table 2 describes consistent results for each value of η (more overhead cranes needed, less redundancy and greater risk impact; see Reference [9] for details), and Fig. 8 shows how the concavity of the projection changes in the risk profile depending on the configuration of the structure of the overhead crane system.

The *Loss Capacity* indicator defined in reference [9, eq. (8)], is a conditional expected value of the convolution product defined in [9, eq. (7)] from the same reference. When we change the structure of the overhead crane system, Y defined in [9, eq. (2)] as the production line capacity, remains the same distribution frequency, but the values are scaled by the total available loading capacity (not affected), and X defined in [9, eq. (5)] as the distribution function of the loading capacity of the overhead crane system, is the impacted variable. Figure 8 shows a particular result; in the full-parallel structure scenario (comparing the scenario with the real structure system analyzed) the overhead crane system is more concentrated in fewer possible states.

As a result, in those possible states (if they are measured or included), the impact on the *Loss Capacity* indicator (conditional expected value) can be greater depending on the η value assigned (see interaction between both scenarios in Fig. 8 at $\eta = 93\%$) because when we increase the value of η, we force to measure all the possible states of the system and, as a consequence, all the area not measured before $\eta = 93\%$, is added afterwards.

Knowing the impact of the change of the series-parallel structure, we can assume that the *loss capacity* indicator measures the changes in the modelling in a coherent way, as we can also see in Reference [12] when analyzing how the data changes (sensitive variable), specifically by simulating the potential impacts when updating the system with new data. That said, the following discussed results and conclusions related to the impacts of dependencies will also remain consistent due to the change in the structure of the system.

Returning to the discussion on dependencies, the copula approach is a well-defined way to model, for instance, identical system or components (overhead cranes in our case) working in parallel with similar operational exploitation parameters and maintenance diagnostic and performance process (same manufacturer and exploitation environment), and in the following discussion, we describe why.

Now, extending the analysis at the system level and using the *Loss Capacity* indicator to measure impacts and a multivariate Gaussian copula to model dependencies, where the dimension d depends on the number of overhead cranes involved in the analysis, we

Table 2. Full parallel impact.

Scenario	η (%)	Base structure		Full-parallel	
		Capacity Loss (tons/year)	Sample Size	Capacity Loss (tons/year)	Sample Size
1	95	19830.9	202	26830.2	117
2	94	15809.6	205	19095.9	128
3	93	12926.1	211	13553.4	138
4	92	10161.8	224	8580.3	210
5	91	7730.1	232	4600.8	341
6	90	5499.6	294	2635.6	575
7	89	3827.6	384	1179.1	1395
8	88	2717.2	645	743.2	1652
9	87	1648.5	1111	419.2	2357
10	86	1161.6	1214	237.9	3705
11	85	782.2	1462	123.5	7269
12	80	146.1	3779	3.6	89053

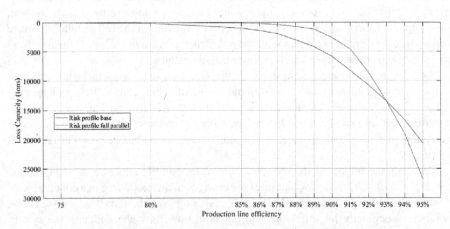

Fig. 8. Risk profile of the overhead crane system with a full parallel structure.

set all pairwise correlation parameters ρ, now a matrix with $d \times d$ dimension, to $\rho =$ 0.2, 0.5 and 0.8, respectively.

Figure 9 shows the impacts when we try to capture the dependencies in the system analyzed. Even with high redundancy in the system structure, when marginals are simulated considering the dependencies, the risk profile of the system changes.

Particularly interesting and remarkable in Fig. 9 and Table 3 (tabular view of the results), are the differences within correlated scenarios. The *Loss Capacity* indicator is a conditional expected value; therefore, rarely can capture the extreme values simulated

Table 3. Dependencies impacts.

Scenario	η (%)	Base structure		$\rho = 0.2$	
		Capacity Loss (tons/year)	Sample Size	Capacity Loss (tons/year)	Sample Size
1	95	19830.88	202	28360.49	316
2	94	15809.63	205	22755.94	353
3	93	12926.06	211	18838.37	380
4	92	10161.75	224	15024.07	411
5	91	7730.12	232	11653.31	436
6	90	5499.55	294	8504.73	580
7	89	3827.58	384	6247.86	856
8	88	2717.24	645	4683.82	1004
9	87	1648.54	1111	3226.29	1441
10	86	1161.59	1214	2352.45	1578
11	85	782.20	1462	1689.70	1834
		$\rho = 0.5$		$\rho = 0.8$	
		Capacity Loss (tons/year)	Sample Size	Capacity Loss (tons/year)	Sample Size
1	95	28502.58	557	28721.84	730
2	94	22944.94	585	23061.31	788
3	93	18978.60	615	19082.23	809
4	92	15128.58	647	15314.00	856
5	91	11725.16	683	11908.94	907
6	90	8716.29	907	8852.07	1127
7	89	6375.80	1201	6458.66	1453
8	88	4803.00	1445	4901.25	1844
9	87	3308.12	1930	3403.50	2525
10	86	2412.90	2066	2500.49	2792
11	85	1720.41	2334	1797.46	3173

and measure the real differences between the correlated scenarios, but as Table 3 shows, the variance is higher when the pairwise correlation increases (see sample size values needed to estimate an accurate *Loss Capacity* indicator).

So far in this section, the impact of considering dependencies between marginals of degradation data at system level is visible. The main impact is due to the change in methodology. The results achieved show a strong statement related with the modelling process; however, the small the dependencies are, the impact on the system analyzed is perceptible.

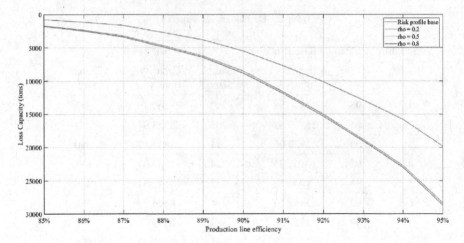

Fig. 9. Dependencies impact on Loss Capacity indicator.

4 Conclusions

The main purpose of this paper is addressed because we challenge the assumption of dependencies in the degradation data of the overhead cranes, finding potential impacts on the modelling of marginals at component and system levels.

First, at the component level, when the correlation parameter ρ increases, the symmetric structure in the generated random values is more visible and the generated *TTF* values are also more aggregated, measuring the desired common failures between the components. As a consequence, if no dependencies are modelled, the simulation will remain independent. And second, at the system level, when the parameters of the pairwise correlation matrix parameters ρ increase, the *Loss Capacity* indicator (metric used to assess the impact) increases, although the greatest impact is due to the change in methodology, that is, between non-dependencies and whatever dependencies are.

Given the results achieved so far, copula theory is a robust and consistent approach to describe dependencies between historical degradation data of overhead cranes considered in the system, and the presented paper leaves the ground ready to analyze, in the next research step, the impact of actual dependencies (using the real data collected) on the model [8, 9].

Acknowledgement. The work has been financially supported by the Polish Ministry of Education and Science.

References

1. Villalonga, A., et al.: A decision-making framework for dynamic scheduling of cyber-physical production systems based on digital twins. Annu. Rev. Control. **51**, 357–373 (2021)
2. Zhu, W.: A spatial decision-making model of smart transportation and urban planning based on coupling principle and Internet of Things. Comput. Electr. Eng. **102**, 108222 (2022)

3. Jun, L., Jun, W.: Cloud computing based solution to decision making. Procedia Eng. **15**, 1822–1826 (2011)
4. Wong, P.-M., Chui, C.-K.: Cognitive engine for augmented human decision-making in manufacturing process control. J. Manuf. Syst. **65**, 115–129 (2022)
5. Dong, Y., Sun, C., Han, Y., Liu, Q.: Intelligent optimization: A novel framework to automatize multi-objective optimization of building daylighting and energy performances. J. Build. Eng. **43**, 102804 (2021)
6. Zimmermann, E., Mezgebe, T.T., El Haouzi, H.B.R.I.L., Thomas, P., Pannequin, R., Noyel, M.: Multicriteria decision-making method for scheduling problem based on smart batches and their quality prediction capability. Comput. Indust. **133**, 103549 (2021)
7. Jun, C., Lee, J.Y., Kim, B.H., Noh, S.D.: Automatized modeling of a human engineering simulation using Kinect. Robot. Comput.-Integrat. Manufact. **55**(Part B), 259–264 (2019)
8. Szpytko, J., Salgado Duarte, Y.: Integrated maintenance platform for critical cranes under operation: Database for maintenance purposes. In: 4th IFAC Workshop on Advanced Maintenance Engineering, Services, and Technologies, Cambridge (2020)
9. Szpytko, J., Salgado Duarte, Y.: Exploitation efficiency system of crane based on risk management. In: Proceeding of the International Conference on Innovative Intelligent Industrial Production and Logistics, IN4PL 2020, 2–4 November 2020 (2020)
10. Sun, F., Fangyou, F., Liao, H., Dan, X.: Analysis of multivariate-dependent accelerated degradation data using a random-effect general Wiener process and D-vine Copula. Reliab. Eng. Syst. Saf. **204**, 107168 (2020)
11. Qifa, X., Fan, Z., Jia, W., Jiang, C.: Fault detection of wind turbines via multivariate process monitoring based on vine copulas. Renewab. Energy **161**, 939–955 (2020)
12. Szpytko, J., Salgado Duarte, Y.: Technical devices degradation self-analysis for self-maintenance strategy: Crane case study. In: Proceedings of INCOM 2021, June 2021, 17th IFAC Symposium on Information Control Problems in Manufacturing (2021)

Design of Ambient Conditions Control Capability in Retail

Jānis Grabis[1]([⊠]) [iD], Kristina Jegorova[2], and Krišjānis Pinka[1]

[1] Department of Management Information Technology, Riga Technical University, Kalku 1, Riga, Latvia
{grabis,krisjanis.pinka}@rtu.lv
[2] Baltech Study Center, Riga, Latvia

Abstract. The ambient conditions have profound impact on customer satisfaction. The paper proposes a systematic approach to control the ambient conditions at retail stores to maximize sales performance. The ambient conditions control solution is developed using the Capability Driven Development method, which is suitable for development of adaptive systems. The problem domain model defining the pertinent concepts is created and used to configure the adaptive solution. The model also quantifies relationships among the ambient conditions and the sales performance. The relationships are derived using the case data provided by a large retail chain. The adaptive solution is implemented on the basis of a model driven capability delivery platform. The platform is used to monitor the ambient conditions in retail stores, to evaluate a need for improving the conditions as well as to enact improvement by passing them over to a building management system.

Keywords: Ambient conditions · IoT · Retail · Capability

1 Introduction

The ambient conditions such as temperature, air quality, noise and odor have profound impact on customer satisfaction, and there are several ways to measure the customer responses such as duration of stay, money spend and return [1]. Modern computing and data processing technologies provide opportunities for measuring and improving the ambient conditions. Internet of Things (IoT) is one the technologies allowing to measure conditions at retailing facilities and data analytics processes these measurements to suggest solutions for improving the customer satisfaction. IoT helps businesses to harness and to process data to improve operations and to increase the customer satisfaction [2]. According to the measurements, the ambient conditions can be adapted to achieve desired customer response.

However, deployment of IoT devices and supporting data analytical solutions is a complex endeavorment and requires sophisticated technological platforms [3]. The solution should be setup-up according to the results of data analysis and continuously operated to monitor conditions at retailing facilities and to enact improvements. This paper proposes to use capability driven development (CDD) [4] to design and to deploy

A. Smirnov et al. (Eds.): IN4PL 2020/IN4PL 2021, CCIS 1855, pp. 36–49, 2023.
https://doi.org/10.1007/978-3-031-37228-5_3

an adaptive solution for management of ambient conditions at retail facilities. CDD is a method for design and delivery of adaptive solutions on the basis of data analysis. It is employed to define an ambient conditions control capability. Capabilities are defined as an ability to deliver business services in volatile environments. The capability driven approach uses enterprise modeling techniques to capture the impact of contextual information on business service execution and to adapt the capability delivery according to the business performance and context. The models developed are used to configure information systems supporting capability delivery.

The objective of this paper is to design a solution for adaptive control of the ambient conditions at retail facilities by using the CDD method and its supporting tools. The solution consists of the capability model, context processing models and implementation. The capability model formally describes the problem domain. The context processing models mathematically define dependence of the customer response on the ambient conditions. These models are derived from statistical data analysis of data accumulated at a large retail chain. The implementation is performed in a model driven manner according to the capability model by configuring the capability delivery platform [5]. The paper extends the initial work on identification of relations among the ambient conditions and the customer response [6]. The contribution of this paper is to provide a systematic approach for designing and implementing the adaptive ambient conditions control solutions.

The rest of the paper is structured as follows. Background information on ambient conditions management and capability driven development is provided in Sect. 2. The ambient conditions control capability is designed in Sect. 3. Section 4 describes platform based implementation of the capability delivery solution. Section 5 concludes.

2   Background

The ambient conditions management capability is design using the CDD method. This section reviews selected existing solutions for ambient conditions management and briefly describes the key concepts of capability driven development.

2.1   Ambient Conditions Management

There is a variety of variables characterizing ambient conditions and customer satisfaction. These can be classified as external, general interior, layout and design, point-of-purchase and decoration as well as human variables, and they affect customer enjoyment, time at store, items examined, information acquired, purchases and satisfaction [7]. Many of the general interior variables can be measured using IoT devices [8]. IoT can also be used to appraise customer satisfaction (i.e., duration of the stay at store) [9] while point-sales systems and enterprise resources planning systems record hard data on purchases.

The sensory data are used to control Heating, Ventilation and Air-conditioning (HVAC) devices and optimization of their operational parameters are essential to achieve cost-efficiency [10]. Much of the existing research focuses on optimization and adaptation of environmental parameters to control HVAC units or ambient conditions [11,

12] though the direct link to customer satisfaction is missing if measured by financial returns (e.g., purchases) in particular.

Several recent works address technical aspects of IoT based control of the ambient conditions. The need to interpret measurements received from sensors is emphasized [13]. The measurements are combined to define indoor ventilation states, and this information is used to generate user alerts and to control the ventilation rate. Handling of emergency events is another application where real-time decisions are made to control HVAC and refrigeration systems [14]. A centralized event stream processing engine based solution is replaced with an IoT edge solution to expedite decision-making.

The analysis of the existing work suggests that there is a need to strengthen integration among the ambient conditions management and analysis of customer response. This aspect is addressed by an integrated ambient conditions control approach outlined in Fig. 1. The ambient conditions or environment are measured using IoT devices. The customer response is captured in a point-of-sales system (POS), i.e. higher customer satisfaction with the ambient conditions must result as increased sales. The environment and customer response data are merged and processed using an analytical data integration platform. The platform instructs a building management system (BMS) to improve the ambient conditions. The data integration might help to optimize operations of the BMS and HVAC with respect to the sales performance and to devise dynamic pricing strategies to maximize sales in relation to the ambient conditions if these cannot be changed with ease.

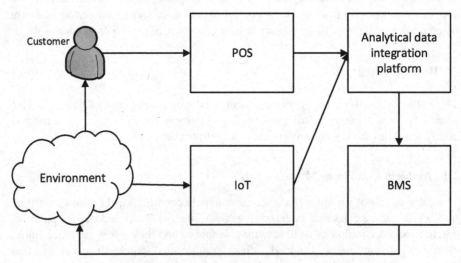

Fig. 1. The overall approach to integrated ambient conditions control.

2.2 Capability Driven Development

The CDD method is a method suited for development of data-driven adaptive information systems. Capabilities are defined as an ability to deliver business services in volatile environments. The capability driven approach uses enterprise modeling techniques to capture the impact of contextual information on business service execution and to adapt the capability delivery according to the business performance and context. The models developed are used to configure information systems supporting capability delivery.

The key concepts of the CDD meta-model [15] are shown Fig. 2. Goals are business objectives the capability allows to achieve. They are measured by Key Performance Indicators (KPI). The context elements are used to describe the relevant environment factors affecting the capability delivery and they drive decision-making of adaptations need to ensure that the goals are achieved. The context elements take values from a context range and jointly define a context set (not shown in the figure) describing the area of capability suitability. The context is measured using measurable properties, which are actual observations of some phenomena.

The service element specifies a capability delivery solution. The capability model does not model the whole delivery solution but only focuses on context dependent and adaptive features. The delivery solution is designed and implemented following the organization and platform specific engineering process. In this case, the capability delivery service is BMS. In order to ensure that capability is delivered as expected in different contextual situations, adjustments are used to adapt capability delivery. The adjustments take context data and KPI as input and evaluate potential changes in capability delivery. They are also used to implement complex context-dependent decision-making logics. The capability designs are aimed to be reusable across organizations. The reusable components are represented by patterns. The patterns provide solutions to capability design and delivery problems observed in similar contexts.

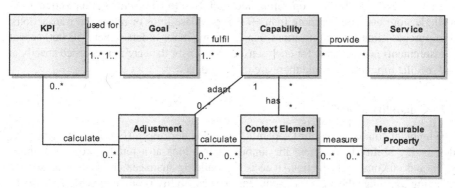

Fig. 2. Key concepts the capability driven development.

3 Capability Design

The ambient conditions control capability is designed. The relevant concepts are identified from the literature review and the retail chain case study.

3.1 Motivational Case

The ambient conditions control capability is design for a case provided by a large retail chain (more than 2000 stores and 30.000 employees), which have accumulated sensor measurements in their stores are well as sales data [16]. The company aims to interpret the effect of the ambient conditions at the stores on customer behaviour [16]. The main question for the analysis is about the effect of lighting conditions, temperature and humidity on the customer basket size. That involves determining thresholds for unfavourable ambient conditions. The company also expects to have a technological solution in the form of a decision support system that can analyse the IoT data along with the transactions in the store. The sensor data provided include measurements of air quality (higher values correspond to worse air quality), humidity, lighting and temperature. These can be used to control the affective and sensory aspects of customer satisfaction. All customer transactions are recorded and the following sales performance measurements are considered in this investigation:

- Number of items (N) – number of different products purchased by a customer in one store visit (i.e., number of items in shopping basket);
- Weight of purchases (W) – weight of all products purchased by a customer in one store visit;
- Quantity of items (Q) – quantity of items of all products (summed across all types of products) purchased by a customer in one store visit.

Historical data are used to analyzed relations among the customer response and the ambient conditions. The data are gathered over the period from February 25th, 2019 till March 3rd, 2019 with store's operating hours 8:00 am to 10:00 pm. The data come from a single store and contain more than 60 000 purchase lines or registered transactions. The purchase lines belong to more than 7000 purchase orders. Over 150 000 sensor measurements are available for each sensor. The sensor data are not recorded strictly at the specific time intervals and there are missing data.

3.2 Capability Model

The ambient conditions control capability model is developed (Fig. 3.). The capability defines the ability to maintain the ambient conditions at a retail store to maximize sales and customer satisfaction. It uses the building management system as service allowing to change the ambient conditions. The capability is ought to achieve the goals of increasing sales and proving enjoyable customer experience. Additionally, the goal to limit crowding is added to represent social distancing rules. These goals are measured by suitable KPIs. The KPIs are derived from the measures used in the case study. KPI2-KPI4 are extracted from the POS system in real-time. The goals are mutually contradicting and the control of ambient conditions is a multi-objective search problem.

The measurable properties are also determined according to the sensory data available in the case study and these primarily are humidity, temperature, air quality and lightning sensors. These are used to evaluate corresponding context elements. The context elements can be expressed as numerical values or categorical values and they have clear business interpretation to drive adaptation of the capability delivery. The afore-mentioned context elements can be evaluated in a relatively straight-forward manner. The customer number context element on the other hand is evaluated out of several measurable properties to account for potential irregularities, and analysis of customer movement video stream requires a relatively complex processing.

The adjustments define adaptions to be invoked in response to changes in the context or unsatisfactory performance. The primary adjustment is Regulate environment settings. It uses the context elements and KPI as inputs and determines the necessary changes in the ambient conditions. The adjustment has a triggering condition and an implementation. The triggering condition specifies context situations the adjustment should be invoked. The implementation specifies the context and performance dependent adaptation logics. From the implementation view-point, the adjustment invokes suitable actuators of the BMS to change the ambient conditions. The Regulate environment settings interacts with the BMS to change operating parameters of HVAC devices and adjusts lighting. The Regulate customer flow adjustment uses information about the number of customers to limit customer access to the store if the Customer per square meter KPI is not satisfied.

The capability model provides a clear and reusable representation of the concepts pertinent to the ambient conditions control. It is used to configure the capability delivery solution as described in Sect. 4.

3.3   Context Processing

The capability model defines data and information needs for adjustment of capability delivery according to the changes in context. Values of the context elements are calculated from the measurable properties. The statistical data are analyzed to elaborate a model for calculation of the context elements. A regression model was fitted to characterize relations between the ambient conditions and sales [6]. However, the model had relatively low explanatory capability due to various other unknown factors affecting sales.

Therefore, the sensor measurements are factorized in quintiles of equal number of observations and dependence of the number of items purchased on the quantiles of the ambient conditions is analyzed (Fig. 4). The analysis suggests that the number of items purchased decreases if the air quality is low. The number of items purchased is by approximately 50% smaller in the 5th quintile than in the 2nd quintile. The relative decline of the number of items purchased in the 1st quintile (the best air quality) can be explained by interactions between the air quality and hour of the day factors. It can also be used as guidance to reduce HVAC power without adverse effect on sales. The number of items purchased is relatively stable according to the humidity factor in all quintiles but the fifth. Improved lighting gradually increases the number of items purchased. Concerning the temperature, the customers dot not like either too cold or hot conditions. The number of items purchased is the largest if temperature is in the fourth quintile.

These observations are used to define the context element and to formulate implement adjustments defined in the capability model. This is illustrated using the Air quality level context element and the Regulate environmental settings adjustment.

The Carbon dioxide measurable property is used to evaluate the Air quality level context element:

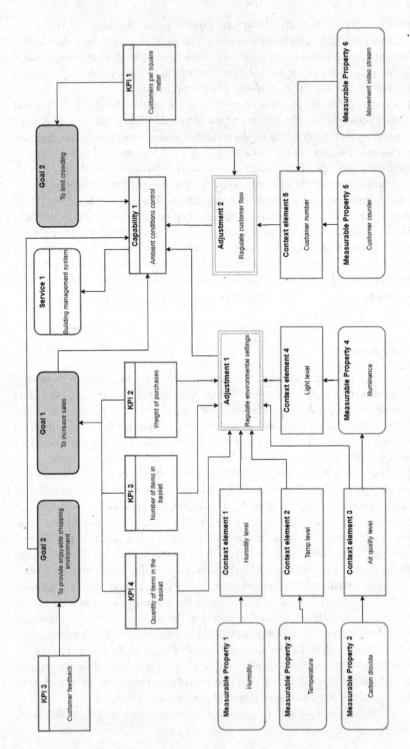

Fig. 3. The ambient conditions control capability model.

```
               CarbonDioxide = "Normal"
if CarbonDioxide < 264 then AirQualityLevel = "Too low"
   if CarbonDioxide > 283 AND CarbonDioxide< 298 then
               AirQualityLevel = "Optimal"
  if CarbonDioxide < 120 then AirQualityLevel = "Too low"
 if CarbonDioxide > 316 then AirQualityLevel = "Too high"
```

The partial definition of the Regulate Environmental Settings adjustment is:

```
if AirQualityLevel = "Too high" then InvokeBMS(Increase
               HVAC power)
```

InvokeBMS (Increase HVAC power) is an abstract function calling the BMS to improve the air quality. This abstract function is specified during the implementation of the ambient conditions control solution.

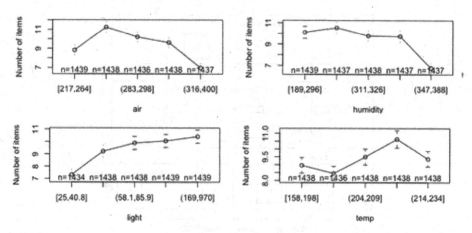

Fig. 4. The average number of items N according to the quintile of sensory measurements [6].

4 Implementation

The adaptive ambient conditions control solution is implemented using a capability delivery platform also referred as to the BaSeCaaS platform [5]. The platform is configured according to the capability model and the context processing models. It continuously receives data from IoT sensors, processes these data and invokes the building management system to alter the ambient conditions if needed.

4.1 Platform

The main components of the BaSeCaaS platform are shown in Fig. 5. Stream processing units K_m are responsible for receiving raw data from data providers (1) and handling internal data streams. A dedicated unit is created for every data stream representing individual measurable properties and context elements. The archiving jobs store the data in persistence storage and evaluation jobs use the raw data to evaluate the ambient conditions and the evaluation results are sent to internal stream processing (4), where they are forwarded for evaluation by triggering jobs used to invoke improvement actions (6). If triggering conditions are met (7), an improvement action is generated and posted to BMS (8, 9). All potentially computationally intensive tasks are executed in dedicated containers in a cluster to ensure high performance. The stream processing is implemented using Apache Kafka streaming platform. The evaluation jobs are built using the Apache Spark big data analytics engine and the adaption engine is based on Docker containers. The infrastructure is provided using CloudStack cloud infrastructure tools.

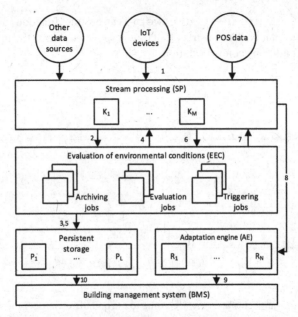

Fig. 5. Components of IoT data analytics platform [6].

There are various alternatives to the proposed platform and comprehensive comparison is beyond the scope of this paper. The main advantages of the platform are the use of open technologies, ability to integrate various data providers, decoupling of information requirements from data supply and separation of IoT analytics from the core BMS system. The decoupling allows to setup the system in various stores in a large chain, where different types of sensors might be used. The separation allows delegation of computationally intensive tasks to the platform without overloading BMS and using the IoT analytics with various types of BMS as well as other systems used in customer relationships management. The platform is horizontally scalable for application in large retail chains and can benefit from data exchange among the stores.

4.2 Setup

The capability model is used to configure the capability delivery platform. The entity model is created in the platform (Fig. 6). While the capability model is dimension-less, the entity model explicitly defines dimensions of the concepts defined in the capability model. The dimensions are determined by the entities. The entities represent specific objects characterized by measurable properties or context elements. The main entity is a retail store ("Veikals" in in the figure). The figure shows that the retail store belongs to retail chain and the store is divided into sections and aisles. This way the platform can be used to manage the ambient conditions at the store level or, for example, the section level if supported by the BMS. The entity model allows to attribute, for example, temperature measurements to a particular store or section.

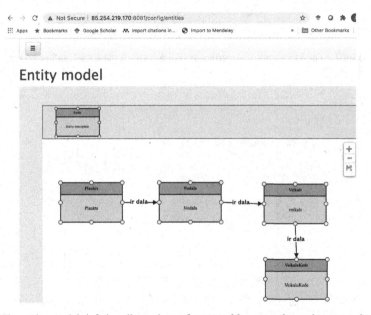

Fig. 6. The entity model defining dimensions of measurable properties and context elements.

The measurable properties are created in the platform according to the capability model (Fig. 7). The dimensions of the measurable properties are specified in the Schema section. Similarly, the context elements are also created. That includes definition of the schema (i.e., dimensions) and composition from the measurable properties. Giving the volatile data streams, raw data can aggregate and several data streams can be combined. As an example, Fig. 8 shows calculation the Air quality level context element. The calculation is defined according to the context processing results as described in Sect. 3.3. The sample calculation uses a set of rules to transform the raw measurements in the air quality levels.

The context data are used to evaluate the necessary adjustments. Figure 9 shows the Regulate environmental settings adjustment. The trigger composition defines context

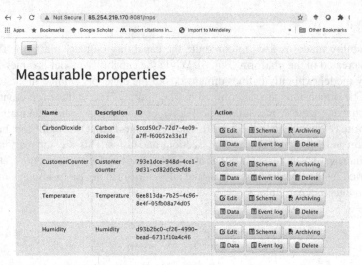

Fig. 7. The measurable properties as represented in the BaSeCaaS platform.

Fig. 8. The calculation of the Air quality level context element.

elements used to evaluate the need for adjustment. The need for adjustment is defined in the Trigger rule. In this case, the adjustment is triggered if the Air quality level context element is either Too high or Too low. The Implement section programmatically defines the adjustment, which invokes the BMS to change the ambient conditions.

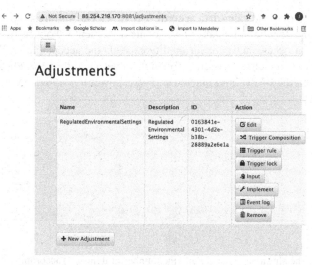

Fig. 9. The Regulate environmental settings adjustment.

The data stream processing jobs are created for the concepts in the capability models (Fig. 10). During the capability delivery (or run-time), the jobs are started and continuously run to process incoming data and perform the necessary adjustments.

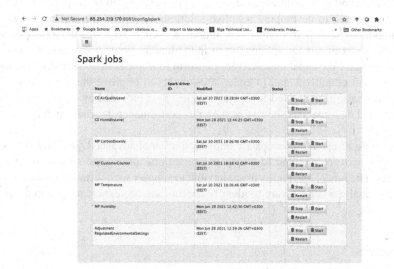

Fig. 10. The data processing jobs created in the BaSeCaaS platform.

4.3 Execution

Once the platform is configured it continuously measures the ambient conditions and evaluates the need for any adjustments. The monitoring example is shown in Fig. 11. It shows the air quality and sales data according to time. The air threshold line represents the lower bound for the Air quality level context element's `Too high` value. It can be observed that occasionally the air quality exceeds the acceptable level, i.e., the Air quality level context element assumes Too high value. Therefore, the adjustment should be triggered and the BMS should increase HVAC power to avoid decreased sales.

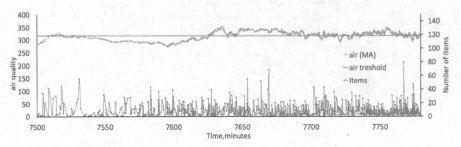

Fig. 11. The air quality changes and the number of items (N) according to time [6].

5   Conclusion

The ambient conditions control capability has been elaborated in the paper. It provides a formal approach to developing adaptive solutions to control the ambient conditions and to maximize sales performance. The model can be reused across the retail chain and it can also be extended for application to individual sections in the store. It has been used to configure the capability delivery platform to implement continuous monitoring of the ambient conditions and to enact adjustments to improve these conditions. The adjustments have been derived from the statistical data provided by a large retail chain. The statistical data analysis shows that the sales performance depends upon the ambient conditions.

The future research directions are implementation of advanced adjustments to maximize sales performance and to consider interactions among the various measurable properties. The model and platform are flexible to support such features. However, additional data analysis is necessary to identify appropriate context elements and to specify adjustments.

References

1. Bitner, M.J.: Servicescapes: The impact of physical surroundings on customers and employees. J. Mark. **56**(2), 57–71 (1992). https://doi.org/10.2307/1252042
2. Shrikanth, G.: The IoT Disruption. Dataquest **34**(12), 12–17 (2016)
3. Weyrich, M., Ebert, C.: Reference architectures for the internet of things. IEEE Softw. **33**(1), 112–116 (2016)
4. Sandkuhl, K., Stirna, J. (eds.): Capability Management in Digital Enterprises. Springer International Publishing, Cham (2018). https://doi.org/10.1007/978-3-319-90424-5

5. Kampars, J., Grabis, J.: Near Real-Time Big-Data Processing for Data Driven Applications. In: Proceedings - 2017 International Conference on Big Data Innovations and Applications, Innovate-Data 2017. pp. 35–42 (2018)
6. Grabis, J., Jegorova, K. Pinka, K.: IoT Data Analytics in Retail: Framework and Implementation. In: Proceedings of the International Conference on Innovative Intelligent Industrial Production and Logistics - Volume 1: IN4PL, pp. 93–100 (2020)
7. Turley, L.W., Milliman, R.E.: Atmospheric effects on shopping behavior: A review of the experimental evidence. J. Bus. Res. **49**(2), 193–211 (2000). https://doi.org/10.1016/S0148-2963(99)00010-7
8. Afolaranmi, S.O., et al.: Technology review: prototyping platforms for monitoring ambient conditions. Int. J. Environ. Health Res. **28**(3), 253–279 (2018). https://doi.org/10.1080/096 03123.2018.1468423
9. Patil, K.: Retail adoption of Internet of Things: applying TAM model. Int. Conf. Comput. Anal. Secur. Trends CAST **2016**, 404 (2017)
10. Woradechjumroen, D., et al.: Analysis of HVAC system oversizing in commercial buildings through field measurements. Energy Build. **69**, 131–143 (2014). https://doi.org/10.1016/j.enb uild.2013.10.015
11. Yang, S., et al.: Model predictive control with adaptive machine-learning-based model for building energy efficiency and comfort optimization. Appl. Energy. **271**, 115147 (2020). https://doi.org/10.1016/j.apenergy.2020.115147
12. Mazar, M.M., Rezaeizadeh, A.: Adaptive model predictive climate control of multi-unit buildings using weather forecast data. J. Build. Eng. **32**, 101449 (2020). https://doi.org/10.1016/j.jobe.2020.101449
13. Rastogi, K., Lohani, D.: An Internet of Things Framework to Forecast Indoor Air Quality Using Machine Learning. In: Thampi, S., Trajkovic, L., Li, KC., Das, S., Wozniak, M., Berretti, S. (eds) Machine Learning and Metaheuristics Algorithms, and Applications. SoMMA 2019. CCIS, vol 1203. Springer, Singapore (2020). https://doi.org/10.1007/978-981-15-4301-2_8
14. Karthikeyan, R.R., Raghu, B.: Design of event management system for smart retail stores with iot edge. Int. J. Eng. Trends Technol. **68**(11), 81–88 (2020). https://doi.org/10.14445/22315381/IJETT-V68I11P210
15. Bērziša, S., et al.: Capability driven development: an approach to designing digital enterprises. Bus. Inf. Syst. Eng. **57**(1), 15–25 (2015). https://doi.org/10.1007/s12599-014-0362-0
16. EDI Consortium. IoT in Retail (2019). https://edincubator.eu/2019/03/13/iot-in-retail/

HyDensity: A Hyper-Volume-Based Density Metric for Automatic Cluster Evaluation

Dylan Molinié[✉][iD], Kurosh Madani, and Abdennasser Chebira

LISSI Laboratory EA 3956, Université Paris-Est Créteil, Sénart-FB Institute of Technology, Campus de Sénart, 36-37 Rue Georges Charpak, 77567 Lieusaint, France
{dylan.molinie,kurosh.madani,abdennasser.chebira}@u-pec.fr

Abstract. As the systems produce ever more, becoming more and more complex and universal, the time spent on product validation narrows. The main alternative to the examination of every final product is a statistical study, with a confidence interval; another solution may be an automated validation, possibly integrated to the system's core. Some works addressed this topic using unsupervised learning, and especially clustering, but one challenge remains, that of supporting the information brought by these blind, automatized techniques. In this chapter, we address this problem of cluster validation using a data-driven metric, based on the hyper-volume theory, to estimate the clusters' density, so as to estimate how representative they are. We apply this metric to real industrial data, and show how resilient and representative this metric is, and we extend it to two other metrics from literature to provide a hybrid quantifier, which allows to automatically validate or reject a cluster. The accepted clusters can eventually be assimilated to true regions of the feature space, whose representativeness and meaningfulness are given by this hybrid quantifier.

Keywords: Unsupervised clustering · Knowledge extraction · Automatic characterization · Cluster density · Hyper-volume theory

1 Introduction

With the ever increasing amount of data generated, collected and finally stored, it becomes less and less feasible to correctly analyze them all. More data means higher processing-time, more energy, and, perhaps, lower interpretable results (but with a higher representiveness) [16]. This is not new though, and many policies have been developed to reduce the processing time: on-the-fly processing [1], dimensionality reduction [8], off-line processing [12], etc.; but the many more data now require innovative ways to help analyze them rapidly and accurately, to make the most of them.

In the past, the only one way to deal with data was by a manual expertize; this is generally more accurate (since an expert asserts every information drawn), but is long, expensive, and less and less feasible due to the increasing amount of information [3]. To compensate that, a new trend has been gaining ground for the four last decades with the emergence and generalization of the Machine Learning paradigm, and its related fields [4].

© The Author(s), under exclusive license to Springer Nature Switzerland AG 2023
A. Smirnov et al. (Eds.): IN4PL 2020/IN4PL 2021, CCIS 1855, pp. 50–69, 2023.
https://doi.org/10.1007/978-3-031-37228-5_4

The one which interests us the most here is Data Mining, a field of research which consists in digging into data so as to extract some sort of information from them, whether automatically (unsupervised learning) or driven by any sort of expert (supervised learning) [19]. Among a thousand tools, unsupervised clustering is one of the most useful to provide a first insight on the data, by automatically and blindly gathering them into compact and homogeneous groups, within which they share some similarities, but not from a group to another; notice that clustering can also be supervised, but is essentially used to find a fine border between already-known classes, and, to this end, requires much information upstream [11].

Actually, unsupervised clustering can help understand better the system, by discovering non-salient information or patterns, and can also be used to simplify the analysis of its data, by diminishing their number (while keeping their representativeness) or just acting as a pretreatment to rough out the system [13].

Nonetheless, the fact that unsupervised learning needs no reference to operate is both its strongest advantage and its greatest weakness. Indeed, if one already knows the system, there is no need to use such knowledge extraction tools, since that knowledge would already be accessible; such knowledge is often long and hard to build though, whence the recourse to unsupervised learning. However, operating in a blind context makes the validation harder, since there is no way to confirm the validity and representiveness of the extracted knowledge [20].

Focusing on unsupervised clustering only, blindly asserting a cluster is not an easy task, due to the absence of already-defined objectives to which compare the clusters to; however, the clusters must be asserted in some fashion, to estimate their quality (outliers, overlaps, etc.) and representativeness (clear, distinct and distant borders, and meaningful cluster, i.e., a cluster represents something real in the system) [28]. This estimation must be done in some fashion, and since there is no reference to which compare the clusters, it should be done by unsupervised and automatic metrics/quantifiers. This becomes clearly noticeable when dealing with real data, issued from complex and nonlinear systems, such as the industrial systems for instance; as an example, [5, 21] used clustering to identify the real behaviors of systems, and asserted the clusters through such metrics.

From literature, some of such quantifiers have been proposed so far to estimate the quality of the clusters, either based on their homogeneity, compactness, isolation, etc. In [22], we proposed a new metric, based on the hyper-volume theory so as to define and compute the "density" of n-dimensional groups of data, which serves as a compactness indicator. In this present chapter, we continue that work, by generalizing this metric and by applying it to real industrial data (related to Industry 4.0) so as to test it in real situations.

This chapter is organized as follows: Sect. 2 introduces the most common quantifiers from literature, Sect. 3 describes our methodology and the proposed density-based metric, Sect. 4 consists of a set of applications to show the benefit of using this metric, and Sect. 5 eventually concludes this chapter.

2 State-of-the-Art

This present work aims to assess the quality of groups of data, and especially that produced by unsupervised clustering. As a consequence, the very first matter to discuss is clustering *sensu stricto*. It is a powerful tool, which optimizes the inner organization of a dataset; its aim is to gather data into compact groups, whose inner-distances (i.e., the distance from a data to another inside the same group) should be as small as possible, whilst the outer-distances (i.e., the distance from a data of a given group to another in a different one) should be as large as possible. Therefore, the main challenge of unsupervised clustering is to automatically find the optimal borders between the groups of data, so as to minimize the sum of all the intra-cluster distances, whilst maximizing the sum of all the inter-cluster distances, both at the same time.

From a mathematical point of view, clustering is a matter of optimization; however, one must keep in mind that clustering should also have a real meaning: the clusters should represent the intrinsic properties of a system. As an example, clustering was used in [23] to identify the real behaviors (and possible failures) of real industrial systems, by gathering data with similar states over time.

As a mathematical optimizer, one may quite confidently trust a clustering algorithm, for it was designed to solve that optimization problem with great intelligence; of course, some are poorly or naively designed, but many carry out their task with brio. The quality and representativeness of the clusters depend on two major elements: the data complexity and the considered feature space.

Regarding the former, it is quite natural: some algorithms are elementary, and just linearly separate the data, which gives good results with simple and linearly separable datasets, but less with more complex and nonlinear ones.

Concerning the feature space, it is a little less evident: the feature space is a very important key parameter of clustering, since two data might be close to some extent in a given feature space, while also being very distant in another. Consider for instance a sheet of paper: if laid flat, two corners are very distant from one another, but if folded up on itself, the two corners are stuck to one another. This simple example illustrates the difference between a Cartesian space (flat sheet) and a folded up space (folded up sheet). The outputted clusters will manifestly not be the same in these two feature spaces.

Even tough that is not a rule by itself, a possible feature space for a real industrial system can be that whose basis is composed by its different sensors; the problem is that such system typically comprises hundreds of sensors, which implies that the corresponding feature space has a very large dimensionality, making greatly harder the interpretation of the clusters. As such, it is unfortunately not always easy to interpret the outputted results, for it is all about the considered feature space; it may be simple to understand why some data have been gathered when only two dimensions are considered, but that becomes more blurry as the dimensionality and the complexity in the data increase.

There exist many clustering algorithms (Neural Gases [18], Region Growing [25], Correlation Clustering [2], etc.), all with their advantages, drawbacks, and dedicated contexts. Since we will deal with real industrial data in this chapter, we will discuss some previous works conducted on that topic, in order to select an appropriate unsupervised clustering method for our experiments.

In [21], three methods were investigated and compared: the K-Means (KMs) [17], the Kernel K-Means (KKMs) [7] and the Self-Organizing Maps (SOMs) [14]; applied to real industrial data, the experiments showed that the SOMs achieved great accuracy in pointing out the real behaviors of the system, followed by the KKMs, and the KMs eventually provided the poorest results.

Following a similar methodology, [20] introduced the Bi-Level Self-Organizing Maps (BSOMs), a two-level clustering method based on the stratification of several SOMs; compared to the original SOMs and to the K-Means, the BSOMs seemed more resilient and robust in the identification of the system's behaviors. It is this last method that will be used in the rest of this chapter to build the clusters and eventually estimate their quality with the proposed metric.

When only considering unsupervised clustering algorithms, their common problem is the validation of the outputted clusters; indeed, in the absence of reference, how to estimate the quality and representativeness of a cluster? Several works have addressed this question, by proposing data-driven metrics, quantifying how good is a cluster, in the sense of the considered metric (compactness, homogeneity, isolation, etc.). There exist two categories of indicators: that based on the ground truth, called "extrinsic metrics", and that which only use the data, assuming no previous knowledge, called "intrinsic metrics" [31]. In this chapter, we deal only with unsupervised tools, and assume we have access to as little information as possible, and thus we will only consider the second category.

The first metrics for cluster's quality evaluation were statistical: close to the spirit of clustering itself, the idea was to estimate how near the data within a cluster were, and how far from those of a different cluster they were. The first quantifier was proposed in [9] and is known as Dunn Index: its definition can roughly be the ratio between the minimal inter-cluster distance and the maximal inter-cluster distance; this metric is very simple, but not very representative of the clustering, since it only considers extremal values, and, as such, even with a perfect clustering except one outlier (such as a lone cluster overlapping another), the Dunn Index would be very low. To generalize it a little, [6] proposed the Davies-Bouldin Index, which acts very similarly, except that the minimum and maximum are replaced by means; the idea is, somehow, to average the Dunn Index computed for every pair of clusters, which allows to diminish the impact of an outlier. Finally, a third index was developed in [26], namely the Silhouette Coefficients, more sophisticated, more representative, but also very time-greedy, and hardly applicable to large datasets; these coefficients take into account every pair of data to estimate both their intra-cluster and inter-cluster distances and somehow average all of them and eventually propose a normalized value assessing both cluster's compactness and isolation.

For quite a long time, the Silhouette Coefficients served as the reference for cluster's quality estimation, and few additional works have addressed this problem; it is nonetheless worth mentioning [27] which proposed the Average Standard Deviation, a simple metric based on the computation of the standard deviation within any axis of the feature space, and then a mixture of some kind of all these standard deviations (minimum, maximum, mean, etc.). This metric is not representative of the isolation of the clusters, but indicates their compactness, and is very fast to compute, especially compared to the Silhouettes.

Finally, we proposed a metric based on the density of the clusters, introduced in the original conference paper [22] of which this present chapter consists in a fully revised version; its aims was to provide a definition of the density of n-dimensional groups of data. Several attempts were made to provide such definition, but most stuck to elementary concepts: cluster's span (maximal distance between two points within a cluster), maximal distance to the cluster's barycenter, neighborhood (adjacent data belong to the same cluster, and two clusters are distinct if they have no data distant of a least a certain value), etc. We proposed to stick to the definition of Physics, as the ratio between the number of items (thus data) and the "volume" of the cluster. To define such volume with n-dimensional data, we used the hyper-volume theory, which provides n-dimensional equivalent to the traditional 3D volumes (cube, sphere, etc.). This definition was applied to clusters, and helped characterize them, by attributing them a density score: the higher the denser. This metric proved to be very representative and indicated the very compact clusters, and the "problematic" ones. Nonetheless, it is quite sensitive to outliers, which may produce false positives.

3   Methodology

The core of this chapter is the automatic evaluation of groups of data, in order to provide some criterion indicating their are correctly built, well isolated, compact, dense, etc., and state whether a further refinement is needed or not. If a cluster obtains bad scores, it may be worth being reworked in some fashion (refinement, outliers removal, new clustering, etc.); on the contrary, if the indicators are good, the cluster should be assumed to be representative and meaningful, and, as such, should not be selected for further refinement.

This should be seen as a pretreatment for any algorithm which would rely on clustering as a first step. An example can be found with the Multi-Modeling of systems [29]: it consists in splitting a dynamic system into pieces and then propose local models, eventually connected in some fashion. The system splitting can be manually done, but clustering its feature space can be a good, cheaper and faster alternative: as an example, with a real industrial system, clustering may help point out and isolate its distinct regular states, which can be seen as its "behaviors". As a consequence, the multi-model would be a complex and dynamic combination of the behaviors of the system, which can serve several purposes, among which modeling, monitoring or even prediction.

In this chapter, we will consider three intrinsic metrics introduced in Sect. 2, namely the Average Standard Deviation (AvStd), the Silhouette Coefficients (SCs) and the proposed one, that based on the hyper-volume theory and the physical density, that we will refer to as Hyper-Density (HyDensity). Each method will be explained in detail, and will be used within Sect. 4.

In all the following, we will refer to the database as $\mathcal{D} = \{x_i\}_{i \in [1,N]}$ with $N = |\mathcal{D}| = \text{card}(\mathcal{D})$ the size of the database, and n the data dimensionality, to $\mathcal{C} = \{\mathcal{C}_k\}_{k \in [1,K]}$ the set of clusters, with K the total number of clusters, and to d as a mathematical distance.

3.1   Already-Existing Metrics

In this subsection, we detail two already existing metrics, namely the Silhouette Coefficients and the Average Standard Deviation, to which the proposed density-based metric will be compared for validation in the next section.

Silhouettes. [26]: these coefficients can be seen as an evolution of the Davies-Bouldin Index, which is itself an ameliorated version of the older Dunn Index. The idea is similar for all three: estimate how close the data within a cluster are, and how distant the data from different clusters are. The Dunn Index only considers the extremal values, and is thus lowly representative, since easily confused by outliers; notice there is one unique score for the whole clustering. Similarly, the Davies-Bouldin Index provides a unique score for a full set of clusters, but it considers the mean interactions between each, and, as such, it averages the outliers. Finally, that which interests us the most, the Silhouette Coefficients (or just Silhouettes) are a dynamic comparison between any pair of data; this comparison is exhaustive, accurate, but also long, since the number of pairs is quadratic with respect to the number of data. There is one Silhouette Coefficient per pair of data, and the final score of the clustering is given by a mixture of any kind of all these coefficients. They are obtained in three steps:

1. For any data x_i, compute its average distance $\text{avg}(x_i)$ to any of its neighbors in the same cluster $\mathcal{C}_k$ (1); that measures the compactness of the clusters, i.e., if the data contained within are close from one another: the lower, the more compact, with 0 the best case (data overlay).

$$\forall x_i \in \mathcal{C}_k, \ \text{avg}(x_i) = \frac{1}{|\mathcal{C}_k| - 1} \sum_{x_j \in \mathcal{C}_k \backslash \{x_i\}} \text{d}(x_i, x_j) \qquad (1)$$

2. For every different cluster $\mathcal{C}_{k'}, _{k' \neq k}$, compute the mean distance between x_i and any data belonging to $\mathcal{C}_{k'}$: the minimal value is the dissimilarity score $\text{dis}(x_i)$ of x_i (2); that represents the isolation of the clusters, i.e., if the data of a given cluster are far from that of the other clusters: the higher, the more distant and, thus, the better (clear borders), with 0 the worst case.

$$\forall x_i \in \mathcal{C}_k, \ \text{dis}(x_i) = \min_{\substack{k' \in [\![1,K]\!] \\ k' \neq k}} \left\{ \frac{1}{|\mathcal{C}_{k'}|} \sum_{x_j \in \mathcal{C}_{k'}} \text{d}(x_i, x_j) \right\} \qquad (2)$$

3. The Silhouette Coefficient $\text{sil}(x_i)$ of x_i is finally obtained by subtracting the average distance $\text{avg}(x_i)$ from the dissimilarity $\text{dis}(x_i)$, and by dividing this value by the maximum among both indexes (3).

$$\forall x_i \in \mathcal{C}_k, \ \text{sil}(x_i) = \frac{\text{dis}(x_i) - \text{avg}(x_i)}{\max\{\text{dis}(x_i), \text{avg}(x_i)\}} \qquad (3)$$

A Silhouette measures how correctly a data is classified; it can somehow be interpreted as a regulated dissimilarity measure, reduced by the average distance as a penalty: for a given cluster, this measure is higher if the data contained within are near from each other (avg), whilst being far from that of the other clusters (dis), and vice-versa. The division by the maximum among the two scores has a normalization purpose, so as to bring the Silhouettes in the interval $[-1, +1]$; this eases the interpretation: -1 means x_i is closer to the data of another cluster than its own, and $+1$ means x_i overlays its same cluster's neighbors and is far from the other clusters; as such, the closer to $+1$, the better.

AvStd. [27]: when dealing with statistics, the notion of mathematical moments should spontaneously come in mind, and especially the mean and variance; they are the two most common tools to study a dataset, to inform the user about its inner organization [30]. In particular, the standard deviation informs on data scattering, to know how closely centered around their mean they are. This information is highly valuable, especially when one wants to evaluate the compactness of the group of data, but it unfortunately works only in one dimension. This is not totally true, since a standard deviation relies on a distance, which can easily be n-dimensional, but this indicator is poorly representative when considering several dimensions at the same time, since data may be scattered along an axis, but not along another; the true challenge is to find a way to apply the second mathematical moment to a basis with n axes. A piece of solution was proposed by [27], by computing the standard deviation in every dimension and eventually merging these n values in some fashion rather than directly computing it in that n-dimensional space. This simple change avoids some aberrations, since it is possible to detect that there is a problem along a given axis, but not along another. There are several ways to merge a set of values (the n standard deviations), and three were tested: the minimum, mean and maximum; the author came to the conclusion that their mean is generally the most representative choice, and provides a good (and very fast) estimate of cluster's quality, fairly enough for a quick validation, or with simple databases. This metric was named AvStd after Average Standard Deviation, for it uses the mean of the standard deviations, computed along each dimension. This metric diminishes the impact of the outliers, but is more an indicator of data scattering than anything else. Assuming the center m of a group of data $\mathcal{D}$ is given by (4), the standard deviation $\sigma^{(j)}$ along axis $j \in [\![1, n]\!]$ is defined by (5), and the AvStd measure of the dataset $\mathcal{D}$ is finally given by (6).

$$m = \frac{1}{|\mathcal{D}|} \sum_{x_i \in \mathcal{D}} x_i \tag{4}$$

$$\sigma^{(j)} = \frac{1}{|\mathcal{D}|} \sum_{x_i \in \mathcal{D}} \left(m^{(j)} - x_i^{(j)} \right)^2 \tag{5}$$

$$\text{AvStd} = \overline{\sigma} = \frac{1}{n} \sum_{i=1}^{n} \sigma^{(j)} \tag{6}$$

3.2   Proposed Metric: HyDensity

The notion of density can be found in different contexts: Physics, Chemistry, Human sciences, etc., each coming with its own definition. Nonetheless, it can widely be defined as the ratio between the number of things (mass, particles, people, etc.) and the space these items occupy (surface, volume, land, etc.) [10]. More specifically to Physics, to be a true density, this value must be divided by a reference, so as to normalize it and cancel its units [15,24]; otherwise, one should rather talk about specific mass.

In our case, the specific mass ρ' of a dataset can be given by the ratio between the number N of data instances contained within, and its volume V; the density ρ is that specific mass divided by a reference ρ_{ref}, as expressed by (7).

$$\rho' = \frac{N}{V} \quad \text{and} \quad \rho = \frac{\rho'}{\rho_{ref}} \tag{7}$$

The notion of volume is a little ambiguous though, since there is no universal definition for it in computer science. It may be the sum of the distances between any pair of data within, the maximal span of the cluster, or else the shape which covers all these data. Since we dealt with experimental data in [22], we rejected a too strict definition, and preferred to use a more traditional and more universal one. For these reasons, we decided to represent datasets by regular shapes, such as cubes or spheres, and then assimilate the cluster's volume to that of its surrounding and representative shape.

This works fine with 3 dimensions, since there is no ambiguity to define a volume there; but that becomes less common as dimensionality increases. A piece of solution may come along the hyper-volume theory, which provides n-dimension equivalents to the regular 3D volumes (tetrahedron, cube, prism, pyramid, sphere, etc.); for each, a n-dimension equivalent exists, even though it may be hard to mathematically formalize them all. The remaining challenge is to select that which represents best the data.

Nonetheless, two shapes stand out: the cube and sphere, for they are natural. Indeed, if one wants to fulfill a Cartesian space, leaving no uncovered areas, cubes should be considered; this is for instance the reason why the moving boxes are squared. Nevertheless, Nature does not really agree: its elementary shape is the sphere, as can be seen with the celestial bodies and atoms; it is very relevant due to its democratic aspect: any point on its surface is at the exact same distance from its center. Actually, if there is no particular reason to give a certain shape to something, a sphere-like one is probably the most universal choice.

In our previous work, we searched for the smallest hypersphere containing the whole dataset, and then assimilate their respective volumes. The volume of the n-hypersphere of radius r is given by (8), where Γ is the Gamma function.

$$V^{(n)}(r) = r^n V^{(n)}(r=1) = \frac{r^n . \pi^{n/2}}{\Gamma(\frac{n}{2}+1)} \tag{8}$$

Unfortunately, a group of data is rarely perfectly regular, thus it remains to evaluate the radius r of that hypersphere; the most natural value may be the maximal distance separating two of its points, which can be seen as the cluster's span, but this is heavy to compute (complexity of $\mathcal{O}(N^2)$). Instead, we proposed to use an intermediate (but representative nonetheless) value for the radius: we preferred the maximal distance between any point and a reference (we chose the dataset's barycenter); this allows to reduce the complexity to $\mathcal{O}(N)$. The cluster's span corresponds to the true smallest

hypersphere containing the cluster, whilst the maximal radius provides an upper estimate of the cluster's volume, but is easier and faster to compute. Moreover, a cluster's
barycenter is essentially a region of influence, which only depends on the recorded
data: tomorrow, a data belonging to a given class could slightly differ from its historical
neighbors; therefore, an estimate by excess is not a so strong assumption in that case.
The radius r of cluster $C_k \subset D$, whose mean is m, is given by (9); the span s can be
estimated as the double of that radius r.

$$\forall C_k \subset D, \ r^{(mean)} = \max_{x_i \in C_k} \big\{ d(x_i, m) \big\} \tag{9}$$

Notice that this estimate is sensitive to outliers, since the radius is defined by the
most distant points from the center; to decrease the impact they may have, one may
identify several outermost points, and then compute their average.

The density metric estimates the compactness of a cluster, and thus its homogeneity:
the higher, the better. It may take any value between 0 and $+\infty$, thus it may be difficult
to interpret the results. As consequence, and similarly to the Silhouette Coefficients,
the idea is to normalize that value by a reference, which would bring back the density
measure into the standard interval of $[0, 1]$, with 0 the worst case, and 1 the best case.
A possible candidate may be the dataset's density itself, but a more judicious reference
is the maximal density found within the clusters, ensuring that the maximal normalized
value is 1.

Indeed, since this metric serves to characterize clusters, one may assume that at least
one of them is well-built and compact. This cluster can thus serve as a reference, and
its own density can be used as a candidate for ρ_{ref} in (7).

As a consequence, we finally define HyDensity (standing for Hyper-Volume-based
Density, or just Hyper-Density) as the normalized specific mass ρ'_k of cluster C_k, i.e.,
divided by the maximal of these specific masses among of the clusters, as given by (10).

$$\text{HyDensity}(C_k) = \rho_k = \frac{\rho'_k}{\max\limits_{\substack{k' \in [\![1,K]\!] \\ k' \neq k}} \{\rho'_{k'}\}} \tag{10}$$

Notice that, for comparison, we will also consider the hyper-sphere defined by the
real cluster's span, i.e., the maximal distance between any pair of its points, as defined
by (11).

$$\forall C_k \subset D, \ r^{(span)} = \frac{1}{2} \max_{x_i, x_j \in C_k} \{d(x_i, x_j)\} \tag{11}$$

Therefore, we define $\rho^{(mean)}$ the Hyper-Density based on $r^{(mean)}$, and $\rho^{(span)}$ that
which uses $r^{(span)}$ instead.

3.3 Hybridization of the Metrics

Following our works in [22] and [23], and with respect to all what have been said
concerning the three metrics discussed above (SCs, AvStd and HyDensity), we propose
a hybridized version of them, which uses the strength of each and overcomes their
respective weak spots.

Ironically, what a metric sees is often what another misses, and vice-versa; nevertheless, nothing prevents us from merging them within a decision tree. HyDensity informs on the density of a cluster, i.e., if its data are numerous and close from one another: if yes, it is probably compact and of good quality, but, on the contrary, a low score means the presence of outliers or of scattered data. AvStd indicates if the data are centered around their mean or if they spread over a large area; combined to HyDensity, it tells if a problematic cluster is only due to the presence of some outliers, or if it contains few, highly scattered data. Additionally, the Silhouettes inform on the cluster's isolation and homogeneity.

Both HyDensity and AvStd inform on the intrinsic quality of the dataset, i.e., if their data are compact and homogeneous, whilst the Silhouettes indicate if it is clearly distinguishable (separated) from the others. If a cluster is of good quality and distant from the others, a real group of data, with an intrinsic meaning (i.e., a true class), is detected. On the contrary, depending on the scores of the metrics, the cluster may be worth being reworked or just left alone for further usage. This hierarchy is summarized as a decision tree and presented as of Fig. 1.

To keep it clear and understandable, we will refer to this metric as HyDAS, for Hybridized Density-AvStd-Silhouettes-based metric.

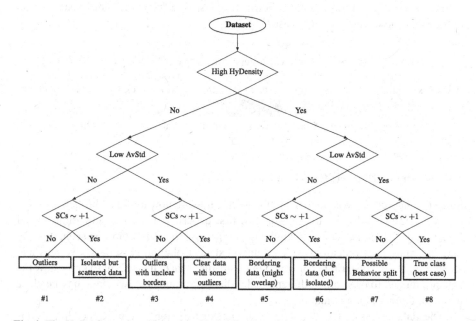

Fig. 1. The HyDAS metric, a hierarchical hybridization of the three considered metrics. The number #X below every leaf is the case number (for indexation).

4   Application to Industrial Data

In the original work [22], the cluster's density was assessed on academic datasets. These datasets were clustered using Self-Organizing Maps, and the proposed metric proved to be meaningful, accurate and helped identify both correct and problematic clusters. In this present chapter, we extend the experiments to real industrial data, we test the two radius estimations (max-to-mean and max-span) to compare their respective accuracy, we confront HyDensity with both AvStd and Silhouettes, and we assess the validity of the hybridized metric HyDAS.

Notice that the scoring of AvStd is the reverse of that of HyDensity and Silhouettes: for the latter, the higher the better, whilst it is the other way around for the former. In order to standardize the interpretation, we will consider the reverse of AvStd instead, so as to have the three metrics behave the same way: the higher the better. Moreover, similarly to HyDensity and to Silhouettes, having a normalized value is easier to interpret; for that reason, we divide by the maximal reversed value among all the clusters to obtain the final, normalized measure. By denoting the original AvStd measure of cluster $\mathcal{C}_k$ by $\overline{\sigma}'_k$, the corrected measure, that we use in all the following, is given by (12).

$$\overline{\sigma}_k^{-1} = \frac{1/\overline{\sigma}'_k}{\max_{\substack{k' \in [1,K] \\ k' \neq k}} \{1/\overline{\sigma}'_{k'}\}} \tag{12}$$

In all the following, we will refer to the identified clusters by a unique color; this color scheme is given as of Table 1. For instance, saying "clt1" or "blue cluster" refers to the exact same cluster in both cases.

Table 1. Clusters' color scheme.

Clusters	clt1	clt2	clt3	clt4	clt5	clt6	clt7	clt8	clt9
Colors									
	Blue	Orange	Green	Red	Purple	Pink	Gray	Olive	Cyan

4.1 Academic Dataset: Gaussian Distributions

Since the methodology is not trivial, it is worth showing how it works through a simple and didactic example; for this reason, we first experiment a set of low-dimensional Gaussian distributions. These small datasets represent the most common scenarios one may encounter when dealing with groups of data: isolation, closeness, overlaps and stretching. Since clustering is operated in the feature space, it is useful to know how the data are related to each other, dimension by dimension; indeed, two data may be close in one of them, but not in another.

The database is a set of twelve Gaussian distributions, along three dimensions (denoted as x, y and z); each set comprises 250 data and, for each dimension, is randomly attributed a mean between 0 and 1 and a standard deviation of 0.05. This database has been clustered using a BSOM, with 10 SOMs of size 3×3, resulting in seven nonempty clusters; the corresponding clustered database is depicted on Fig. 2, where the data are projected onto the three plans formed by any pair of the basis' axes, and where every color represents a unique cluster (consistent within the graphs). Notice that "[au]" stands for "Arbitrary Unit", for the intrinsic values and physical dimension of the axes do not matter here.

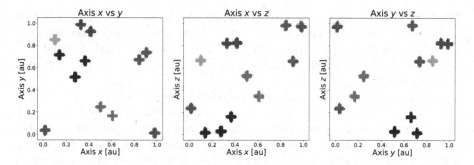

Fig. 2. The twelve Gaussian distributions, clustered by a 3×3 BSOM. (Color figure online)

On that figure, four types of clusters appear: 1) The quite close sets, but scattered though, not completely isolated from the other groups (blue); 2) The sets close in only one or two dimensions (orange and red); 3) The gathering of several sets, close and isolated in any dimension (green); 4) The lone sets, compact, dense and isolated (purple, brown and pink).

For all these clusters, their corresponding quantifiers are regrouped within Table 2. As a remainder, $\overline{\sigma}^{-1}$ is the normalized reversed AvStd, SCs are the mean Silhouette Coefficients, $\rho^{(mean)}$ is HyDensity using the mean-to-max distance as hypersphere's radius and $\rho^{(span)}$ is that using the maximal cluster's span, and HyDAS is the hybridized metric. All the quantifiers are normalized between 0 (worst) and 1 (best), with no physical dimension, and the HyDASes are a score from 1 to 8, corresponding to the different cases explained on Fig. 1. The results computed over the database have been added for comparison, with its SCs set to 0 by default (as there is one unique dataset, there is no dissimilarity measure, thus the Silhouettes can not by applied to a lone dataset).

Table 2. Normalized metrics of the Gaussian clusters.

Clusters	$\rho^{(mean)}$	$\rho^{(span)}$	$\overline{\sigma}^{-1}$	SCs	HyDAS (mean)	HyDAS (span)
dba	0.44	0.47	0.02	0.00	1	1
clt1	0.67	0.68	0.07	0.74	1	1
clt2	0.69	0.68	0.09	0.82	2	2
clt3	0.81	0.80	0.20	0.83	6	6
clt4	0.63	0.62	0.07	0.72	1	1
clt5	0.97	0.99	1.00	1.00	8	8
clt6	0.94	0.96	0.92	1.00	8	8
clt7	1.00	1.00	0.91	0.98	8	8

Beginning with the database, its quantifiers (with the exception of the SCs, which can not be computed there) achieved poor results, both regarding its HyDensty and its

AvStd: the data are scattered and lowly compact; this is not surprising though, with respect to the original database: there are many empty spaces, and the Gaussian sets are locally distributed, *ipso facto* leading to scattered (low $\overline{\sigma}^{-1}$) and stretched (low $\rho^{(mean/span)}$) data. It is with no surprise that the HyDAS scores are 1 in each case, indicating non-homogeneous data.

Regarding the clusters issued from the BSOM, there is much to say. First, as observed in the introduction of the database and of the clusters, that which comprise several local Gaussian sets, and that we consider as non-compact, got poor results. For instance, clt1 comprises three quite close, but not overlapping though, sets of data: there is an empty space between them, in every of the three dimensions. As a consequence, it is with no surprise that the three quantifiers got intermediate values, for it depends on the tolerance one accepts: the three sets are quite close, thus they may be considered as representatives of the same class; but they are scattered nonetheless, thus if the tolerance is low, this previous assertion should be rejected, and the cluster should be reworked. This is exactly that the HyDensities (mean and span alike) and the SCs tell us; notice that the corrected AvStd is very bad. Actually, it is the HyDensities and Silhouettes which are right there: the cluster is not perfect, but it may represent a unique class nonetheless, if the tolerance on the classification is reduced a little.

These observations work equally for clt2 and clt4, which share the same state than clt1: two Gaussian sets, not so distant but not touching tough, and quite correctly isolated from the others, thus they may be assimilated to unique classes if the tolerance is, anew, reduced, but if one wants a very accurate clustering, they should be reworked, as indicated by HyDAS. On the contrary, clt3 is a good example where HyDensity and the SCs overcame AvStd: indeed, the two former ones got very good results, but not the latter, although the green cluster comprises two very close sets, even overlapping in two of the three dimensions. This cluster is clearly isolated from the others, and is compact and dense, thus this assimilation is very likely a good thing there, even though AvStd tells not, which is probably a mistake here. Anyway, HyDAS gives a good score nonetheless, indicating the cluster may be worth being left alone for possible future usage.

Finally, the last clusters, i.e., the three correctly identified (one cluster for one set), namely clt5, clt6 and clt7, got the highest results, very close to 1 for every quantifier, which is actually true, since there is only one cluster for one unique set (thus class). For the three, HyDAS got the highest score, indicating that the clusters are of very good quality, compact, dense, homogeneous and isolated from the others, and should *ipso facto* be assimilated to true classes, which is actually true.

Notice that the two first columns of Table 2, i.e., the two versions of the HyDensity measure, got very close results; the max-to-mean version generally achieved slightly lower values, due to the estimation by excess of the hyper-sphere's volume, leading to a slightly lower density compared to a finer radius obtained with the maximal span. Here, in every case, both versions stated the exact same thing on every cluster, but the max-to-mean version is easier and faster to compute, thus this emphasizes that this version is a good candidate for the computation of the Hyper-Density of the clusters.

Finally, which are the conclusions drawable from this academic example? First, the metrics globally helped identify both correct and problematic datasets; when one cluster contained compact and homogeneous data, the three quantifiers got very high values (close to 1), indicating a correct clustering, and the HyDAS score confirmed that as well; on the contrary, when the data were scattered and/or stretched, the quantifiers got lower values, indicating non-compact groups of data, which is actually true, confirmed by the HyDAS scores (0 or 1). Moreover, AvStd mistook only once, whilst both HyDensity and the Silhouettes were correct with the seven clusters. The main conclusion may be that AvStd is a good estimation for validation, but the most trustful metrics are undoubtedly HyDensity and Silhouettes, but the first is greatly faster to compute, and, therefore, may be the first candidate for cluster characterization.

4.2   Real Industrial Dataset

Now that the metrics are assessed over an academic example, it is time to test them in real situation; to that purpose, we apply them to the automatic characterization of a blind clustering operated over real industrial data.

This work takes place in the European project HyperCOG, whose aim is to study the cognitive plant, with an Industry 4.0 vision. This project acts on two levers: a cyber-physical system which should link all the production units and control systems, so as to have an oversight on the whole plant, and control almost anything from anywhere; and highly intelligent tools and algorithms, able to analyze and interpret the evolution of the different systems and react in case of need. This book chapter focuses on the second part of the project, i.e., the cognitive and intelligent framework oriented toward the cognitive plant.

To test the works, several industrialists provided us with their factory's data; one of them is Solvay®, a chemical company developing and producing many specialty products. The database they provided comprises two hundreds of sensors, containing 105,120 samples each (recorded one per minute). Dealing with blind data is often tricky, thus we asked them to diminish the number of sensors, by pointing out the most representative ones, reducing the database to fifteen sensors of major importance (situated at key stages in the production chain); we will only consider these sensors to ease the interpretation. Five of them are depicted on Fig. 3; the ten others are not represented for the sake of clarity. Each sensor is compared to the others to show their interactions.

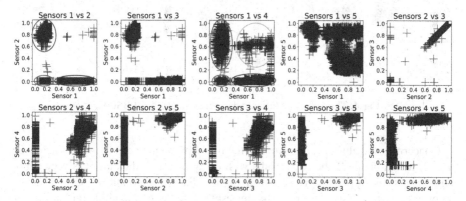

Fig. 3. Five sensors of the Solvay's database and their feature space's compact regions.

On the sub-figures, some groups of data appear: they are colored circled to stand them out. With respect to the work presented in [23], these different groups correspond to the real behaviors of the system, in the sense of its regular and expected states. In this chapter, we do not consider them this way, and we just want to know if these groups can be identified by unsupervised clustering, and validated using the quantifiers introduced in Sect. 3. The purpose is not so much isolating the clusters as estimating their intrinsic quality, in order to blindly state on their relevance and representativeness.

To that purpose, the database is clustered using a BSOM (comprising anew ten 3×3 SOMs), resulting in four nonempty clusters, all depicted on Fig. 4. Globally, the expected groups of data are identified as unique clusters, even though overlaps exist. For instance, the blue cluster mostly corresponds to the red circle on Fig. 3, but it also comprises the data of the yellow circle; that being said, this may have an intrinsic meaning by itself, which is actually true with respect to the closeness of the blue cluster in most of the dimensions.

The quantifiers of both database and clusters are regrouped within Table 3; anew, the database's Silhouettes are set to 0 as default values. The first thing to notice is its very low AvStd, whilst its densities (both versions) are quite high. Actually, the former result can be explained by the data scattering across all dimensions, as evidenced by the gaps between the Fig. 3's colored circles. The latter can be explained by the large number of data contained in a fixed hyper-volume; indeed, the data are repeating themselves through time, thus there are more points, although the feature space remains the same. This last remark may be a great drawback of HyDensity, since redundant samples might confuse it (even though that is also true for the two other metrics).

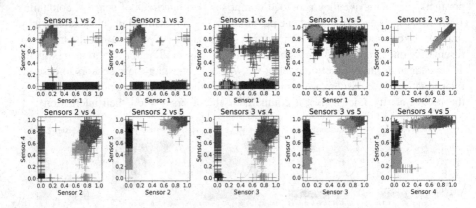

Fig. 4. The Solvay's clustered database using a 3×3 BSOM.

Concerning the clusters *sensu stricto*, the first thing to notice is the values achieved by clt2, which obtained the best results with every metric, indicating it is very dense and compact; its HyDAS score is 8, meaning it is likely representative of a real class. According to Fig. 4, this cluster mostly corresponds to the purple circle (at least a part of it). The classification as a unique class may be both right and wrong, depending on the tolerance one has on the separation of the system's behaviors. Here, the green and orange clusters actually correspond to two steps of a unique behavior: its initialization and its steady-state, respectively, thus if one wants a fine grain partitioning, having two clusters is acceptable, but maybe not with a coarser grain. In any case, the green cluster, clt3, also achieved honorable results, also obtaining a HyDAS score of 8, as clt2, indicating another unique class (actually the other part of the clt2's). Their inner quality is too high to not assimilate them as real classes on their own.

On the contrary, the two other clusters, clt1 and clt4, achieved poor results, with low HyDAS scores (1 and 2, respectively). Indeed, the blue cluster contains data close in some dimensions ("Sensors 1 vs 2" for instance), but not in others ("Sensors 2 vs 4" for instance), resulting in scattered data according to AvStd, whence its very low score. Moreover, due to the high proximity (almost overlaps) of the blue and red clusters in most dimensions, its Silhouette Coefficients are very low, and even negative, indicating a poor clustering; that being said, these bad results are not so much due to the proximity with another cluster as due to a real presence of several sub-classes within, fact that is pointed out by HyDensity, which achieved intermediate results, not so low than AvStd and the Silhouettes. In this present case, it is more a question of coarse clustering rather than true overlapping or mis-classification, fact that is detected by HyDensity only.

It is about the reverse that happens with clt4, for which HyDensity is low, but not AvStd and SCs (the last ones are even good). Actually, the cluster is quite meaningful, and representative to a real behavior of the system, but the low HyDensity score is due to the presence of outliers (borderline data), especially visible on "Sensors 2 vs 4" and "Sensors 3 vs 4", at values around 0.8 in abscissa, and 0 in ordinate for both. The small groups are distant from the cluster's core, greatly increasing the cluster's maximal intra-distance (span), decreasing *ipso facto* its Hyper-Density, whence the low values obtained. These small outliers may be worth being isolated, or, perhaps, purely removed, thing that SCs missed, but not AvStd nor HyDensity (and especially the max-to-mean variant).

Therefore, what can we draw from that experiment on real industrial data? First, the Silhouette Coefficients are very meaningful, but may sometimes be mistaken, cases when the two other metrics often indicated something else, and especially HyDensity. This last metric, the proposed one, proved to be meaningful in all of the encountered cases, and was never wrong. Moreover, the HyDAS scoring proved also to be resilient, and attributed low scores to issuing clusters, either due to the presence of outliers or due to another, close cluster.

Table 3. Normalized metrics of the Solvay's clusters.

Clusters	$\rho^{(mean)}$	$\rho^{(span)}$	$\overline{\sigma}^{-1}$	SCs	HyDAS (mean)	HyDAS (span)
dba	0.72	0.70	0.15	0.00	1	1
clt1	0.59	0.69	0.23	-0.21	1	1
clt2	1.00	1.00	1.00	1.00	8	8
clt3	0.87	0.84	0.86	0.87	8	8
clt4	0.42	0.55	0.62	0.80	2	2

5   Conclusion

In this chapter, we proposed Hyper-Density (HyDensity), a blind quantification metric for cluster validation, based on the Physics' definition of the relative density, i.e., the ratio of the specific mass of a body to its volume. As we operated in multi-dimensional spaces, we proposed to use the theory of the hyper-volumes, which defines multi-dimensional equivalents to the more traditional 3D volumes (cube, sphere, etc.); the proposed metric is therefore defined as the ratio of the number of data instances and their related volume, defined as the smallest hyper-sphere containing them all.

To that end, we first partitioned the database using unsupervised clustering; we chose BSOM, a clustering technique consisting in a projection of several Self-Organizing Maps onto a unique, final one. This method proved to be resilient in the identification of the behaviors of industrial systems.

We confronted HyDensity to two other metrics from literature, namely the Average Standard Deviation[1] and the Silhouette Coefficients. Additionally, we also proposed the Hybridized Density-AvStd-Silhouettes-based metric (HyDAS), a hybrid quantifier based on the three previous ones, specifically crafted so as to give a score to a group of data, and represent its quality and meaningfulness.

We first applied these metrics to an academic example consisting of several 3D Gaussian distributions to test how representative and trustful they are. Applied to the characterization of the clusters outputted by a BSOM, they proved to be meaningful and highlighted both correct and problematic clusters, even though AvStd was sometimes wrong, whilst the Silhouettes and HyDensity were rarely.

Once these quantifiers, and especially HyDensity, tested over this intuitive dataset to explain the results in detail, we applied them to real industrial data, provided by a partner involved in the HyperCOG project. After having clustered the database with a BSOM, the quantifiers were computed to automatically characterize the outputted results. They helped identify two problematic clusters (that which may be worth being reworked or split further) and two correct ones (real system's behaviors, thus the corresponding clusters should be left alone). Actually, we saw that the results' meaningfulness is more a matter of user's tolerance regarding the grain of the partitioning. HyDensity was always correct, but both AvStd and the Silhouettes confused at least once. That being said, this is not to say that this metric is a thousand times better than any other, but this strengthens the feeling that it is very representative and trustful in the characterization and identification of both correct and problematic clusters.

We also tested two ways to evaluate the smallest hyper-sphere containing all data: half the maximal distance between two of them, and the maximal distance between their mean and any of them. The former is slightly finer, but longer to compute; the results of both the academic and real databases showed that both versions led to close results in the computation of HyDensity, thus the mean-to-max version may be a perfectly acceptable candidate so as to speed up the algorithms, at the cost of a potential small sacrifice in accuracy.

Finally, the HyDAS metric showed to be a good indicator of cluster's quality, and of what to do according to its score, as detailed in the tree structure of Fig. 1. According

---

[1] Precisely, we used our revised, reversed version of it to standardize its interpretation.

to the studies, HyDensity appears to be the most trustful, then come the Silhouettes, and eventually AvStd, thus so should be the HyDAS's hierarchy, to organize the scores in ascending order of cluster's quality. In current version, AvStd is at the second place, thus more weight is put on it, which may confuse a little the scoring. That was made on purpose, since the Silhouettes are generally long to compute (or just impossible, as with a lone database for instance); putting them in the leaves of the hierarchy allows to remove them with ease if required, without changing the tree, so as to work only with HyDensity and AvStd.

As a summary, we introduced HyDensity, a density-based metric for automatic characterization of clusters, which proved to be accurate and resilient in most of the tested cases. Compared to AvStd and the Silhouettes, it showed to be superior to the former, and equivalent to the latter (or even superior), but has the great advantage of being greatly faster to compute. We also presented HyDAS, a hybrid score evaluating the state of the cluster and what to do with it to improve it, by just reading and comparing the three considered metrics.

One very interesting purpose of this metric may be the hierarchical characterization of clusters, by indicating the issuing ones, i.e., that which may be worth being reworked further, so as to obtain a finer clustering. It may therefore be used in a split-and-merge fashion so as to find back the real objective clusters, which can be very helpful in blind and unsupervised contexts in which very few things about the system are known.

Acknowledgements. This paper received funding from the European Union's Horizon 2020 research and innovation program under grant agreement No 869886 (project HyperCOG-869886). Authors would thank Solvay and especially Mr. Marc Legros for their fruitful discussions. Authors also wish to express their gratitude to the EU 2020 program for supporting the presented works.

References

1. Bavay, M., Fierz, C., Nitu, R.: Data access made easy: flexible, on the fly data standardization and processing. In: EGU General Assembly 2022, Vienna, Austria (May 2022). https://doi.org/10.5194/egusphere-egu22-8262,
2. Becker, H.: A survey of correlation clustering. In: Advanced Topics in Computational Learning Theory, pp. 1–10 (2005)
3. Ben-David, A., Frank, E.: Accuracy of machine learning models versus "hand crafted" expert systems - a credit scoring case study. Expert Syst. Appli. **36**(3, Part 1), 5264–5271 (2009). https://doi.org/10.1016/j.eswa.2008.06.071
4. Buchanan, B.: Can machine learning offer anything to expert systems? Mach. Learn. **4**, 251–254 (1989). https://doi.org/10.1007/BF00130712
5. Calvo-Bascones, P., Sanz-Bobi, M.A., Álvarez Tejedo, T.: Method for condition characterization of industrial components by dynamic discovering of their pattern behaviour. In: ESREL 2020 (November 2020)
6. Davies, D., Bouldin, D.: A cluster separation measure. IEEE Trans. Pattern Anal. Mach. Intell. PAMI **1**, 224–227 (1979). https://doi.org/10.1109/TPAMI.1979.4766909
7. Dhillon, I., Guan, Y., Kulis, B.: Kernel k-means, spectral clustering and normalized cuts. In: KDD-2004 - Proceedings of the Tenth ACM SIGKDD International Conference on Knowledge Discovery and Data Mining, pp. 551–556 (July 2004). https://doi.org/10.1145/1014052.1014118

8. Dong, H., Chen, X., Dusmanu, M., Larsson, V., Pollefeys, M., Stachniss, C.: Learning-based dimensionality reduction for computing compact and effective local feature descriptors (2022). https://doi.org/10.48550/ARXIV.2209.13586

9. Dunn, J.: Well-separated clusters and optimal fuzzy partitions. Cybern. Syst. **4**, 95–104 (1974). https://doi.org/10.1080/01969727408546059

10. Encyclopedia Britannica: Density. https://www.britannica.com/science/density, online (last update 02 February 2021). (Accessed 04 October 2022)

11. Ezugwu, A.E., et al.: A comprehensive survey of clustering algorithms: State-of-the-art machine learning applications, taxonomy, challenges, and future research prospects. Eng. Appl. Artif. Intell. **110**, 104743 (2022). https://doi.org/10.1016/j.engappai.2022.104743

12. Gan, Y., Dai, X., Li, D.: Off-line programming techniques for multirobot cooperation system. Int. J. Adv. Rob. Syst. **10**(7), 282 (2013). https://doi.org/10.5772/56506

13. Golalipour, K., Akbari, E., Hamidi, S.S., Lee, M., Enayatifar, R.: From clustering to clustering ensemble selection: A review. Eng. Appl. Artif. Intell. **104**, 104388 (2021). https://doi.org/10.1016/j.engappai.2021.104388

14. Kohonen, T.: Self-organized formation of topologically correct feature maps. Biol. Cybern. **43**(1), 59–69 (1982). https://doi.org/10.1007/BF00337288

15. Kriegel, H.P., Kröger, P., Sander, J., Zimek, A.: Density-based clustering. Wiley Interdisciplinary Rev. Data Mining Knowl. Dis. **1**(3), 231–240 (2011)

16. Lezoche, M.: Formalisation models and knowledge extraction: Application to heterogeneous data sources in the context of the Industry of the Future. Habilitation à diriger des recherches, Université de Lorraine (January 2021). https://hal.univ-lorraine.fr/tel-03178698

17. Lloyd, S.P.: Least squares quantization in pcm. IEEE Trans. Inf. Theory **28**, 129–136 (1982)

18. Martinetz, T., Schulten, K.: A "neural-gas" network learns topologies. Artifi. Neural Netw. **1**, 397–402 (1991)

19. Mikut, R., Reischl, M.: Data mining tools. Wiley Interdisciplinary Rev. Data Mining Knowl. Dis. **1**(5), 431–443 (2011)

20. Molinié, D., Madani, K.: Bsom: A two-level clustering method based on the efficient self-organizing maps. In: 6th International Conference on Control, Automation and Diagnosis (ICCAD) (July 2022), [Accepted but not published by 15 October 2022]

21. Molinié, D., Madani, K., Amarger, C.: Identifying the behaviors of an industrial plant: Application to industry 4.0. In: Proceedings of the 11th International Conference on Intelligent Data Acquisition and Advanced Computing Systems: Technology and Applications (IDAACS), vol. 2, pp. 802–807 (September 2021). https://doi.org/10.1109/IDAACS53288.2021.9661018

22. Molinié, D., Madani, K.: Characterizing n-dimension data clusters: A density-based metric for compactness and homogeneity evaluation. In: Proceedings of the 2nd International Conference on Innovative Intelligent Industrial Production and Logistics (IN4PL), vol. 1, pp. 13–24. INSTICC, SciTePress (October 2021). https://doi.org/10.5220/0010657500003062

23. Molinié, D., Madani, K., Amarger, V.: Clustering at the disposal of industry 4.0: Automatic extraction of plant behaviors. Sensors **22**(8) (2022). https://doi.org/10.3390/s22082939

24. National Aeronautics and Space Administration (NASA): Gas density. https://www.grc.nasa.gov/WWW/BGH/fluden.html, online, (last update 07 May 2021). (Accessed 04 October 2022)

25. Rabbani, T., Heuvel, F., Vosselman, G.: Segmentation of point clouds using smoothness constraint. In: International Archives of Photogrammetry, Remote Sensing and Spatial Information Sciences, vol. 36 (January 2006)

26. Rousseeuw, P.: Silhouettes: A graphical aid to the interpretation and validation of cluster analysis. J. Comput. Appl. Math. **20**, 53–65 (1987). https://doi.org/10.1016/0377-0427(87)90125-7

27. Rybnik, M.: Contribution to the modelling and the exploitation of hybrid multiple neural networks systems: application to intelligent processing of information. Ph.D. thesis, University Paris-Est XII, France (December 2004)
28. Shivakumar, A., Alfstad, T., Niet, T.: A clustering approach to improve spatial representation in water-energy-food models. Environ. Res. Lett. **16**(11), 114027 (2021)
29. Thiaw, L.: Identification of non linear dynamical system by neural networks and multiple models. Ph.D. thesis, University Paris-Est XII, France (2008), (in French)
30. Wan, X., Wang, W., Liu, J., Tong, T.: Estimating the sample mean and standard deviation from the sample size, median, range and/or interquartile range. BMC Med. Res. Methodol. **14**(1), 1–13 (2014). https://doi.org/10.1186/1471-2288-14-135
31. Wang, S., Yu, L., Li, C., Fu, C.-W., Heng, P.-A.: Learning from extrinsic and intrinsic supervisions for domain generalization. In: Vedaldi, A., Bischof, H., Brox, T., Frahm, J.-M. (eds.) ECCV 2020. LNCS, vol. 12354, pp. 159–176. Springer, Cham (2020). https://doi.org/10.1007/978-3-030-58545-7_10

Synchronizing Devices Using Asset Administration Shells

Stephan Schäfer, Dirk Schöttke[✉], Thomas Kämpfe, Oliver Lachmann, and Aaron Zielstorff

Hochschule für Technik und Wirtschaft (HTW) Berlin, 12459 Wilhelminenhofstraße 75A, Berlin, Germany
{Stephan.Schaefer,Dirk.Schoettke}@htw-berlin.de

Abstract. Flexible production systems are characterized by the fact, that they can be reconfigured at ever shorter intervals in order to respond to changing production processes in a time and cost-minimizing manner. Reconfiguring the existing system architecture consisting of process control systems and industrial controllers here referred to as Programmable Logical Controllers (PLCs), which communicate with each other via proprietary bus systems, requires considerable engineering efforts both at the field level of the PLC and at the control level. Therefore, this article shows a method of synchronizing PLCs with corresponding Asset Administration Shells (AASs), in which changing data within the PLC is automatically updated in the connected AAS using the Packaging Machine Language (PackML) standard to synchronize the processes. To use AAS in a production environment, infrastructure is needed, which is provided by the Open Source Eclipse BaSyx Framework. Therefore, this paper gives a brief insight into the required infrastructure components of the framework and ends with the presentation of a responsive Web GUI that can be used to monitor and control devices and plant segment.

Keywords: Asset Administration Shell · Digital twin · PackML

1 Introduction

In order to migrate existing plants into I4.0 plants with the desired flexibility, different approaches are possible in the implementation. At the IN4PL 2021 congress [22], the authors prepared this process of migration for the use case of type testing of thermal switches. The challenge of implementing the research project "OpenBasys 4.0" [17] and the possibility of generic preparation of digital representatives were discussed. Building on these foundations, the current paper discusses the use of the generated Asset Administration Shell. This concerns the possibility of synchronizing resources on the part of the controller via the generated Asset Administration Shell and the use of a generic frontend for the visualization of information from the Asset Administration Shell.

For better comprehensibility, an explanation of the essential terms and definitions, which are in the context of the implementation, is given first.

2 Asset

According to IEC TS 62443-1-1:2009 [12] an asset is an entity which is owned by or under the custodial duties of an organization, having either a perceived or actual value to the organization. [9, 12] . In other words, an asset is an entity in the real world, that requires a connection to an Industrie 4.0 solution [10].

It could be a physical or logical object that is owned or managed by an organization and that has an actual or perceived value to the organization. The standard primarily considers the use phase of such assets and the associated factory facilities, i.e. their design, construction, commissioning, operation and maintenance. Also, machines, products or controllers are considered as assets. For the identification, the standard uses identifiers according to ISO/TS 29002-5 [1]. Assets can also be identified via other identifiers (e.g. URI).

3 Digital Twin

In Industry Internet of Things Vocabulary [3] a digital twin is defined as a "digital model of one or more real world entities that is synchronized with those entities at a specified frequency and fidelity".

Fig. 1. Pallet and three dimensional model for mounting thermal switches.

According to Gardner [10] a digital twin is a digital representation of a real world entity or system. The implementation of a digital twin is an encapsulated software object or model that mirrors a unique physical object, process, organization, person or other abstraction. Data from multiple digital twins can be aggregated for a composite view across a number of real world entities, such as a power plant or a city, and their related processes. A digital twin concept requires at least four elements: digital model, linked data, identification and real-time monitoring capabilities.

According to Tao a digital twin, shows the following characteristics:

(1) Real-time reflection. Two spaces exist in digital twin, physical space and virtual space. The virtual space is the real reflection of the physical space, and it can keep ultra-high synchronization and fidelity with the physical space.
(2) Interaction and convergence. This characteristic can be explained from three aspects.
  (a) Interaction and convergence in physical space. Digital twin is a kind of full-flow, full-element, and full-service integration. So the data generated in various phases in physical space can connect with each other.

(b) Interaction and convergence between historical data and real-time data. Digital twin data is more comprehensive. It not only depends on expert knowledge but also collects data from all deployed systems in real time. Therefore, the data can be mined deeply and used more fully through the convergence.

(c) Interaction and convergence between physical space and virtual space. The physical space and virtual space are not isolated in digital twin [23].

4   Asset Administration Shells

According to [24] an Asset Administration Shell (AAS), as defined in the context of the Reference Architecture Model Industrie 4.0 (RAMI 4.0) [5], is a practical embodiment of a digital twin, and can be realized with the integration of operation technologies and information and communication technologies. AAS offer an inter-operable way to capture key information pertaining to assets, such as intrinsic properties, operational parameters, and technical functionalities, and to enable straightforward interaction over standardized, secure communication with other Industrie 4.0 components [24]. But the AAS goes beyond the typical digital twin in that essential features and properties such as its structure, behavior and interfaces are already standardized in the IEC 63278-1 [4]. This simplifies interoperability enormously. The standard facilitates cross-manufacturer interoperability for both intelligent and non-intelligent systems. AAS also represents a lifecycle model that can accompany the asset across manufacturers throughout its entire life-cycle to allow end-to-end value chains. A comprehensive introduction to the use of an AAS as a digital twin in the context of a service-badged architecture is given by [15]. There is also an introduction to a framework that enables the use of AAS as digital twins. We will return to this framework in Sect. 7.3.

4.1   Structure of the Asset Administration Shell

The structure of Asset Administration Shells can be derived from the following figure. An AAS consists of a header and body. The header contains information to uniquely identify the Asset Administration Shell. This identification can therefore also serve as a root entry point for an application programming interface (API) to browse for information and functionalities. The header contains also the identification of one or multiple assets that are described by the Asset Administration Shell. The header also indicates if these assets are asset types or asset instances. The body contains information about the asset(s) and describes functionalities that are associated with the asset(s) or the Asset Administration Shell. The information can concern asset type(s) and/ or asset instance(s). Thus, the body serves as the actual carrier of information and functionality.

According to the platform Industrie 4.0 an AAS includes Submodels, that are used to structure the information and functionality of an Asset Administration Shell into distinguishable parts. Each submodel refers to a well-defined domain or subject matter. Submodels can become standardized and thus become submodels types. An Asset Administration Shell of an asset can refer to a submodel type, causing this submodel instance to feature a guaranteed set of properties and functions [8]. The following class diagram (Fig. 3) provides a detailed impression of the structure of the AAS.

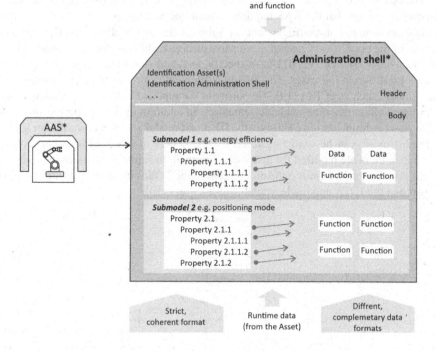

Fig. 2. Structure of the Asset Administration Shell [8].

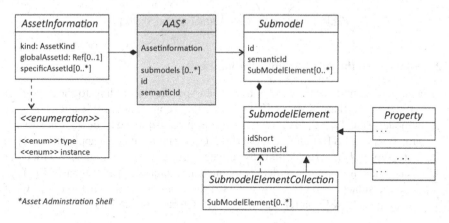

Fig. 3. Excerpt of a class diagram representing the structure of AASs [9].

The asset is linked to the AAS via an aggregation as a special case of an association. This means that an AAS can at most be derived from an asset. However, an AAS can also exist without an asset. Furthermore, the structure of the AAS is also explained in more detail in [18, 19].

The fact that the AAS is connected to the Submodel via a composition, i.e. a stronger association, means that the AAS requires at least one Submodel for its existence. Submodels can contain SubmodElelements or SubmodelElementCollections. These are the carriers of the properties. Currently, extensive efforts are taking place in Industrial Digital Twin Association e. V. (IDTA) to specify, test, and subsequently standardize submodels for different use cases. The SubmodelElement is already found in standardized data formats such as eCl@ss [9]. The attribute "semanticid" identifies elements of the AAS that contain machine-readable semantics. In addition to the unique identification of the Asset Administration Shells via the ID, a part model also receives a unique global identification. It can be used to reference part models in other information models. These identifiers are required for distributed automation solutions in order to be able to access the resources of the Asset Administration Shell. Various submodels are currently prepared in the IDTA and made available to the users [13].

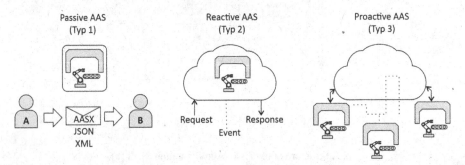

Fig. 4. Interfaces of Asset Administration Shells [9].

4.2   Interface of the Asset Administration Shell

So far, three different types of AAS have been specified according to the following Fig. 4. Type one AAS are XML or JSON files (Fig. 5) containing serializations of AAS and submodel data. Type 2 AAS are runtime instances deployed to devices or servers. They provide http/REST or OPC-UA interfaces to communicate with applications. Type 3 AAS are Type 2 AAS that additionally initiate actions. They communicate with other AAS to negotiate, for example, orders or maintenance intervals. The languages for Type 3 AAS are the subject of current research [15]. In addition, for the creation of AAS of Type 1 with the AASX Explorer the binary AASX format is required.

4.3   Behaviour of Asset Administration Shells

In our research project, which provides the basis for this paper, we have investigated different state machines for the synchronization of processes within devices such as Programmable Logical Controllers (PLCs) but also for the synchronization of the communication between AAS and the devices connected to them. We have chosen to implement the Process control with Packaging Machine Language (PackML). PackML is an automation standard developed by the Organization for Machine Automation and Control (OMAC) and adopted by ISA as TR88.00.02.

```
„embeddedDataSpecifications": [
    {
      "dataSpecification": {
      "keys": [
        ...
      ]
    },
      "dataSpecificationContent": {
      "preferredName": [
        {
          "language": "de",
          „text": "maximales Drehmoment"
        },
        {
          "language": "en",
          „text": "maximal torque"
        }
      ],
      "shortName": [],
      "unit": "Nm",
      „dataType": "INTEGER_MEASURE",
      "definition": []
    }
```

Fig. 5. Asset Administration Shell in .json format.

PackML is widely used in the field of packaging machines, but also in discrete manufacturing automation, that makes it easier to transfer and retrieve consistent machine data. The primary goals of PackML are to encourage a common "look and feel" across a plant floor, and to enable and encourage industry innovation.

The PackML State machine describes up to 17 states (Fig. 6), which are divided into acting-states, wait-states and a hybrid execute-state. These 17 states can be called from the three operating modes, manual, automatic and maintenance. In your own implementation, states may be omitted without violating the standard, but no additional states may be added. PackML defines data points, called PackTags, that can provide the raw data necessary for end users to monitor Key Performance Indicators (KPIs) and machine efficiency in real time. According to PackML V3.0 the model includes four different unit modes as Manual, Maintenance, Production and userdefined modes. The 17 machine states such as Stopped, Starting, Execute, Aborting, etc. can be used to handle the machine states within an operating mode.

Acting states are the states with an "ing" at the end. In acting states the machine is processing some form of an activity. The acting states are leaved when the state is completed (SC). Wait states: identify that the machine has achieved a defined set of conditions (end user determined). In addition to the states and operating modes, the standard also defines variables with the socalled PackTags, which are available for exchange with other systems [2]. In our application, a PLC was required for monitoring and controlling a sorting process. In order to be able to make changes in the PLC without manual intervention in the connected AAS. Another example in which PackML has already been used in combination with AAS can also be found in [11]. The PackML templates

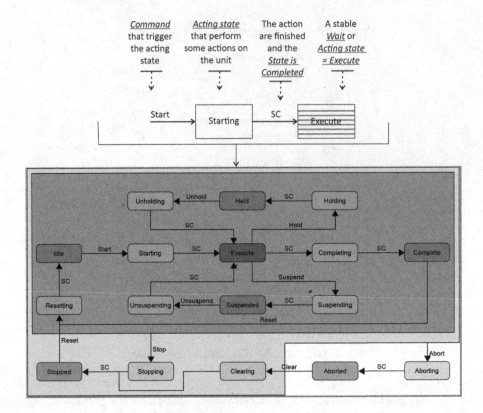

Fig. 6. The PackML state machine [20].

provided by the PLC manufacturers were adapted in such a way that adjustments can be made to the system, so that machines, plant areas or even processes can be booked in or out at run-time. Structured process information was also provided for later use in Asset Administration Shell or other applications.

5   Infrastructure

To use the AAS in operations, a suitable infrastructure is required. Here, the Industrie 4.0 base system (BaSys 4.0), is an open platform for the fourth industrial revolution, that provides a middleware for the usage of AAS. Therefore, BaSys 4 defines a reference architecture for production systems that enables the transformation to Industrie 4.0. The open source middleware Eclipse BaSyx is a reference implementation of the concepts of BaSys 4.

BaSys 4.0 control components provide a harmonized interface to device services, and shield native device communication from users.

The same physical device may provide several device control components at different network communication endpoints to control independent device services. The

BaSyx device interface defines a generic interface to all control components, i.e. device control components and group control components [6].

BaSyx components are structured into four layers:

Field Level: The field level consists of automation devices, sensors, and actuators without a specific BaSys conforming interface.

Device Level: The device level consists of automation devices that offer a BaSys 4.0 conforming interface. Bridging devices that implement BaSys 4.0 conforming interfaces for field devices, that do not provide a conforming interface by themselves are part of the device level as well.

Middleware Level: The middleware level consists of reuseable Industrie 4.0 components that implement required generic, and plant-independent capabilities for Industrie 4.0 production lines. Registry and Discovery services, protocol gateways, and Asset Administration Shell providers for example reside on the middleware level.

Plant Level: The plant level consists of high-level plant components that manage, optimize, and monitor the production.

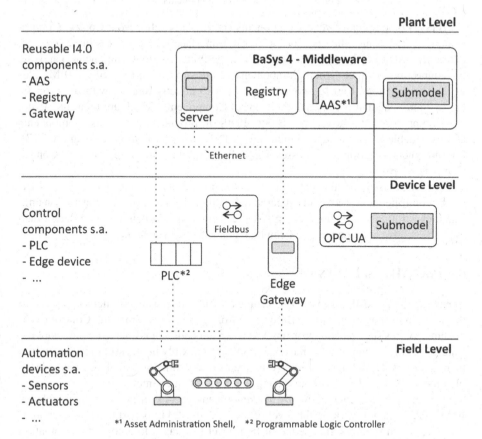

Fig. 7. Infrastructure oriented of the Exlipse BaSyx Framework [7].

Control Components are typically programmed via standardized PLC programming paradigms. IEC61131-3 defines five languages for programming PLCs and its standardization was first published in December 1993 (the most recent standard was published in February 2013). 3S is for example implementing an IEC61131-3 development and runtime environment called CodeSys.

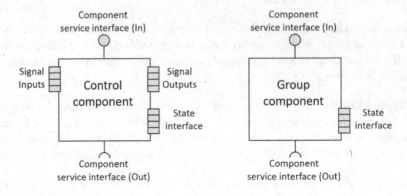

Fig. 8. Group and control components [6].

BaSys4.0 compliant Group Components significantly differ from Control Components (Fig. 8) because they do not have an IO interface to the process under control, but rather two network interfaces, one to the underlying Control Component(s) and one for connecting to other Group Components or the services in the BaSys4.0 Middleware. The function of such a component is not to directly interact with the process, but to coordinate and orchestrate the Control Components, which are then interacting with the process [7]. The Eclipse BaSyx Platform provides ready-to-use components and extendable software development kits (SDK) for Java, Python, C++ and C# [7]. For the synchronization of processes The Eclipse BaSyx Platform provides a "Control Component" [6].

This allows individual capabilities to be mapped in a state machine. Each process can be controlled uniformly and triggered individually by a user or an orchestration unit. The orchestration can be done by an AAS or a controller, which has been determined to be the control component. Itself can be represented by a state machine.

6   PackML vs. BaSyx CC

The use of the PackML standard has become established but shows deficits compared to the solution proposed in [16] by BaSyx Control Components. Since the Control Component accesses state machines on any level, e.g. allocation, it is able to display booking states. This means that it is no longer a problem to flexibly book asset parts and assign them to orders. Higher-level GroupComponents or coordinators can thus create a flexible production landscape without having to resort to human intervention.

However, the implementation by automation engineers is difficult on the field level. BaSyx CC does not work on the level of the PLC itself, but is part of the BaSyx middleware, which requires knowledge of high-level languages to embed it. Automation

Table 1. Overview of PackML extensions.

	PackML - Template	PackML extension
diverse modes	yes	yes
Superior State Machine	no	yes
SubUnits	no	yes
Booking	no	yes
similar structures to submodels	no	yes
seperation in SMCs	no	yes
properties	no	yes
changing properties	no	yes
interface to AAS	no	yes

engineers cannot always access these resources, which reduces the level of adoption of BaSyx CCs.

The authors therefore take the approach of adapting the already existing PackML structure and making it equal to a BaSyx CC. Likewise structures are implemented, which help to be able to generate AAS automatically. The PackML is thereby embedded with similar functions on a PLC and can be booked and used by higher-level coordinators of any kind. In addition, structures of the AAS are available as templetes, which can be modified by a technically authorized person and meet the structure of an AAS. Furthermore, BaSyx CC uses a so-called GroupComponent. This is used to coordinate other ControlComponents. The PackML template from e.g. Beckhoff also lacks such superimposed structures. However, these are ideal for coordinating subordinate plant components.

To meet the BaSyx approach, a kind of GroupComponent must be developed. This in turn should be able to be implemented on the PLC and control or coordinate subordinate units. Among other things, the booking process is to be handled via this component. In addition, it provides subordinate resources, which indirectly indicates that a PLC is in operation and that its resources can be accessed. Table 1 shows a comparison of the existing solution based on PackML V3 from Beckhoff and the solution implemented by the authors.

7 Explanation of the Practical Use Case

The application case is taken from a concrete problem of a medium-sized company that manufactures very high-quality thermal switches that are used in the automotive sector, among others.

7.1 Initial Situation in the Use Case

Since an individual type test is prescribed for the thermoswitches, they are subjected to an extensive thermal test in a highprecision test furnace after being placed on a special pallet carrier. The test is used to check whether the manufactured thermoswitches comply with the technical specification. As this is an individual testing of products, the

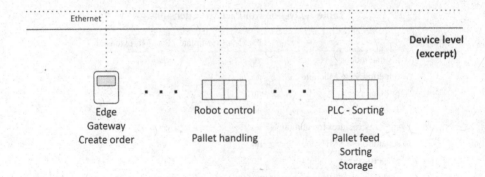

Fig. 9. Instrumentation - existing plant (without AAS) - initial situation.

respective parameters of the testing process have to be provided and evaluated according to the product batch.

After completion of the test process, the pallet carrier is released and removed. The pallet carrier is removed from the test furnace by an industrial robot and transferred to the subsequent processes. This concerns the process of sorting the topic switches, as well as the subsequent provision of the pallet carrier for a new placement process. The process of sorting involves the removal and filing of the thermoswitches according to the assigned result of their testing. The existing heterogeneous instrumentation (Fig. 9) of the existing plant includes controls from different manufacturers, as well as industrial robots for handling.

This means that the available resources must be coordinated in their future use. The coordination of resources can take place within a control system or through a higher-level process.

Since essential components of the plant were implemented in an IEC 61131-3-compliant Codesys environment, the question arose of transferring components to a future I4.0 environment. Among other things, a large number of function libraries and various communication protocols can be used in this platform. However, there are no solutions that enable simple integration into an I4.0 environment and synchronization via AAS.

7.2   Discussion of the Requirements

The challenge lies in the effort-reduced realization of a digital representative as I4.0 components and their integration [14]. These can be mapped in the form of a AAS. The available variants of asset adminsitration shell and their structure were discussed in paragraph 3. The discussion of the use case results in the necessity of both migrating the inventory of industrial controllers to the future environment and implementing their representation in the form of Asset Administration Shell at a reduced cost.

With the implementation of the PackML on the controllers and necessary extensions, which corresponds to the range of functions with the "Control Component", a number of advantages arise with the gradual migration. These include the booking of resources, the synchronization of the processes and the possibility of equalizing the migration over time.

A key aspect is the future use and configuration of plant components independent of separate software environments (programming environment) with any end devices. Only with a generic preparation of a suitable user interface (GUI) and their individual configuration the desired advantages in engineering result. For example, a management component for synchronizing the components must currently still be implemented manually on the basis of the IDTA templates. This template is currently only available in the SDK version (Java/C++), which limits its distribution for synchronization.

In many cases, there are also not enough employees with the necessary knowledge available in the company. However, automation engineers are already employed for the existing machinery and equipment, who are responsible for the support of the plant, among other things. Their knowledge and skills can be drawn upon with regard to the design of solutions. This also applies to the coordination/synchronization of processes. Since the manual creation of AAS is widely established, this will not be considered in detail in this article. Instead, the question arises as to how the user of industrial control is enabled to use Asset Administration Shells in the industrial environment.

One option is the largely generic preparation and use of AAS without knowledge of the SDK environment. Prerequisites for this should only be the description of the asset as AAS type 1 and the adaptation of the necessary interfaces in the control software.

Since the software development process goes through several phases, it makes sense to establish the generation of the AAS online with the controller, as well as offline without the controller but with a defined data model and communication protocol. Thus, a generated AAS (offline variant) can already be evaluated via its interfaces with a test application even without a controller.

7.3   Implementation

The possibility of a largely generic preparation of Asset Administration Shells was presented by the authors at the IN4PL 2021 congress. The generic approach was implemented in the "OpenBasys 4.0" project and, in addition to simplifying software development, enables a reduction in the time required and possible malfunctions.

The prerequisites for using the AAS generator are the use of the data model created by the authors on the part of the controller and the established communication channel. For this purpose, corresponding adjustments must be made in the respective application of the control system. This mainly concerns the data model used and the communication channel, since the AAS generator in the current version accesses defined global variable tables. Templates with the global variable tables are available for various Codesys implementations.

The process of the AAS generation can be initiated over the control, as well as over the user - interface of the AAS generator. The following is a description of the interface to the AAS and the generation process. After generation, an associated AAS type 2 exists for each control component, which can be used by a higher-level coordinator for process control. The schematic representation of the instrumentation is shown with Fig. 10.

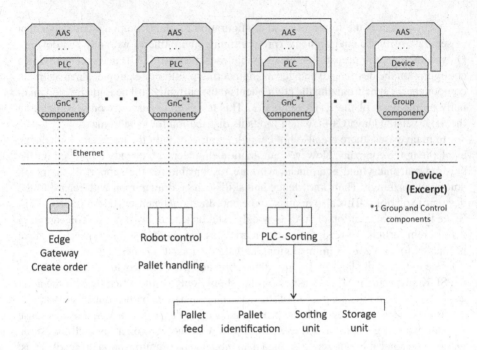

Fig. 10. Instrumentation - with AAS assignment.

7.4 Interface to AAS

The metamodel requires a subdivision of submodels in an AAS into so-called SubModelCollections. Such an implementation is not available on the control side, which is why a solution must be found for efficiently storing engineering data in the AAS.

It must be possible to assign technical descriptions and engineering data to information from the process events. This applies to new plants as well as to existing plants. In the existing system environment, various structures are integrated for this purpose, which provide information. One such structure is UnitInfo (Fig. 11), which provides information on the system boundaries and the technical framework conditions and makes them visible to the person responsible for the plant. For the manipulation of system states another structure, UnitController, is embedded. Via this, commands from outside are forwarded to the system. This is made available to the user via the GVL and can be interpreted by an external process, among others.

Both structures, UnitInfo and UnitController, are specially adapted to the application of the developed PackML State Machine. If this is not used and the user of the template wants to use his own state machine, a similar structure is available to him via the GVL "Process". Both GVL are considered in the process of generation. After the generation process, all structures are stored in the form of Submodels and SubmodelCollections and can be processed on any device via a GUI (Front End).

In the proposed solution, units are individual assets, such as a sort or an articulated robot. The presented application maps a Unit as a delimited subprocess from the asset. Processes can then be requested, posted, and blocked from other processes by the

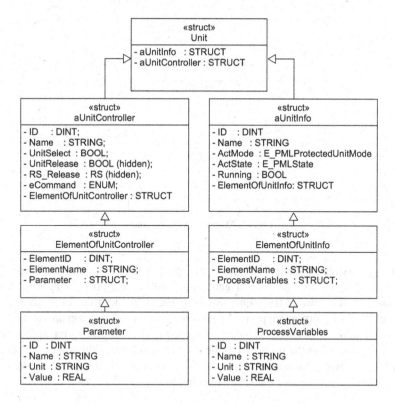

Fig. 11. Unit structure (aUnitInfo and aUnitController).

UnitSelect variable. The state is controlled by the command eCommand, which can be influenced by an OPC UA interface as well as by internal signals. ElementOfUnitController provides various parameterization options. It is responsible for the overall control of the plant, while ElementOfUnitInfo provides information about the plant status and the individual processes. As a result, an OPC UA client only has read authorization and cannot manipulate information. They are supplemented by the programmer when configuring the plant. Supplementary information that cannot be added in the lower-level state machine is embedded in the "Process" structure.

8 Generating Process

A functioning I4.0 system requires at least a minimal environment (see Fig. 12). In our application case, this consists of a registry, as a directory in which the type 2 Asset Administration Shells can register with their submodels, and the AAS generator, which converts type 1 Asset Administration Shells into type 2 Asset Administration Shells. The AAS generator has a database in which type 1 Asset Administration Shells have already been stored for later use. Furthermore, a generic user interface (GUI) is provided.

The sequence diagram shown in Fig. 13 explains the generation process for creating an Asset Administration Shell and the required communication interfaces. In order to

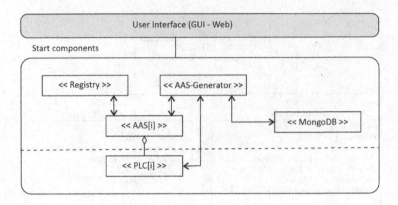

Fig. 12. Minimal environment.

convert administration shells from type 1 to type 2 AAS, the required AAS generator has been developed. The process of generation and configuration of future AAS can be initiated as described in the requirements by the controller itself or by using it user interfaces. For this purpose, appropriate possibilities of configuration on the part of the GUI are available. This concerns the reference to the general description in form of the AAS type 1, as well as the reference to the used protocol and addressing of the control. The AAS generator is from its structure itself a type 3 AAS. In the following the phases of the generation process are explained exemplarily.

Variant 1 - Request by User. In the user-initiated preparation of an AAS generation (see Fig. 13), the user must ensure that the relevant controller is accessible and contains the appropriate application as a boot project. After entering the relevant information/parameters, the process of generation is started and it is checked whether the relevant AAS type 1 is available to describe the asset. Currently there is no check of the structure of the description and used submodel here. In future versions, a test for correctness of the template will be performed here. If there are errors in the description provided, not all elements may be embedded in the generation. In the second phase, the accessibility of the controller via the selected communication channel is checked. For example, in the case of OPC UA communication, the AAS generator creates a session as OPC client and establishes a connection to the PLC acting as OPC server. Now all information stored in the respective data structure is read in by the AAS generator and prepared for future use in the associated AAS. After the generation process has been completed, the created AAS is registered. Subsequently, the digital representation (AAS) is available for use by the control system. With the data from the registry, it can be configured or booked via the user interface.

Variant 2 - Request by Controller. In an AAS generation initiated by the control system, the control system must have a rest interface and be assigned the information on the accessibility of the AAS in the project planning phase. Likewise, the AAS type 1 references must be included so that a unique assignment can be made in the generation process.

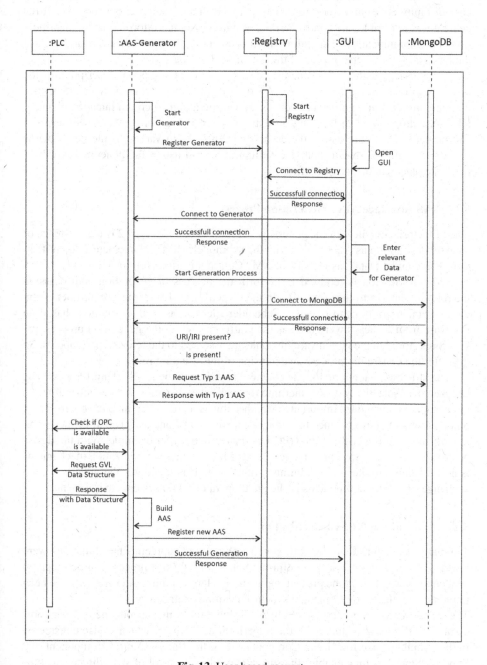

Fig. 13. User based request.

The controller first checks the availability of the generator by sending a request. In case of faulty communication, a timeout is received and the process is aborted. If the generator is reachable, the controller then provides essential information for identification and communication. This information is essential, because otherwise no check of the reach ability and preparation of the data model can be done.

As in variant 1, the AAS generator checks whether the general description of the asset is available in the form of an AAS type 1. Then the accessibility of the control via the communication channel is checked. Via the assigned communication channel, all information stored in the relevant data structure is read in by the AAS generator and prepared for future use in the associated AAS. As in variant 1, the new AAS is registered. With the registration, the configuration and use of the generated AAS can thus take place via the user interface.

8.1   AAS Interface After Generation Process

One of the prerequisites for the generic generation of an AAS type 2 is the existence of an asset description as AAS type 1 with the submodels (SM) "Nameplate", "Identification", "Technical Data", as well as the SM "Communication" (option) (Fig. 14).

This information is required to perform the process of generation and to assign the relevant data from the controller. In the "OpenBasys 4.0" project, controllers from the manufacturers Beckhoff, Wago, Schneider Electric, as well as solutions based on firmware from Codesys were used as the platform. During the generation process, the structures stored in the global variable table are assigned to the relevant part models. So that after the generation process an extension of the structure results.

The structures mentioned in the chapter "Interface to the AAS" (Unit, Process) can be taken over selectively or together into the new asset structure. For the generator, it is in principle of secondary importance whether this is a controller, an edge controller or other automation device, since the submodels are created and assigned after successful identification on the basis of the OPC UA data structure, for example. With the designated data structures, the entire range of Pack ML with its synchronization mechanisms is now available to the Asset Administration Shell. This facilitates the integration and exchange of system components in the plant operator's I4.0 system environment.

8.2   Precondition for Synchronization

Templates with embedded PackML state machines and supplementary functions were prepared for different Codesys platforms. Since not only one process can be prepared on a controller but, as in the present application, a large number of processes have been implemented, their structuring and synchronization is mandatory.

The encapsulation of processes in SubUnit-SM was taken into account here. Their coordination and release is done with the SuperiorStateMachine, which is also considered in the template. Like the Group Component from the BaSyx Control Component, the Superior State Machine enables the superimposed use/control of subordinate capabilities.

The initialization process including the booking of resources is shown as an example in Fig. 15. The individual states are offered in the templates according to the selected

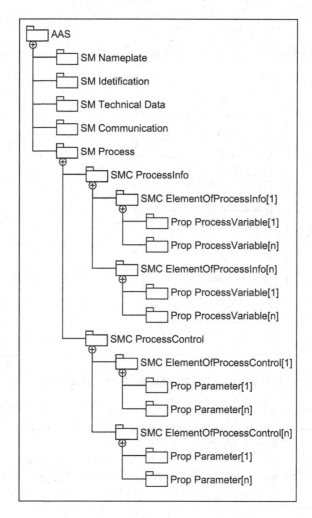

Fig. 14. Extract from the generated AAS structure.

mode in the form of methods. Thus, at the level of the Asset Administration Shells, it is always apparent in which mode and which state the plant components/processes are.

Since all information is stored in the associated global variable table (unit) and is available as an image in the Asset Administration Shell, it can also be visualized via the user interface. For further information from the plant environment, a supplementary global variable table is currently available in the Asset Administration Shell. This is also visualized via the user interface.

9   Web GUI

The web GUI should enable the user to interpret and use the information from the AAS in a comprehensible form. For this purpose, a generic approach is also followed, which

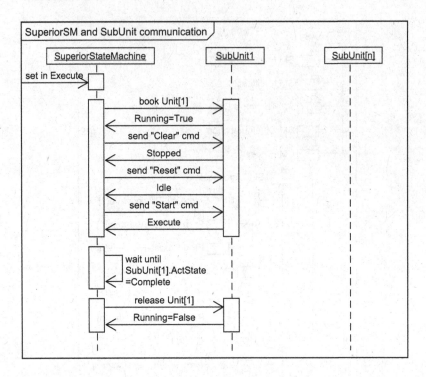

Fig. 15. INIT process of the PackML state machine (excerpt of [21]).

accesses the AAS as an information source (BackEnd) and automatically realizes the interpretation of the data as a front.

In the current version of the Web GUI, contents of the AAS Type 1 (JSON format) are provided to the user in a user-friendly representation (for an excerpt, see Fig. 16). Furthermore, all AAS addressed and accessible in the registry can be displayed regardless of the end device.

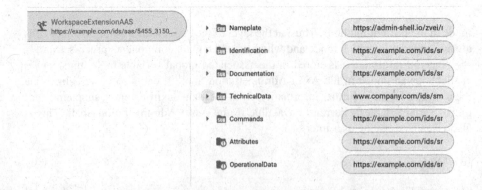

Fig. 16. Interpretation of a type 1 AAS.

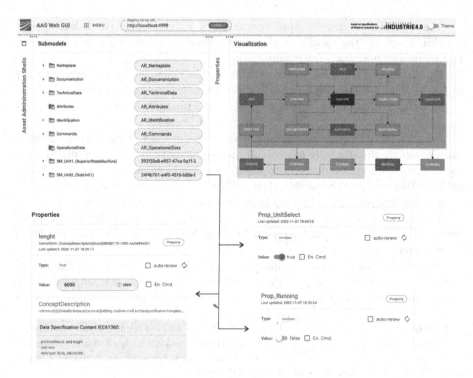

Fig. 17. Interpretation of a type 2 AAS.

The following Fig. 17 shows the responsive web GUI developed in our research project, which dynamically adapts to the graphical capabilities of the respective devices. On the left side, the respective AAS are displayed. The second column from the left shows the submodels selected in the respective AAS. The selection of the property of a submodel shows the current state. The right column shows the active states of the state machine. In addition, the representation shows the status of resources. Furthermore, the possibility of booking implemented resources on the part of the PLC was explained in the article. The booking and the current state of the resource (SubUnit) is shown exemplarily with the "Prop_Unitselect" and "Prop_Running". Likewise the technical specification, the configuration and the states of the selected asset are visible for the user at any time with appropriate availability.

10   Conclusion and Outlook

Digital twins in their form as Asset Administration Shells are a good way to integrate PLCs into I4.0 environments.

This paper explains the basic concepts of AAS and provides the context for its successful use in industry using the open source Eclipse framework BaSyx.

The article illustrates the synchronization of different plant segments using a PackML template. The focus was placed on ensuring that existing plants in particular can meet an Industrie 4.0 standard.

By embedding individual subunits within a PLC they can be orchestrated via a higher-level unit. The BaSyx Control Component follows a similar pattern.

However, since these do not yet correspond to a generally applicable standard, this contribution is oriented to the ISA 88 state machine (PackML).

In order to correspond to the conditions of a Control Component according to BaSyx, various changes were made to an existing template, which cover almost all of its functions. Different skills were managed by a SuperiorStateMachine. Furthermore each SubUnit gets its own PackML state machine, which is also passed on to the AAS. Thus, a uniform synchronization can be achieved across all plant segments.

Through the agile combination of different skills leads to a high degree of changeability of the system that can be achieved without having to carry out timeconsuming programming work.

This article ends with the presentation of a web application, which both displays the current plant status independent of the respective end device and enables the possibility of controlling the plant via the AAS.

Acknowledgment. This research work called 'OpenBasys 4.0' has been funded by the Federal Ministry of Education and Research - BMBF (01IS1900A) and is a BaSys 4 satellite project for application oriented projects. The effort of this work was made possible by the Basys 4 framework. The authors thank for the support of the BaSys 4 team.

References

1. Industrial automation systems and integration - exchange of characteristic data - part 5: Identification scheme. Standard, Geneva, CH
2. ANSI/ISA-TR88.00.02-2015: Machine and unit states: An implementation example of ansi/isa-88.00.01. Standard ANSI/ISA-TR88.00.02-2015, International Society of Automation, Durham, USA (2015). https://www.isa.org/products/ansi-isa-tr88-00-02-2015-machine-and-unit-states-a
3. Baudoin, C., Bournival, E., Buchheit, M., Simmon, E., Zarkout, B.: Industry internet of things vocabulary: An industry iot consortium framework publication. Tech. rep., Industry IoT Consortium (2022). https://www.iiconsortium.org/wp-content/uploads/sites/2/2022/04/Industry-IoT-Vocabulary.pdf
4. DIN En IEC 63278–1:2022–07 - Draft: Asset administration shell for industrial applications - part 1: Asset administration shell structure. Standard DIN EN IEC 63278–1:2022–07 - Draft, Deutsches Institut für Normung, Berlin, DE (2022), https://www.beuth.de/en/draft-standard/din-en-iec-63278-1/354882246
5. DIN Spec 91345:2016–04: Reference architecture model industrie 4.0 (rami4.0). Standard DIN SPEC 91345:2016–04, Deutsches Institut für Normung, Berlin, DE (2016). https://www.beuth.de/de/technische-regel/din-spec-91345/250940128
6. Eclipse BaSyx: Eclipse BaSyx / Documentation / API / ControlComponent. https://wiki.eclipse.org/BaSyx_/_Documentation_/_API_/ (2021)
7. Eclipse BaSyx: Eclipse BaSyx Platform. https://www.eclipse.org/basyx/ (2021), [Online]

8. Federal Ministry for Economic Affairs and Energy (BMWi): Structure of the administration shell - trilateral perspectives from france, italy and germany. Tech. rep., Berlin (2018). https://www.plattform-i40.de/IP/Redaktion/DE/Downloads/Publikation/hm-2018-trilaterale-coop.html

9. Federal Ministry for Economic Affairs and Energy (BMWi): Details of the Asset Administration Shell : Part 1 - The exchange of information between partners in the value chain of Industrie 4.0; Version 2.0.1. Tech. rep., Berlin (2020). https://publications.rwth-aachen.de/record/791889

10. Gartner Inc: Gartner glossary. https://www.gartner.com/en/information-technology/glossary/digital-twin (2022)

11. Grüner, S., Hoernicke, M., Thies, M., Fachinger, G., Torres, N.C., Kleinert, T.: A reference architecture for modular industrial automation systems. In: 2021 26th IEEE International Conference on Emerging Technologies and Factory Automation (ETFA), pp. 1–8 (2021). https://doi.org/10.1109/ETFA45728.2021.9613203

12. IEC Ts 62443-1-1:2009: Industrial communication networks - network and system security - Part 1–1: Terminology, concepts and models. Standard IEC TS 62443-1-1:2009, International Electrotechnical Commission, Geneva, CH (2009). https://webstore.iec.ch/publication/7029

13. Industrial Digital Twin Association e. V.: IDTA - working together to promote the Digital Twin. https://industrialdigitaltwin.org/en/ (2022)

14. Koulamas, C., Kalogeras, A.: Cyber-physical systems and digital twins in the industrial internet of things [cyber-physical systems]. Computer 51(11), 95–98 (2018). https://doi.org/10.1109/MC.2018.2876181

15. Kuhn, T., Schnicke, F., Oliveira Antonino, P.: Service-based architectures in production systems: Challenges, solutions & experiences, pp. 1–7 (12 2020). https://doi.org/10.23919/ITUK50268.2020.9303207

16. Lüder, A., Behnert, A.K., Rinker, F., Biffl, S.: Generating industry 4.0 asset administration shells with data from engineering data logistics. In: 2020 25th IEEE International Conference on Emerging Technologies and Factory Automation (ETFA). vol. 1, pp. 867–874 (2020). https://doi.org/10.1109/ETFA46521.2020.9212149

17. OpenBasys 4.0: BaSys 4.0 in der Anwendung. https://www.softwaresysteme.dlr-pt.de/media/content/Projektblatt_OpenBaSys40.pdf (2021)

18. di Orio, G., Maló, P., Barata, J.: Novaas: A reference implementation of industrie4.0 asset administration shell with best-of-breed practices from it engineering. In: IECON 2019 - 45th Annual Conference of the IEEE Industrial Electronics Society. vol. 1, pp. 5505–5512 (2019). https://doi.org/10.1109/IECON.2019.8927081

19. Plattform Industrie 4.0: VWS-Referenzmodellierung : Exemplarische Modellierung einer fertigungstechnischen Anlage mit AASX Package Explorer auf Basis des VWS-Metamodells : Diskussionspapier; Stand April 2021. Tech. rep., Berlin (2021). https://publications.rwth-aachen.de/record/819250

20. Schäfer., S., Schöttke., D., Kämpfe., T., Lachmann., O., Zielstorff., A., Tauber., B.: Industrial controls and asset administration shells: An approach to the synchronization of plant segments. In: Proceedings of the 3rd International Conference on Innovative Intelligent Industrial Production and Logistics - IN4PL, pp. 75–84. INSTICC, SciTePress (2022). https://doi.org/10.5220/0011527200003329

21. Schäfer, S., Schöttke, D., Kämpfe, T., Lachmann, O., Zielstorff, A., Tauber, B.: Migration and synchronization of plant segments with asset administration shells. In: 2022 IEEE 27th International Conference on Emerging Technologies and Factory Automation (ETFA), pp. 1–8 (2022). https://doi.org/10.1109/ETFA52439.2022.9921595

22. Schäfer, S., Schöttke, D., Kämpfe, T., Ralinovski, K., Tauber, B., Lehmann, R.: Design and deployment of digital twins for programmable logic controllers in existing plants. In: Proceedings of the 2nd International Conference on Innovative Intelligent Industrial Production and Logistics - IN4PL, pp. 145–150. INSTICC, SciTePress (2021). https://doi.org/10.5220/0010711000003062
23. Tao, F., Cheng, J., Qi, Q., Zhang, M., Zhang, H., Sui, F.: Digital twin-driven product design, manufacturing and service with big data. Int. J. Adv. Manufact. Technol. **94** (02 2018). https://doi.org/10.1007/s00170-017-0233-1
24. Ye, X., Hong, S.H., Song, W.S., Kim, Y.C., Zhang, X.: An industry 4.0 asset administration shell-enabled digital solution for robot-based manufacturing systems. IEEE Access 9, 154448–154459 (2021). https://doi.org/10.1109/ACCESS.2021.3128580

A Family of Digital T Workflows and Architectures: Exploring Two Cases

Randy Paredis[1] , Cláudio Gomes[2] , and Hans Vangheluwe[1,3(✉)]

[1] Department of Computer Science, University of Antwerp, Middelheimlaan 1,
Antwerp, Belgium
`Hans.Vangheluwe@uantwerpen.be`

[2] DIGIT, Department of Electrical and Computer Engineering, Aarhus University, Åbogade 34,
Aarhus N, Denmark

[3] Flanders Make@UAntwerp, Antwerp, Belgium

Abstract. Digital Models/Shadows/Twins/... have been given numerous definitions and descriptions in the literature. There is no consensus on terminology, nor a comprehensive description of workflows nor architectures. In this paper, we use the catch-all "Digital T" (pronounced "Digital Twinning") to refer to all concepts, techniques, architectures, ... related to the "twinning" paradigm. In this paradigm, virtual instances, known as twins, of a System under Study (SuS) are continually updated with the SuS's health, performance, and maintenance status, over its entire life-cycle. Digital T can be used for monitoring, analysis, optimization, and adaptation of complex engineered systems, in particular after these systems have been deployed. Digital T makes full use of both historical knowledge and of streaming data from sensors. Following Multi-Paradigm Modelling (MPM) principles, this paper proposes to explicitly model construction/use workflows as well as architectures and deployment of Digital T. Applying product family modelling allows for the de-/re-construction of the different Digital T variants in a principled, reproducible and partially automatable manner. Two small illustrative cases are discussed: a Line-Following Robot and an Incubator. These are representative for respectively an Automated Guided Vehicle and an Industrial Convection Oven, both important in an industrial context.

Keywords: Digital model · Digital shadow · Digital twin · Architecture · Workflow · Variability modelling

1 Introduction

Digital Twins (DTs) are increasingly used in Industry 4.0 and industrial processes for purposes such as condition monitoring, analysis, and optimization. While their definition has changed throughout the years, the concept of "twinning" has stayed the same: there exists a digital counterpart of a real-world (realized) system that provides information about this system.

Academic and industrial interest in DTs has grown steadily, as they allow the acceleration through digitization that is at the heart of Industry 4.0. Digital Twins are made possible by technologies such as the Internet of Things (IoT), Augmented Reality (AR), and Product Lifecycle Management (PLM).

© The Author(s), under exclusive license to Springer Nature Switzerland AG 2023
A. Smirnov et al. (Eds.): IN4PL 2020/IN4PL 2021, CCIS 1855, pp. 93–109, 2023.
https://doi.org/10.1007/978-3-031-37228-5_6

Despite the many surveys on the topic [1, 3–5, 12, 13, 15, 17, 23, 26, 28, 30], there is no general consensus on what characterizes a Digital Twin, let alone how it is constructed. Some researchers state that a DT encompasses only the virtual counterpart of the system, while for others, it encompasses both virtual and real-world systems as well as the architecture connecting them. For example, Lin and Low [14] define DT as *"a virtual representation of the physical objects, processes and real-time data involved throughout a product life-cycle"*, whereas Park et al. [23] define DT as *"an ultra-realistic virtual counterpart of a real-world object"*. The ISO 23247 standard "Automation systems and integration - Digital twin framework for manufacturing" defines a DT for manufacturing as a *"fit for purpose digital representation of an observable manufacturing element with a means to enable convergence between the element and its digital representation at an appropriate rate of synchronization"* [9]. Rumpe [27] observes that there are at least 118 different definitions in the literature that concern Digital Twins.

Additionally, many commonly used concepts such as Digital Shadows, Digital Models, Digital Passports, Digital Avatars, Digital Cockpits and Digital Threads, are closely related to "twinning".

In this paper, we introduce the catch-all "Digital T" (pronounced as "Digital Twinning") to refer to all concepts, techniques, architectures, ... related to the "twinning" paradigm. In this paradigm, one or more virtual instances, know as twins, of a System under Study (SuS) are continually updated with the SuS's health, performance, and maintenance status, and this over its entire life-cycle [16].

Our work focuses on the variability that appears when creating and managing Digital T systems, by unifying the most common definitions and viewpoints in the form of *product families* of problems solved by, and conceptual architectures and possible deployments for, Digital T. This allows for the de- and re-construction of the different Digital T variants in a principled, reproducible and partially automatable manner.

In order to illustrate our approach, we apply our approach to the development of Digital T systems for two complementary and small, but representative, use cases, a Line-Following Robot and an Incubator. Our approach is a first step towards generalization to relevant industrial systems.

The rest of this paper is structured as follows. Section 2 discusses variability and product family modelling. Section 3 introduces two simple examples that are representative for industrial systems. Next, Sect. 4 discusses the possible variations that may occur at the exploration stage. Section 5 then focuses on the design of a Digital T system and introduces some conceptual architecture models. In Sect. 6, possible deployment architectures are shown for both example cases. Section 7 presents a generic workflow for constructing Digital T systems. Finally, Sect. 8 concludes the paper.

2   Variability Modelling

It is common for multiple *variants* of a product to exist. These variants share some *common* parts/aspects/features/... but do *vary* in others. In the automotive industry for example, it is common for all sold cars to be (often subtly) different due to small differences in salient *features*. Such variants can often be seen as different *configurations*.

Feature Modelling [11] is widely accepted as a way to explicitly model variability. One possible representation to capture variability in a product family is by means of a Feature Tree (also known as a Feature Model or Feature Diagram). It is a hierarchical diagram that depicts the features that characterize a product in groups of increasing levels of detail. At each level, constraints in a Feature Tree model indicate which features are mandatory and which are optional. Traversing a Feature Tree from its root downwards, features are selected conforming to the constraints encoded in the Feature Tree model. This feature selection leads to a configuration which uniquely identifies an element of the product family. Note that Feature Trees are not the only way to model product families. Wizards can be used to traverse a decision tree. In case the variability is mostly structural, with many complex constraints, Domain-Specific Languages may be used [6].

The notion of a *product family* is used to denote the often vast collection of variants. Product families appear at multiple stages of a development process. The following will describe variability in the goal exploration stage, in the design stage and in the deployment stage.

To illustrate our proposed approach, we apply it to the two simple use cases of Sect. 3.

3   Example Cases

As this work is meant to guide the creation of Digital T systems in a multitude of contexts, two cases are included as running examples: a Line-Following Robot and an Incubator. These cases were chosen as representative (*i.e.*, exhibiting the essential complexity) for their industrial counterparts, an Automated Guided Vehicle and an industrial oven, respectively.

3.1   Line-Following Robot

An *Automated Guided Vehicle* (AGV) is a simple transportation device in an industrial setting. It is a computer-steered vehicle that allows the transportation of materials, resources and people. For the purposes of this use case, a *Line-Following Robot* (LFR) is used as a simplification of an AGV. The LFR drives over a surface that contains a line (which can be painted, reflective, fluorescent, magnetized, ...), with the sole purpose of following that line as closely as possible. However, unexpected situations (*e.g.*, the robot cannot find the line anymore, a forklift is blocking the robot's trajectory, ...) are difficult to all accommodate for during the (LFR controller) design phase. Unforeseen changes in the LFR's environment is one of the scenarios where twinning provides a solution as it may help detect the anomaly, identify its cause, and suggest adaptation.

Using AGVs reduces the need for conveyor belts, while being highly configurable at the same time. It is an easy-to-understand system that still provides enough essential complexity.

Our LFR is a *nonholonomic, wheeled, differential-drive robot* [25]. Nonholonomicity is due to the fact that the robot has only two controls, but its configuration space is three dimensional. The "differential-drive" (DD) aspect indicates that the robot has two wheels next to each other, driven by two distinct motors. In the middle of the LFR, there is a sensor that is able to detect the colour of the surface underneath the robot. From this information, it is possible to infer whether or not the LFR is on the line. The LFR is shown in Fig. 1. It was described in detail in [21].

Fig. 1. The Line Following Robot.

The robot drives on a flat surface following a line. In Fig. 2, trajectory data for this system are shown.

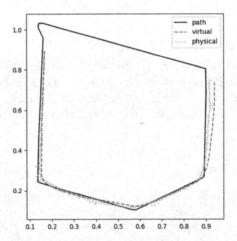

Fig. 2. Trace of an LFR experiment, as shown in a dashboard. Taken from [21]. (Color figure online)

The blue, full line represents the path to follow, as marked on the floor, the orange, striped line identifies the twin's simulation trace and the green, dotted line represents a trace of the Physical Object's position. This position is obtained using machine vision on the data received from a depth vision camera, mounted statically in a harness above the surface at such a height as to allow the camera's field of view to capture the entire driving range.

3.2 Incubator

A *heating chamber* (*i.e.,* an *industrial oven*) is commonly used in industry for curing, drying, baking, reflow,... It introduces high-temperature processes to the creation of a product. Some ovens allow this product to be transported through the heating chamber on a conveyor belt (or even an AGV).

The temperature in an industrial oven needs to be regulated, as a change in temperature could damage the product. For instance, glazed ceramics could have a completely different colour when baked at the wrong temperature. Additionally, such a system has to react to unpredictable changes in its environment (*e.g.,* complete a safety shutdown when a person enters the chamber during the baking process). This makes an industrial oven an excellent example for the use of a Digital T system.

Similar to the previous use case, a simplification of such a device is made for the purposes of this paper, to focus on the essential Digital T workflows and architectures. An incubator is a device that is able to maintain a specific temperature (or profile over time) within an insulated container. With an appropriate temperature profiel, microbiological or cell cultures can be grown and maintained.

The incubator (see Fig. 3) consists of five main components: a thermally insulated container, a heatbed (for raising the temperature), a fan (for circulating the airflow, which, through air convention, allows a uniformly distributed temperature when in steady-state), three temperature sensors (two are used to measure the internal heat, one is used to measure the temperature outside the container – the environment, which is outside our control) and a controller. In our example this controller is similar to a *bang-bang* (or *on/off*) controller, but has to wait after each actuation, to ensure that the temperature is raised gradually.

Fig. 3. The Incubator (with lid removed).

In [8], a full description of this incubator is given. Figure 4, adapted from [8], shows an example scenario where the lid of the incubator is opened. This is detected as an anomaly by a Kalman (tracking) filter [10] (the purple temperature trajectory is the result of the Kalman filter; the blue trajectory is the real temperature as measured inside the incubator.). The Kalman filter uses a model for the prediction of the temperature. Such a model does not consider the thermal dynamics when the lid is open. As a result, when the lid is opened, the predictions start to perform poorly, a fact that can be the basis for anomaly detection. Note that the figure also shows a simulation that runs completely independently of the measured data. The reason the Kalman filter does not perform as poorly as this simulation is because it still takes into account real sensor data. This, in contrast to the simulation, which uses a model of the environment. Also note that, compared to the simulation, after the lid is closed, the simulation has difficulty returning to normal, whereas the Kalman filter, because it uses the measured data, quickly returns to tracking the system behaviour.

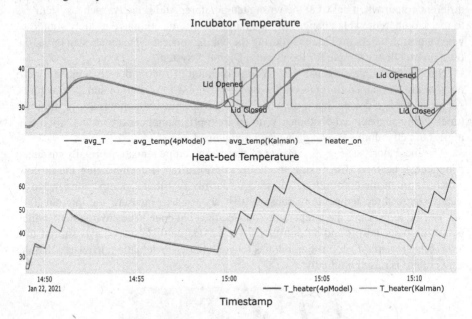

Fig. 4. Example experiment where an anomaly is detected using the Kalman filter. Adapted from [8].

4 Exploration Stage

Based on our experience with the two use cases and on the extensive Digital T litera-ture, we built feature models for each of the development stages in creating Digital T systems. Note that these are by no means complete, but are rather meant as a starting point, to illustrate our approach. They can therefore be seen as a "base" feature model that can be critiqued and extended by others.

When creating a solution for a problem (that is to be solved by twinning), it is impor-tant to first describe the individual *Properties of Interest* (PoIs) for the problem. These PoIs are attributes (or descriptors) of an artifact that are either logical (*i.e.,* the LFR has wheels) or numerical (*i.e.,* the LFR has 2 wheels). They can be *computed* (or derived) from other artifacts, or *specified* (*i.e.,* defined by a user) [24]. These PoIs describe the *goals* of the system that will solve the problem. Each specific goal corresponds to a specific choice in the variability models for that system. They define the problem space.

A (sub)set of the most common Goals for a Digital T system is shown in Fig. 5. Notice the separation of the mandatory "*Observe*" and the optional "*Observe and Mod-ify*". This separation identifies the split between analysis, whereby the real-world system is not modified, and adaptation, where it is.

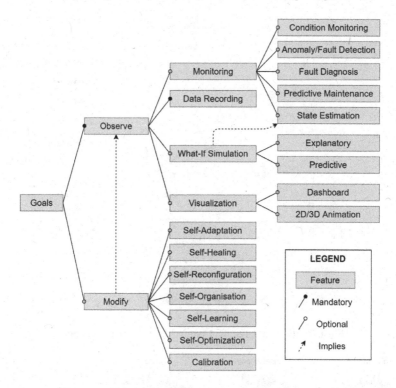

Fig. 5. Feature model of the Goals of a Digital T System.

While the LFR case allows for additional PoIs to be added, we will only focus on the "Dashboard" section for the purposes of this work. The incubator case also supports "Anomaly Detection".

In addition to the selection of the Goals, there is also the Context in which the Digital T system is to be used. This is shown in the feature model of Fig. 6. In the first layer, under Context, all features are mandatory. There is always some User, always a Scale, always a Product Lifecycle Stage, ... This is an indication that these are orthogonal dimensions. Feature choices in each of these dimensions can be combined. Note that the context in which the Digital T system is active constrains downstream choices in the Solution Space.

The LFR case focuses on "Customers", only requires "Monitor Time" and is a "Single Digital T System". The "Connection" is not critical, and the Digital T system is meant to work at the "Usage PLM Stage". The incubator case focuses on "Customers", requires a certain "Response Time" and is also a "Single Digital T System". The "Speed" of the "Connection" is important, as it must adapt to anomalies in a timely manner. It is also meant to be used at the "Usage PLM Stage".

Many different Ilities can be listed and discussed. According to [29], the Ilities are desired properties of systems, such as flexibility or maintainability (usually but not always ending in "ility"), that often manifest themselves after a system has been put to its initial use. These properties are not the primary functional requirements of a system's performance, but typically concern wider system impacts with respect to time and stakeholders than are embodied in those primary functional requirements.

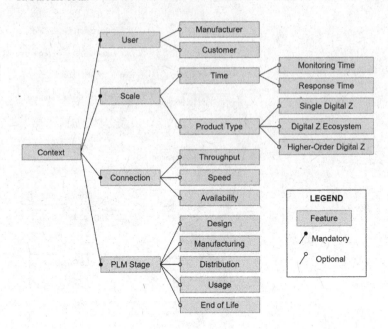

Fig. 6. Feature model of the Contexts for a Digital T System.

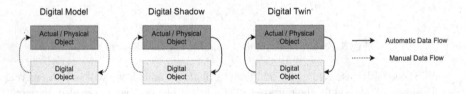

Fig. 7. Three main Design variants of DTs, adapted from [12].

The main Ilities to be focused on in our example cases are "Testability", "Repeatability", "Replicability" and "Usability".

5   Design Stage

There is variability in the kind of Digital T system we wish to build. [12] defines three Digital T variations, as outlined in Fig. 7.

As shown in the figure, each variant contains a *Physical Object* (PO) and a *Digital Object* (DO). The PO represents the System under Study (SuS) within its Environment. The DO represents a virtual copy of the SuS (often in the form of a real-time simulator), trying to mimic its behaviour, *assuming* it is active in the same Environment as the PO. Depending on one's viewpoint and on the application domain, *"physical"* may be an ambiguous term as not all SuS are constructed from what we typically call physical (mechanical, hydraulic, ...) components. The SuS may for example also contain software components. Hence, the more general term *"Realized Object"* (RO) will be used. The same logic can be applied to the DO. For instance, a DO of a train may be modelled

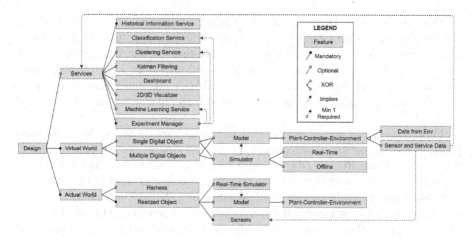

Fig. 8. Variability for the Design of a Digital T System.

using a scale model of the train, instead of a mathematical model used in a simulator. In this case, the DO will be an *"Analog Object"* (AO) or *Analog Twin* instead. For the purpose of this paper, the focus will be on DOs.

The three main Design variants of DTs follow from the nature of the data/information flow between RO and DO. In a *Digital Model* (DM), there is no automated flow of data/information between the objects. The only way data/information is transferred is by a human user. If something changes in the RO, the DO must manually be updated, and vice-versa.

In a *Digital Shadow* (DS) however, the data flow from the RO to the DO becomes automated (*i.e.,* without human intervention). This data, more specifically, is environmental information captured by sensors. This, to ensure that the RO and the DO "see" the same Environment. This is an important step, as it allows the DO to "track" the RO. In Fig. 5, the Observe family of goals leads to a DS solution.

Finally, the *Digital Twin* (DT) closes the loop between RO and DO. If something now changes in the DO, the RO will receive an automated update corresponding to this change. This is usually optimization information, fault tolerance notification, predictive maintenance instructions, etc. Note that in the DT case, automation may also refer to the inferencing and decision making without human intervention.

When building a DT, these variants are typically all traversed in different "stages" in of the Digital T workflow. When a system exists as a DM, the introduction of an appropriate data communication connection yields a DS. When the DO of a DS is now expanded to do system analysis and optimizations (and the RO is able to evolve to allow for system adaptation), we obtain a DT. Note that there needs to be an initial plan to build a DT, so the architecture of the RO can be engineered to allow for adaptation. If there was no original plan to build a DT, modifying an existing RO may be hard. Making the RO configurable from the outside as an afterthought may introduce security risks.

Similar to the Exploration Stage, we present a Feature Tree to model the variability in the conceptual Design of a Digital T system. This is shown in Fig. 8.

Many options exist. Does the realized Digital T system contain a Testing Harness? Is there a single Digital Object in the Virtual World, or are multiple Digital Objects required, one for each Property of Interest. Finally, there are the Services that provide solutions for the Goals presented earlier. There will always be a Historical Information Service (HIS) to store and access historical data of experiments carried out in the past. Additionally, there will be an Experiment Manager that orchestrates Services and Digital Objects.

Figure 7 presents a very high-level view on Digital T architectures. Going into more detail, there must be some component to set up and handle any and all experiments being done with the RO and DO. This will be done by a set of Experiment Managers (EMs) or Assimilation Objects (in case only data if collected from RO and DO). An Experiment can therefore be seen as an execution of a Digital T system such that one or more PoIs can be analyzed. All this information is communicated to the HIS, over which one or more Reasoners may make inferences. Such inferences are important, both in the design of new Digital T systems and in the optimization of future SuS designs.

In Fig. 9, a high-level architecture is shown for the DM. The SuS is modelled containing a *Plant-Controller* feedback loop. Both in the RO and in the DO, this SuS interacts with an *Environment*. For the DO, however, this Environment is a modelled mock-up of the real environment. It should interact with the SuS in exactly the same way as the real environment. In practice, the environment models a typical "duty cycle" of the SuS and is based on historical (measured) data. At the heart of a DO is a *Simulator* to produce behaviour traces from the SuS and mock-up Environment models. Note that there is no direct link between RO and DO (only an indirect one, via the Experiment Managers). Simulation will hence typically not be real-time, but rather as-fast-as-possible.

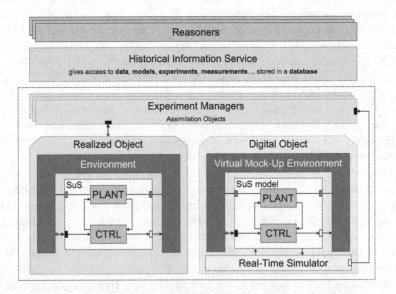

Fig. 9. High-level DM architecture, originally presented in [22].

When taking a closer look at Fig. 10, a high-level architecture for a DS, it becomes clear that (in the DO) the mock-up Environment is now (partially) replaced by a data connection from the input of the SuS in the RO. This provides both RO and DO subsystems with the exact same input and should, therefore, yield identical behaviour in both. Note that deviations are still possible as the plant's behaviour may be influenced by the environment in ways that are not recorded by the sensors in the RO. In that case, the DO still relies on a mock-up (model, possibly based on historical data) of the Environment[1].

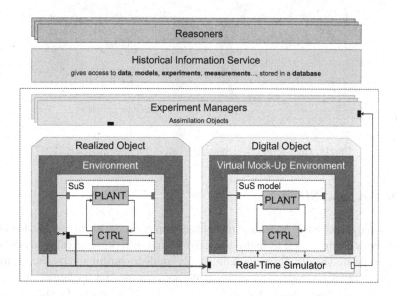

Fig. 10. High-level DS architecture, originally presented in [22].

Figure 11 shows a similar architecture for a DT. Compared to the DS, a connection from the EM goes towards the inputs of both RO and DO of the SuS. If the EO identifies the need for a change in the RO, it will ask the SuSs in both RO and DO to apply this change.

Notice how Figs. 9, 10 and 11 describe variant architectures. They are models in an appropriate Architecture Description Domain-Specific Language (AD DSL). DSLs are more appropriate than Feature Trees when the variability is structural.

---

[1] The authors are grateful to Francis Bordeleau for pointing this out during Dagstuhl Seminar 22362 on Model Driven Engineering of Digital Twins.

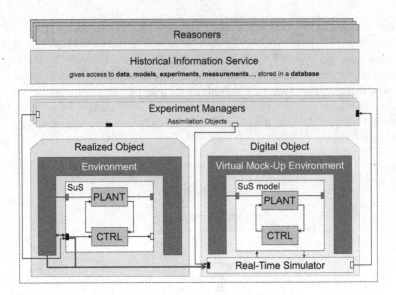

Fig. 11. High-level DT architecture, originally presented in [22].

6 Deployment Stage

For the deployment stage, no feature model has been created. Due to the vast number of possible options, this is left as future work. We plan to still provide feature models, but at an appropriate level of abstraction, in particular, distinguishing between commonly used architectures. Here, deployment diagrams are presented for the current implementation of the two cases. Each component type is the result of a specific choice that has been made in the creation of these systems. Unmarked, dashed arrows denote data flow. For the LFR, the deployment diagram is given in Fig. 12. The LFR was constructed using the *LEGO Mindstorms EV3 Core Set (313131)*, which connects to a *Computer* (for which the specifications are not mentioned here) via a TCP/IP connection. Above the LFR, there is a depth vision camera, whose image needs to be processed before a valid representation of the system can be shown in a Dashboard.

Figure 13 shows the deployment diagram for the incubator case. The core of the incubator is a Raspberry Pi that controls the temperature in a Styrofoam box. Inside, there are two temperature sensors to measure the inside temperature. Additionally, there is one temperature sensor on the outside of the box. Control information is communicated to the heatbed and the fan through a relay. On a *Computer* (for which the specifications are not mentioned), multiple OS applications and processes implement anomaly detection and data management.

Even with only two example cases, some commonality is apparent. This will form the basis for a feature model of the Deployment Stage.

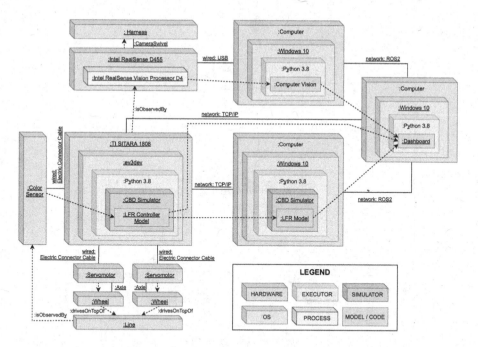

Fig. 12. Deployment mapping diagram for the LFR case.

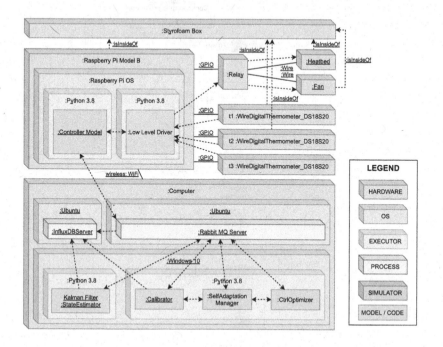

Fig. 13. Deployment mapping diagram for the incubator case.

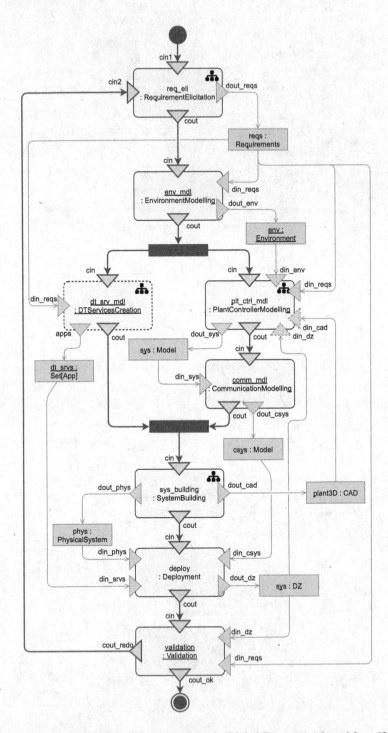

Fig. 14. Workflow model for the construction of a Digital T system. Adapted from [20].

7   Workflow

Section 4 looked at the required setup and features in the problem space and Sect. 5 presented the general architectures of Digital T systems. Finally, the two example cases were deployed as described in Sect. 6. Each of these stages have their own *worflows* and final results. On top of that, the overall creation of the Digital T system also follows a workflow. Such a workflow describes in which order which activities are carried out, on which artifacts. A well-chosen workflow may optimize the overall development time. Note that a workflow or Process Model (PM) follows partly from the constraints imposed by the variability models. Figure 14 shows a PM that yields a Digital T system, going through the previously defined stages. It has been created by analyzing and unifying the workflows followed for both cases from Sect. 3. The PM shown is modelled in a language similar to a UML Activity Diagram, but following the notations defined in [19]. It describes the order of activities (bold, blue control flow), annotated with their in- and output artifacts (thin, green data flow). The blue roundtangles represent the activities carried out and the green rectangles identify the input/output artifacts. All activities and artifacts have a name and a type, denoted as "name : Type". Some of the activities can be automated. This depends on the modelling languages and tools that were used.

In the following, we detail some of the process steps.

First, starting from some "Requirements", the environment in which the Digital T system is active is modelled. Once the environment is available, the plant and controller models can be constructed in the hierarchical "PlantControllerModelling" activity. To allow for more possibilities and variability, no details will be provided on the exact realization of this activity (*i.e.,* , this is a Variant Subsystem). The "CommunicationModelling" activity provides for communicating data to an external instance. At the same time as "CommunicationModelling" and "PlantControllerModelling", it is possible to concern the services required for creating Digital T systems.

Next, the system is built, potentially also resulting in a 3D CAD model as an intermediate artifact. Once the system is built, all components are deployed as described by a corresponding deployment diagram. After deployment, the overall functionality is validated and (if need be) new requirements are constructed for a next iteration of this process.

8   Conclusions and Related Work

This paper has discussed the variability in creating Digital Ts (*e.g.,* (a family of) Digital Models/Shadows/Twins/...) using Multi-Paradigm Modelling principles [2], at the exploration, design and deployment stage. For the design stage, an architecture was also presented. The feasibility of the presented workflow has been demonstrated by means of two distinct, exemplary cases that are simplifications of often used industrial components (potentially used together). We plan to further explore the various product family models introduced here using the recent Cross-Domain Systematic Mapping Study on Software Engineering for Digital Twins [7] as a starting point. In particular, the relationships between the features will be further investigated, with as ultimate goal, to chart and automate as much as possible of the workflow. The link will be made with the Asset Administration Shell (AAS). Oakes et al. [18] provided a mapping of their Digital Twin framework onto the Asset Administration Shell.

Acknowledgements. This research was partially supported by Flanders Make, the strategic research center for the Flemish manufacturing industry and by a doctoral fellowship of the Faculty of Science of the University of Antwerp. In addition, we are grateful to the Poul Due Jensen Foundation, which has supported the establishment of a new Center for Digital Twin Technology at Aarhus University.

References

1. Aivaliotis, P., Georgoulias, K., Alexopoulos, K.: Using digital twin for maintenance applications in manufacturing: state of the art and gap analysis. In: 2019 IEEE International Conference on Engineering, Technology and Innovation (ICE/ITMC), pp. 1–5. IEEE, Valbonne Sophia-Antipolis (2019). https://doi.org/10.1109/ICE.2019.8792613
2. Amrani, M., Blouin, D., Heinrich, R., Rensink, A., Vangheluwe, H., Wortmann, A.: Multiparadigm modelling for cyber–physical systems: a descriptive framework. Softw. Syst. Model. **20**(3), 611–639 (2021). https://doi.org/10.1007/s10270-021-00876-z
3. Bradac, Z., Marcon, P., Zezulka, F., Arm, J., Benesl, T.: Digital twin and AAS in the industry 4.0 framework. In: IOP Conference Series: Materials Science and Engineering, vol. 618, p. 012001 (2019). https://doi.org/10.1088/1757-899X/618/1/012001
4. Cheng, Y., Zhang, Y., Ji, P., Xu, W., Zhou, Z., Tao, F.: Cyber-physical integration for moving digital factories forward towards smart manufacturing: a survey. Int. J. Adv. Manuf. Technol. **97**(1–4), 1209–1221 (2018). https://doi.org/10.1007/s00170-018-2001-2
5. Cimino, C., Negri, E., Fumagalli, L.: Review of digital twin applications in manufacturing. Comput. Ind. **113**, 103130 (2019). https://doi.org/10.1016/j.compind.2019.103130
6. Czarnecki, K.: Overview of generative software development. In: Banâtre, J.-P., Fradet, P., Giavitto, J.-L., Michel, O. (eds.) UPP 2004. LNCS, vol. 3566, pp. 326–341. Springer, Heidelberg (2005). https://doi.org/10.1007/11527800_25
7. Dalibor, M., et al.: A cross-domain systematic mapping study on software engineering for digital twins. J. Syst. Softw. **193**, 111361 (2022). https://doi.org/10.1016/j.jss.2022.111361, https://www.sciencedirect.com/science/article/pii/S0164121222000917
8. Feng, H., Gomes, C.A., Thule, C., Lausdahl, K., Iosifidis, A., Larsen, P.G.: Introduction to digital twin engineering. In: 2021 Annual Modeling and Simulation Conference (ANNSIM) (2021)
9. International Organization for Standardization (ISO/DIS): ISO 23247: Automation systems and integration—Digital Twin framework for manufacturing. Technical report (2020)
10. Kalman, R.E.: A new approach to linear filtering and prediction problems. J. Basic Eng. **82**(1), 35–45 (1960). https://doi.org/10.1115/1.3662552
11. Kang, K.C., Cohen, S.G., Hess, J.A., Novak, W.E., Peterson, A.S.: Feature-oriented domain analysis (FODA) feasibility study. Carnegie-Mellon University, Technical report (1990)
12. Kritzinger, W., Karner, M., Traar, G., Henjes, J., Sihn, W.: Digital twin in manufacturing: a categorical literature review and classification. IFAC-PapersOnLine **51**(11), 1016–1022 (2018). https://doi.org/10.1016/j.ifacol.2018.08.474
13. Kutin, A.A., Bushuev, V.V., Molodtsov, V.V.: Digital twins of mechatronic machine tools for modern manufacturing. In: IOP Conference Series: Materials Science and Engineering, vol. 568, p. 012070 (2019). https://doi.org/10.1088/1757-899X/568/1/012070

14. Lin, W.D., Low, M.Y.H.: Concept and implementation of a cyber-physical digital twin for a SMT line. In: 2019 IEEE International Conference on Industrial Engineering and Engineering Management (IEEM), pp. 1455–1459 (2019). https://doi.org/10.1109/IEEM44572.2019.8978620

15. Lu, Y., Liu, C., Wang, K.I.K., Huang, H., Xu, X.: Digital twin-driven smart manufacturing: connotation, reference model, applications and research issues. Rob. Comput.-Integr. Manuf. **61**, 101837 (2020). https://doi.org/10.1016/j.rcim.2019.101837

16. Madni, A.M., Madni, C.C., Lucero, S.D.: Leveraging digital twin technology in model-based systems engineering. Systems **7**(1), 7 (2019)

17. Negri, E., Fumagalli, L., Macchi, M.: A review of the roles of digital twin in CPS-based production systems. Procedia Manuf. **11**, 939–948 (2017). https://doi.org/10.1016/j.promfg.2017.07.198

18. Oakes, B.J., et al.: A digital twin description framework and its mapping to asset administration shell. arXiv preprint arXiv:2209.12661 (2022)

19. Paredis, R., Exelmans, J., Vangheluwe, H.: Multi-paradigm modelling for model-based systems engineering: extending the FTG+PM. In: 2022 Annual Modeling and Simulation Conference (ANNSIM), SCS (2022)

20. Paredis., R., Gomes., C., Vangheluwe., H.: Towards a family of digital model/shadow/twin workflows and architectures. In: Proceedings of the 2nd International Conference on Innovative Intelligent Industrial Production and Logistics - IN4PL, pp. 174–182. INSTICC, SciTePress (2021). https://doi.org/10.5220/0010717600003062

21. Paredis, R., Vangheluwe, H.: Exploring a digital shadow design workflow by means of a line following robot use-case. In: 2021 Annual Modeling and Simulation Conference (ANNSIM) (2021)

22. Paredis, R., Vangheluwe, H.: Towards a digital Z framework based on a family of architectures and a virtual knowledge graph. In: Proceedings of the 25th International Conference on Model Driven Engineering Languages and Systems (MODELS) (2022)

23. Park, H., Easwaran, A., Andalam, S.: Challenges in digital twin development for cyber-physical production systems. In: Chamberlain, R., Taha, W., Törngren, M. (eds.) CyPhy/WESE -2018. LNCS, vol. 11615, pp. 28–48. Springer, Cham (2019). https://doi.org/10.1007/978-3-030-23703-5_2

24. Qamar, A., Paredis, C.: Dependency modeling and model management in mechatronic design. In: Proceedings of the ASME Design Engineering Technical Conference, Chicago, IL, USA, vol. 2 (2012). https://doi.org/10.1115/DETC2012-70272

25. Rajamani, R.: Vehicle Dynamics and Control. Springer, Heidelberg (2011). https://doi.org/10.1007/978-1-4614-1433-9

26. Rosen, R., von Wichert, G., Lo, G., Bettenhausen, K.D.: About the importance of autonomy and digital twins for the future of manufacturing. IFAC-PapersOnLine **48**(3), 567–572 (2015). https://doi.org/10.1016/j.ifacol.2015.06.141

27. Rumpe, B.: Modelling for and of Digital Twins. Keynote (2021)

28. Tao, F., Zhang, H., Liu, A., Nee, A.Y.C.: Digital twin in industry: state-of-the-art. IEEE Trans. Ind. Inf. **15**(4), 2405–2415 (2019). https://doi.org/10.1109/TII.2018.2873186

29. de Weck, O.L., Roos, D., Magee, C.L., Vest, C.M.: Life-Cycle Properties of Engineering Systems: The Ilities, pp. 65–96. MIT Press, Cambridge (2011)

30. Zhang, H., Ma, L., Sun, J., Lin, H., Thürer, M.: Digital twin in services and industrial product service systems. Procedia CIRP **83**, 57–60 (2019). https://doi.org/10.1016/j.procir.2019.02.131

Online Facility Location Problems Inspired by the COVID-19 Pandemic

Christine Markarian[1]($\boxtimes$) and Peter Khallouf[2]

[1] Department of Engineering and Information Technology, University of Dubai, Dubai, United Arab Emirates
cmarkarian@ud.ac.ae
[2] Data Science - Data and IT, International University of Applied Sciences, Bad Honnef, Germany
peter.khallouf@iubh.de

Abstract. The COVID-19 pandemic has challenged countries to take immediate measures to contain the disease and minimize its spread. Most, if not all, communities faced unprecedented healthcare resource shortages and limitations in hospital capacities. Consequently, leasing facilities and transforming them into health-care service providers were among the common actions taken. Inspired by this situation and the attempt to make wise leasing choices amidst these challenging times, we address in this paper a variant of the well-known *Facility Location* problem, one of the most well-studied optimization problems in computer science, operations research, and combinatorics. Given a collection of facilities, clients, services, and a positive integer $d \geq 2$. Services can be leased for different durations and prices at each facility location. Each service at each facility location is associated with a dormant fee that needs to be paid each time the service is not leased at the facility for d days. In each step, a subset of the clients arrives, each requesting a number of the services. The goal is to connect each client to one or more facility locations jointly offering its requested services. Connecting a client to a facility incurs a connecting cost equal to the distance between the client and facility. The aim is to decide which services to lease, when, and for how long, in order to serve all clients as soon as they appear with minimum costs of leasing, connecting, and dormant fees. This variant is referred to as the *Online Facility Service Leasing with Duration-Specific Dormant Fees* (*d*-OFSL). In this paper, we design online algorithms for the metric and non-metric variants of *d*-OFSL. In the metric variant, facilities and clients are assumed to reside in the metric space. We measure the performance of our algorithms in the competitive analysis framework in which the online algorithm is measured against the optimal offline solution constructed by knowing all the input sequence in advance. The latter is the standard to evaluate online algorithms.

Keywords: Online algorithms · Optimization · Competitive analysis · Metric facility location · Non-metric facility location · Service leasing · Duration-specific dormant fees

1 Introduction

The COVID-19 pandemic has caused severe disruption around the world socially, economically, and educationally. Communities around the world have tried to slow or stop

© The Author(s), under exclusive license to Springer Nature Switzerland AG 2023
A. Smirnov et al. (Eds.): IN4PL 2020/IN4PL 2021, CCIS 1855, pp. 110–123, 2023.
https://doi.org/10.1007/978-3-031-37228-5_7

the spread of the disease by giving recommendations, setting new laws, and mandating behavior changes. There have been supply shortages in many countries. To overcome these shortages, many communities started *leasing* facility locations and transformed them into health-care service providers. Decisions have been challenging in regards to how to distribute patients into health centers and make wise leasing choices. Consequently, a significant number of works addressing such areas from various perspectives appeared in the literature [5, 15, 16, 36, 37]. In a previous work [31], we have introduced a new *Facility Location* variant, known as the *Online Facility Service Leasing* problem (OFSL). OFSL was motivated by leasing scenarios such as the following. A company makes contracts to lease resources at facility locations. Each location offers a number of services that are reserved for the company for as long as stated in the contract. There are a number of lease options to choose from. Each option states the duration and cost of the lease, such that prices respect the economy of scale. That is, a longer lease is more expensive but is cheaper per unit time. For each day on which a facility is not leased, a so-called *dormant fee* must be paid. This is to make sure that the service is reserved. Clients will show up over time. The company will not know how many clients are there and when will they show up. Every arriving client requests a number of services such as treatment, testing, and vaccination. The goal is to make decisions as to *when* to lease, *which* services, *at which* facility locations, such that each client is served by connecting it to multiple facilities jointly offering the requested services and at minimum possible costs of *leasing*, *connecting*, and *dormant fees*.

1.1 Our Results

In this paper, we study a generalization of OFSL in which we are given a parameter d. For each service that is not leased for more than d consecutive days, we need to pay a so-called *dormant fee*. We refer to this variant as the *Online Facility Service Leasing with Duration-Specific Dormant Fees* problem (d-OFSL).

Our study is an extension of our work in [32] in which we address the metric version of d-OFSL. In this paper, we further study the non-metric variant of the problem.

In the metric version, clients and facilities are assumed to reside in the metric space and distances between them respect the triangle inequality. We refer to this variant as metric d-OFSL and the non-metric variant as non-metric d-OFSL. For metric d-OFSL, we design a deterministic online primal-dual algorithm. For non-metric d-OFSL, we design a randomized online algorithm that is similar to the algorithm for OFSL [31].

We analyze our algorithms using the competitive analysis framework [4], a worst-case analysis in which the performance of the online algorithm is measured against the optimal offline solution for all instances of the problem. The optimal offline solution is constructed by an algorithm that is given all the input sequence at once and is optimal. We say that the online algorithm has *competitive ratio* r where r is the worst-case ratio of the cost of the online algorithm to that of the optimal offline solution. The algorithm is referred to as an r-competitive online algorithm. We aim to design online algorithms that have a small r.

Our deterministic online algorithm for metric d-OFSL has an $\mathcal{O}((L + \frac{d}{l_{min}}) \cdot \log l_{max})$-competitive ratio, where:

- L is the number of lease types available

– d is the maximum number of days after which a dormant fee needs to be paid
– l_{min} is the shortest lease duration
– l_{max} is the longest lease duration

Our randomized online algorithm for non-metric d-OFSL has an $\mathcal{O}(\log(n + m \cdot l_{max}) \log(Lm))$ competitive ratio, where:

– n is the total number of clients
– l_{max} is the length of the longest lease duration
– L is the number of lease types available
– m is the total number of facility locations

1.2 Lower Bounds

d-OFSL generalizes the *Parking Permit* problem (PP) [34]. The metric variant of d-OFSL generalizes as well the *Metric Online Facility Location* problem (metric OFL) [33]. The non-metric variant of d-OFSL generalizes as well the *Non-metric Online Facility Location* problem (non-metric OFL) [2]. Hence, we conclude the following lower bounds for metric and non-metric d-OFSL.

There is a lower bound of $\Omega(L + \frac{\log n}{\log \log n})$ on the competitive ratio of any deterministic algorithm for metric d-OFSL, where n is the number of clients and L is the number of available lease types, resulting from the lower bounds for PP [34] and metric OFL [11].

There is a lower bound of $\Omega(\log n \log m + \log L)$ on the competitive ratio of any randomized polynomial-time randomized algorithm for non-metric d-OFSL, assuming $BPP \neq NP$, where n is the number of clients and L is the number of available lease types, resulting from the lower bounds for PP [34] and non-metric OFL [19].

1.3 Outline

The rest of the paper is organized as follows. In Sect. 2, we give an overview of works related to our problem. In Sect. 3, we introduce some preliminaries. In Sects. 4 and 5, we present our results for metric d-OFSL and non-metric d-OFSL, respectively. We conclude in Sect. 6 with some discussion and future works.

2   Literature Review

In this section, we present an overview of works related to the leasing model as well as metric and non-metric Online Facility Location problems.

2.1 Leasing Model

The first theoretical leasing model was introduced by Meyerson with the *Parking Permit* problem (PP) [34]. Meyerson proposed an $\mathcal{O}(L)$-competitive deterministic algorithm and an $\mathcal{O}(\log L)$-competitive randomized algorithm for the problem, along with matching lower bounds, where L is the number of lease types.

Many well-known optimization problems were later studied in this framework [1, 3,28,35]. Extensions to the original model were also known, such as assuming prices of leases change with time, or clients are associated with deadlines and can be served anytime within their deadline, and lease types have dimensions [7–9,21,23].

2.2 Online Facility Location

Meyerson [33] proposed a randomized $\mathcal{O}(\log n)$-competitive online algorithm for the *Metric Online Facility Location* problem (metric OFL), where n is the number of clients. Fotakis [11] improved this bound by proposing an $\mathcal{O}(\log n / \log \log n)$-competitive algorithm and giving a matching lower bound. Many other variants were also studied as in [12,13,38].

Alon *et al.* [2] proposed a randomized $\mathcal{O}(\log n \log m)$-competitive online algorithm for the *Non-metric Online Facility Location* problem (non-metric OFL), where n is the number of clients and m is the number of facilities. Other variants of non-metric OFL were also studied as in [24,25].

In the leasing setting, both metric OFL and non-metric OFL were studied as many variants [1,6,21,27,35]. In these variants, leasing is applied to facilities rather than services. Moreover, unlike in d-OFSL, all clients in these variants can be served by all facilities. d-OFSL generalizes these variants by setting the number of services to one, offered by all facilities, and the number of dormant fees to 0.

3 Preliminaries

We assume the following models, referred to as the *Dormant-Fee-Interval* model and the *Lease-Interval* model for the dormant fees and the lease structures, respectively.

Dormant-Fee-Interval Model. The algorithm pays a dormant fee, if needed, only on days x where $x \mod d \equiv 1$, without affecting the competitive ratio.

Proof. Consider an instance I of the original problem. Let Opt be an optimal solution for I. In the Dormant-Fee Interval model, we are only allowed to pay a dormant fee on days $x : x \mod d \equiv 1$. Let i be an interval of d days at the end of which Opt has paid a dormant fee. Starting from day 0, we will divide the timeline into intervals of length d. Interval i crosses at most two of these intervals. We can create a feasible solution for the Dormant-Fee Interval model by paying the dormant fee associated with the first interval crossed by i. This would not affect the feasibility of the solution constructed. Doing this for all the intervals associated with dormant fees paid by Opt would complete the proof.

Lease-interval Model. Meyerson [34] showed that the following can be assumed by losing only a constant factor in the competitive ratio.

– Leases of the same duration do not overlap.
– All lease durations are power of two.

This model has also been assumed in [31] and many leasing optimization problems studied thus far [1, 21, 22, 35].

Next, we give a formal description of metric/non-metric *Online Facility Service Leasing with Duration-Specific Dormant Fees*(metric/non-metric *d*-OFSL).

Definition 1. *(metric/non-metric* d-*OFSL) Given* m *facility locations and* k *services. Each facility location offers a subset of the* k *services. These services can be leased with L different types, each differing by a duration and price. Given a positive integer* d ≥ 2. *For each service at each facility location, there is a dormant fee that needs to be paid whenever the service is not leased for d consecutive days. There are at most* n *clients which arrive over time. Each day, a subset of the clients arrives, each requesting a subset of the* k *services. The algorithm serves a client by connecting it to a number of facility locations jointly offering the requested services, such that these services are leased at the time of the client's arrival. Connecting a client to a facility location incurs a connecting cost which is equal to the distance between the client and the facility location. To each day, the algorithm reacts by deciding which services to lease at which facility locations with which lease type in order to serve all arriving clients. The goal is to minimize the total leasing costs, connecting costs, and dormant fees.*

4   Metric D-OFSL

In this section, we represent metric *d*-OFSL first as a graphical and then as a primal-dual formulation. Then, we present our primal-dual algorithm and its competitive analysis.

4.1   Graph Formulation of Metric *d*-OFSL

In this section, we formulate metric *d*-OFSL as the following graph-theoretic problem.

- For each client which arrives, we create a node, called *actual client node* at the location of the client. This client needs to be served as soon as it arrives. For each service it is requesting, it needs to be connected to at least one facility location offering the service.
- For each service at each facility, we create a node, called *actual service node* at the location of the facility. This *actual service node* can be leased for L different durations.
- For each service at each facility, we create a node, called *virtual service node* at the location of the facility. This *virtual service node* can be leased only for a duration of a single day and has cost equal to the dormant fee associated with the service. Moreover, it can be leased only on days $x : x \mod d \equiv 0$. Figure 2 shows an example of $d = 5$.
- For each service at each facility, we create a node, called *virtual client node* at the location of the facility. This client appears on days $x : x \mod d \equiv 1$ and requests to be connected either to the *virtual service node* or to the *actual service node* associated with it. Moreover, it can be served on any day starting from the day y it appears until day $y + d - 1$. Figure 2 shows an example of $d = 5$.

The edges are directed and are added as follows.

- We add an edge from an *actual client node* to an *actual service node* if the client corresponding to the client node has requested the service corresponding to the service node. The weight of this edge would be equal to the connecting cost between the client and the facility location.
- From each *virtual client node*, we add two edges, of weight 0, one to its corresponding *actual service node* and another to its corresponding *virtual service node*.

Figure 1 shows an example of three facility locations, each offering one, two, and three services, respectively, and one client requesting one service.

Initially, the algorithm knows all about the facility locations, the services, and the lease prices. The client locations and their requests are revealed over time when clients show up. Each day, the online algorithm reacts to the client nodes created by purchasing from the available leases. Edges correpond to the connecting costs that will be paid upon connecting a client to a facility location. Notice that, a virtual client in our formulation is associated with a deadline that represents whether or not a dormant fee will be paid. Each service at each facility is associated with such a client that appears every d days to ensure that every d days, the algorithm checks whether it is required to pay a dormant fee for the service or not. Figure 1 illustrates the days on which virtual client nodes appear and virtual service nodes are leased.

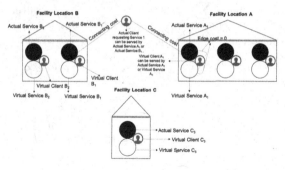

Fig. 1. Three facility locations and a client requesting one service (from [32]).

Fig. 2. Virtual client, virtual service lease days for $d = 5$ (from [32]).

4.2 Primal-dual Formulation of Metric d-OFSL

In this section, we present an integer linear program and the corresponding relaxed dual program for the graph-theoretic problem described above. Figure 3 illustrates this formulation.

The objective function has two parts. The first part represents the costs incurred by leasing services. We denote each service at each facility as a triplet (i, k, t), where i is the service type, k is the lease type, and t is the starting day of the lease. A variable x_{ikt} is assigned to each (i, k, t) indicating whether it is bought or not. c_{ik} is the cost of leasing service i with type k.

A *request* is characterized by a client-service pair, such that for each service requested by a client, we generate a request (js, t, d) referring to client j requesting service s, arriving at time t, and having deadline $t + d$. c_{ijs} is the cost of connecting j to i.

The second part of the objective function represents the costs incurred by connecting each request to a service, such that variable $y_{i,jstd}$ indicates whether request (js, t, d) is connected to service i. Recall that all requests associated with actual client nodes have deadline 0.

The first primal constraint guarantees that each request is connected to at least one service. The second constraint makes sure that each request is only connected to a service that is leased within the arrival time and the deadline of the request. We denote by S the collection of all service triplets and by $\mathcal{R}$ the collection of all request triplets. We denote by S_{js} the collection of service triplets that can serve request js. We call these triplets *nominees*. Let H_n be the nth harmonic number $1 + \frac{1}{2} + ... + \frac{1}{n}$.

$$\min \quad \sum_{(i,k,t) \in S} c_{ik} x_{ikt} + \sum_{(js,t,d) \in \mathcal{R}} \sum_{i \in S_{js}} c_{ijs} y_{i,jstd}$$

$$\text{Subject to:} \quad \sum_{i \in S_{js}} y_{i,jstd} \geq 1 \qquad (js, t, d) \in \mathcal{R}$$

$$\sum x_{ikt'} - y_{i,jstd} \geq 0 \qquad (i, k, t') \in S_{js},$$

$$(js, t, d) \in \mathcal{R}$$

$$y_{i,jstd} \in \{0, 1\} \ i \in S_{js},$$

$$(js, t, d) \in \mathcal{R}$$

$$x_{ikt} \in \{0, 1\} \ (i, k, t) \in S$$

$$\max \quad \sum_{(js,t,d) \in \mathcal{R}} \alpha_{jstd}$$

$$\text{Subject to:} \quad \alpha_{jstd} - \beta_{i,jstd} \leq c_{ijs} \ i \in S_{js},$$

$$(js, t, d) \in \mathcal{R}$$

$$\sum_{(js,t',d) \in \mathcal{R}} \beta_{i,jst'd} \leq c_{ik} \ (i, k, t) \in S_{js}$$

$$\beta_{i,jstd} \geq 0 \quad i \in S_{js},$$

$$(js, t, d) \in \mathcal{R}$$

$$\alpha_{jstd} \geq 0 \quad (js, t, d) \in \mathcal{R}$$

Fig. 3. Linear Programming Formulation of metric d-OFSL (from [32]).

4.3 Primal-dual Algorithm

In this section, we present an online deterministic primal-dual algorithm for metric d-OFSL.

The main idea of the algorithm is that whenever a client arrives and a request is formed, as long as (i) the dual constraints associated with it are not violated and (ii) the request's dual variable is not equal to the distance to a purchased nominee, the algorithm keeps increasing its dual variables. Algorithm 1 illustrates the steps that react to each request formed.

Algorithm 1. Online Primal-Dual Algorithm for metric d-OFSL.

When a request (js, t, d) is generated, we increase its variable α_{jstd} and the variables $\beta_{i,jstd}$ corresponding to its nominees while maintaining $\alpha_{jstd} - \beta_{i,jstd} \geq 0$, until:
(i) either the dual constraint of some nominee $(i, k, t') \in S_{js}$ becomes tight:

$$\sum \beta_{i,jstd} = c_{ik} \colon (js, t, d) \in \mathcal{R}$$

So, we buy (i, k, t') (i.e., we set its primal variable $x_{ikt'}$ to 1).
(ii) or $\alpha_{jstd} = c_{ijs}$ for some bought nominee $(i, k, t') \in S_{js}$
We connect (js, t, d) to the closest bought nominee.

4.4 Competitive Analysis

In this section, we analyze the competitive ratio of our algorithm, based on dual fitting arguments [14, 17, 18].

The proof ideas are based on our previous result in [21]. We partition the timeline into rounds of length l_{max} and conduct the analysis on the first l_{max} time steps only. This has been proven to be sufficient to conclude the competitive ratio of the algorithm [1].

Note that according to the primal-dual formulation, the dormant fees are embedded in the primal-dual program as leasing costs. Hence, they will not appear in the analysis.

Notice that our algorithm outputs a *feasible* primal solution and an *infeasible* dual solution. Consequently, the proof will be composed of two parts. In the first part (Lemma 1), the cost of the primal solution will be bounded by $\mathcal{O}(L + \frac{d}{l_{min}})$ times the cost of the dual solution. In the second part (Lemma 2), the infeasible dual solution constructed will be scaled down by $\mathcal{O}(H_{l_{max}})$ to make it feasible. Using Weak Duality Theorem, we will imply the competitive ratio of the algorithm.

Lemma 1. *The cost of the primal solution constructed by the algorithm is at most* $(L + \frac{2d}{l_{min}}) \cdot \sum_{(js,t,d) \in \mathcal{R}} \alpha_{jstd}$.

Proof. We first show that the sum of the connection costs is at most $\sum_{(js,t,d) \in \mathcal{R}} \alpha_{jstd}$ and then show that the sum of the leasing costs is at most $(L + \frac{2d}{l_{min}}) \cdot \sum_{(js,t,d) \in \mathcal{R}} \alpha_{jstd}$.

A request (js, t, d) is either assigned to an already leased service or it leads to leasing a new service. If it is the first case, then the request has increased only the variable α_{jstd} until $\alpha_{jstd} = c_{ijs}$. If it is the second case, then the request has increased both α_{jstd} and $\beta_{i,jstd}$ as long as $\alpha_{jstd} - \beta_{i,jstd} \leq c_{ijs}$, while maintaining $\alpha_{jstd} - \beta_{i,jstd} \geq 0$. Thus $\alpha_{jstd} \geq c_{ijs}$. We can sum up over all requests and get a total connection cost of $\mathcal{O}(\sum_{(js,t,d) \in \mathcal{R}} \alpha_{jstd})$.

As for the leasing costs, we say a request *contributes* to the leasing cost of a service of type k if it has caused such a service lease to be purchased. The total contribution of request (js, t, d) to service leases of type k can be upper bounded by $\alpha_{jstd} \cdot \frac{d}{l_k}$. This is because the number of nominees of type k does not exceed $\frac{d}{l_k}$ (the maximum is for the virtual clients case). Summing up over all L lease types yields:

$$\sum_{j=1}^{L} \left\lceil \frac{d}{l_j} \right\rceil \le L + d \left[\frac{1}{l_1} \left(\frac{1 - (1/2)^L}{1 - 1/2} \right) \right] = L + d \left[\frac{2}{l_1} \left(1 - (1/2)^L \right) \right]$$

Since $L \ge 1$, we have:

$$L + d \left[\frac{2}{l_1} \left(1 - (1/2)^L \right) \right] \le L + \frac{2d}{l_{min}}$$

The sum of all clients' contributions implies the total leasing costs:

$$\sum_{(js,t,d) \in \mathcal{R}} \alpha_{jstd} \cdot \left(L + \frac{2d}{l_{min}} \right)$$

The following Lemma has been proven in [1,21,35]. It shows that it is sufficient to divide the infeasible dual solution by $2(H_{l_{max}} + 1)$ to yield a feasible dual solution. Its proof is based on repeatedly exploiting the triangle inequality. Moreover, the bound is not based on the number of clients but rather on the number of time steps. That is why the additional number of clients resulting from the virtual client nodes does not appear in the analysis.

Lemma 2. *For any service $(i, k, t) \in S_{js}$ and $\mu = \frac{1}{2(H_{l_{max}}+1)}$, it holds that:*

$$\sum_{(js,t',d) \in \mathcal{R}} \mu \cdot \alpha_{jst'd} - \beta_{i,jst'd} \le c_{ijs}$$

Notice that both bounds do not depend on the number of services and that is why the additional number of clients resulting from the virtual service nodes does not appear in the analysis too.

By combining the two lemmata, we obtain the following theorem.

Theorem 1. *There is an online deterministic $\mathcal{O}((L + \frac{d}{l_{min}}) \cdot \log l_{max})$-competitive algorithm for metric d-OFSL, where L is the number of lease types available, d is the maximum number of days after which a dormant fee needs to be paid, l_{min} is the shortest lease duration, and l_{max} is the longest lease duration.*

5   Non-metric d-OFSL

In this section, we give a graphical formulation of non-metric d-OFSL. Then, we introduce our algorithm and prove its competitive ratio.

5.1   Graph Formulation of Non-metric d-OFSL

In this section, we formulate non-metric d-OFSL as the following graph-theoretic problem.

- For each client which arrives, we create a node, called *actual client node* at the location of the client. This client needs to be served as soon as it arrives.
- For each facility location, we create a node, called *actual facility node*.
- For each service at each facility, we create a node, called *actual facility node*.
- For each facility and each day $x : x \mod d \equiv 1$, we create a *virtual client node* and a *virtual facility node*.

  The edges are directed and are added as follows.

- We add an edge from an *actual client node* to an *actual facility node* if the corresponding client has requested the corresponding service. The weights are added in correspondence to the connecting costs between the client and the facility.
- From each *actual facility node* to each *service node*, we add L directed edges. The weight of each edge is equal to the cost of leasing the corresponding service at the facility location.
- For facility j, we add an edge from the *virtual client node* to the *actual facility node* corresponding to j. We also add an edge from the *virtual client node* to the *virtual facility node* corresponding to j. The weights are set to 0.
- From each *virtual facility node* to each *service node* corresponding to it, we add an edge and set its weight to the dormant fee of the corresponding service at the facility location.

Before clients arrive, the algorithm has information about the facility locations, the services, the leasing costs, and the total number of clients. In each step, a number of clients arrive. The algorithm will know at each step the connecting costs associated with the arriving clients. The job of the algorithm is to serve the clients by connecting them to a number of facilities jointly offering the requested services. These services must be leased on the time step of the client's arrival. For each client, the algorithm needs to find a directed path from the corresponding *actual client node* to each service node requested. Moreover, for each facility, the algorithm needs to find a directed path from the corresponding *virtual client node* to each service node representing the services offered by the facility.

5.2   Online Algorithm

In this section, we present an online randomized algorithm for non-metric d-OFSL.

We denote by w_e the weight of edge e. Each edge is assigned a fractional value v_e. These are set to 0 and will increase over time. The *maximum flow* between two nodes is the smallest total fractional values of edges which disconnect the two nodes if removed. These edges form a *minimum cut*. On a given time step, the algorithm will disregard any edge that has an expired lease.

The randomization approach used by the algorithm is similar to our approach used in [31]. We select a random variable r, the minimum among $2 \lceil \log(n + m \cdot l_{max} + 1) \rceil$

independent random variables. These are uniformly distributed over the interval $[0, 1]$, where the logarithms have base 2.

Algorithm 2 below reacts to each time step as follows. The function *Select-edges* returns a set of edges to be bought by the algorithm, forming a feasible solution.

Algorithm 2. Online Algorithm for non-metric d-OFSL.

If the time step contains a *virtual client node*, select the virtual client node i and for each service s corresponding to it, do the following:
- Buy the edges returned by *Select-edges(i, s)*.

Select each actual client node i and each service s requested
- Buy the edges returned by *Select-edges(i, s)*.

Select-edges (node i, node s)
i. If a directed path from i to s does not exist in the solution, do the following. As long as the maximum flow between i and s is less than 1:
  - Construct a minimum cut $\mathcal{Q}$ between i and s.
  - Increase the value v_e of each edge $e \in \mathcal{Q}$:

$$v_e \leftarrow v_e\left(1 + \frac{1}{w_e}\right) + \frac{1}{|\mathcal{Q}| \cdot w_e}$$

ii. Return edge e if $v_e \geq r$.
iii. If i is still not connected to s, return the edges of a shortest-weight path from i to s.

5.3   Competitive Analysis

We refer the reader to the competitive analysis we have provided for non-metric OFSL in [31], as similar arguments apply here as well.

The analysis leads to the following theorem for non-metric d-OFSL.

Theorem 2. *There is an online randomized $\mathcal{O}(\log(n + m \cdot l_{max}) \log(Lm))$-competitive algorithm for non-metric d-OFSL, where n is the total number of clients, m is the number of facility locations, L is the number of lease types available, and l_{max} is the length of the longest lease duration.*

6   Concluding Remarks

In this paper, we have introduced a generalization of the online facility location problem. The proposed variant may appear as a sub-problem in many real-world leasing scenarios involving serving clients without knowing future clients in advance. Studying other variants of Facility Location Problems such as [10, 20, 24–26, 29, 30] in the model introduced in this paper would make an interesting future work.

Closing the gap between the lower and upper bounds for both the metric and non-metric variants would be a next research direction. One could also target removing the dependency on d in the metric case.

The parameter d in the model is assumed to be fixed for all services and all facilities. In many real-world applications, this does not have to be true. There could be many factors affecting d. For instance, the value of d could depend on how high the demand for the facility or service is. In order to gain customers, a facility might want to limit the restrictions on some periods during which the demand at its location is low.

Dormant fees in our model are also assumed to be fixed for all services and all facilities. This is also not the case in real-world applications. It is not clear whether the proposed algorithms in this paper also work for different dormant fees. It would be interesting to investigate mutiple dormant fee models and design algorithms for them.

Implementing the algorithm and running simulations inspired by real-world applications would be an interesting next step. This way, one can understand the difficulty of the problem from a practical point of view and analyze the performance of the algorithm in scenarios other than worse-case.

References

1. Abshoff, S., Kling, P., Markarian, C., Meyer auf der Heide, F., Pietrzyk, P.: Towards the price of leasing online. J. Combinatorial Optim. **32**(4), 1197–1216 (2016)
2. Alon, N., Awerbuch, B., Azar, Y., Buchbinder, N., Naor, J.: A general approach to online network optimization problems. ACM Trans. Algorithms (TALG) **2**(4), 640–660 (2006)
3. Anthony, B.M., Gupta, A.: Infrastructure leasing problems. In: Fischetti, M., Williamson, D.P. (eds.) IPCO 2007. LNCS, vol. 4513, pp. 424–438. Springer, Heidelberg (2007). https://doi.org/10.1007/978-3-540-72792-7_32
4. Borodin, A., El-Yaniv, R.: Online computation and competitive analysis. cambridge University Press (2005)
5. Choi, T.-M.: Fighting against COVID-19: what operations research can help and the sense-and-respond framework. Ann. Oper. Res. 1–17 (2021). https://doi.org/10.1007/s10479-021-03973-w
6. De Lima, M.S., San Felice, M.C., Lee, O.: Connected facility leasing problems. In: ICTCS/CILC, pp. 162–173 (2017)
7. De Lima, M.S., San Felice, M.C., Lee, O.: On generalizations of the parking permit problem and network leasing problems. Electron. Notes Discrete Math. **62**, 225–230 (2017)
8. De Lima, M.S., San Felice, M.C., Lee, O.: Group parking permit problems. Discret. Appl. Math. **281**, 172–194 (2020)
9. Feldkord, B., Markarian, C., Meyer Auf der Heide, F.: Price fluctuation in online leasing. In: Gao, X., Du, H., Han, M. (eds.) COCOA 2017. LNCS, vol. 10628, pp. 17–31. Springer, Cham (2017). https://doi.org/10.1007/978-3-319-71147-8_2
10. Feldkord, B., Markarian, C., auf der Heide, F.M.: Price fluctuation in online leasing. In: Gao, X., Du, H., Han, M. (eds.) Combinatorial Optimization and Applications - 11th International Conference, COCOA 2017, Shanghai, China, December 16–18, 2017, Proceedings, Part II. Lecture Notes in Computer Science, vol. 10628, pp. 17–31. Springer (2017). https://doi.org/10.1007/978-3-319-71147-8_2, https://doi.org/10.1007/978-3-319-71147-8_2
11. Fotakis, D.: On the competitive ratio for online facility location. In: Baeten, J.C.M., Lenstra, J.K., Parrow, J., Woeginger, G.J. (eds.) Automata, Lang. Program., pp. 637–652. Springer, Berlin Heidelberg, Berlin, Heidelberg (2003)
12. Fotakis, D.: A primal-dual algorithm for online non-uniform facility location. J. Discret. Algorith. **5**(1), 141–148 (2007)

13. Fotakis, D.: Online and incremental algorithms for facility location. ACM SIGACT News **42**(1), 97–131 (2011)
14. Freund, A., Rawitz, D.: Combinatorial interpretations of dual fitting and primal fitting. In: Approximation and Online Algorithms, First International Workshop, WAOA 2003, Budapest, Hungary, September 16–18, 2003, Revised Papers, pp. 137–150 (2003). https://doi.org/10.1007/978-3-540-24592-6_11
15. Howard, M.C.: Who wants to reopen the economy during the covid-19 pandemic? the daring and uncaring. Personality Individ. Differ. **168**, 110335 (2021)
16. Ivanov, D.: Viable supply chain model: integrating agility, resilience and sustainability perspectives-lessons from and thinking beyond the covid-19 pandemic. Annals of Operations Research, pp. 1–21 (2020)
17. Jain, K., Mahdian, M., Markakis, E., Saberi, A., Vazirani, V.V.: Greedy facility location algorithms analyzed using dual fitting with factor-revealing lp. J. ACM 50(6), 795–824 (Nov 2003). http://doi.acm.org/10.1145/950620.950621
18. Jain, K., Vazirani, V.V.: Approximation algorithms for metric facility location and k-median problems using the primal-dual schema and lagrangian relaxation. J. ACM 48(2), 274–296 (Mar 2001). https://doi.org/10.1145/375827.375845, http://doi.acm.org/10.1145/375827.375845
19. Korman, S.: On the use of randomization in the online set cover problem. Weizmann Institute of Science 2 (2004)
20. Li, S., Mäcker, A., Markarian, C., auf der Heide, F.M., Riechers, S.: Towards flexible demands in online leasing problems. In: Xu, D., Du, D., Du, D. (eds.) Computing and Combinatorics - 21st International Conference, COCOON 2015, Beijing, China, August 4–6, 2015, Proceedings. Lecture Notes in Computer Science, vol. 9198, pp. 277–288. Springer (2015). https://doi.org/10.1007/978-3-319-21398-9_22
21. Li, S., Markarian, C., Meyer Auf Der Heide, F.: Towards flexible demands in online leasing problems. Algorithmica **80**(5), 1556–1574 (May 2018). https://doi.org/10.1007/s00453-018-0420-y
22. Markarian, C.: Online resource leasing. Ph.D. thesis, University of Paderborn, Germany (2015)
23. Markarian, C.: Leasing with uncertainty. In: Kliewer, N., Ehmke, J.F., Borndörfer, R. (eds.) Operations Research Proceedings 2017. ORP, pp. 429–434. Springer, Cham (2018). https://doi.org/10.1007/978-3-319-89920-6_57
24. Markarian, C.: Online non-metric facility location with service installation costs. In: Filipe, J., Smialek, M., Brodsky, A., Hammoudi, S. (eds.) Proceedings of the 23rd International Conference on Enterprise Information Systems, ICEIS 2021, Online Streaming, April 26–28, 2021, Volume 1. pp. 737–743. SCITEPRESS (2021). https://doi.org/10.5220/0010469207370743
25. Markarian, C.: Online non-metric facility location with service-quality costs. In: Filipe, J., Smialek, M., Brodsky, A., Hammoudi, S. (eds.) Proceedings of the 24th International Conference on Enterprise Information Systems, ICEIS 2022, Online Streaming, April 25–27, 2022, Volume 1. pp. 616–622. SCITEPRESS (2022). https://doi.org/10.5220/0011101900003179
26. Markarian, C., El-Kassar, A.N.: Algorithmic view of online prize-collecting optimization problems. In: Filipe, J., Smialek, M., Brodsky, A., Hammoudi, S. (eds.) Proceedings of the 23rd International Conference on Enterprise Information Systems, ICEIS 2021, Online Streaming, April 26–28, 2021, Volume 1. pp. 744–751. SCITEPRESS (2021). https://doi.org/10.5220/0010471507440751
27. Markarian, C., Meyer auf der Heide, F.: Online algorithms for leasing vertex cover and leasing non-metric facility location. In: International Conference on Operations Research and Enterprise Systems (ICORES), pp. 315–321 (2019)

28. Markarian, C., Kassar, A.N.: Online deterministic algorithms for connected dominating set & set cover leasing problems. In: International Conference on Operations Research and Enterprise Systems (ICORES), pp. 121–128 (2020)

29. Markarian, C., Kassar, A., Yunis, M.M.: An algorithmic approach to online multi-facility location problems. In: Parlier, G.H., Liberatore, F., Demange, M. (eds.) Proceedings of the 10th International Conference on Operations Research and Enterprise Systems, ICORES 2021, Online Streaming, February 4–6, 2021. pp. 29–35. SCITEPRESS (2021). https://doi.org/10.5220/0010212200290035

30. Markarian, C., Kassar, A., Yunis, M.M.: Algorithmic study of online multi-facility location problems. SN Comput. Sci. 3(4), 296 (2022). https://doi.org/10.1007/s42979-022-01193-y, https://doi.org/10.1007/s42979-022-01193-y

31. Markarian, C., Khallouf, P.: Online facility service leasing inspired by the COVID-19 pandemic. In: Gusikhin, O., Nijmeijer, H., Madani, K. (eds.) Proceedings of the 18th International Conference on Informatics in Control, Automation and Robotics, ICINCO 2021, Online Streaming, July 6–8, 2021. pp. 195–202. SCITEPRESS (2021). https://doi.org/10.5220/0010572601950202

32. Markarian, C., Khallouf, P.: Online metric facility service leasing with duration-specific dormant fees. In: Panetto, H., Macchi, M., Madani, K. (eds.) Proceedings of the 2nd International Conference on Innovative Intelligent Industrial Production and Logistics, IN4PL 2021, October 25–27, 2021. pp. 25–31. SCITEPRESS (2021). https://doi.org/10.5220/0010668600003062

33. Meyerson, A.: Online facility location. In: Proceedings 42nd IEEE Symposium on Foundations of Computer Science, pp. 426–431 (2001). https://doi.org/10.1109/SFCS.2001.959917

34. Meyerson, A.: The parking permit problem. In: 46th Annual IEEE Symposium on Foundations of Computer Science (FOCS'05), pp. 274–282. IEEE (2005)

35. Nagarajan, C., Williamson, D.P.: Offline and online facility leasing. Discret. Optim. 10(4), 361–370 (2013). https://doi.org/10.1016/j.disopt.2013.10.001, https://www.sciencedirect.com/science/article/pii/S1572528613000509

36. Nikolopoulos, K., Punia, S., Schäfers, A., Tsinopoulos, C., Vasilakis, C.: Forecasting and planning during a pandemic: Covid-19 growth rates, supply chain disruptions, and governmental decisions. Eur. J. Oper. Res. 290(1), 99–115 (2021)

37. Queiroz, M.M., Ivanov, D., Dolgui, A., Fosso Wamba, S.: Impacts of epidemic outbreaks on supply chains: mapping a research agenda amid the COVID-19 pandemic through a structured literature review. Ann. Oper. Res. 1–38 (2020). https://doi.org/10.1007/s10479-020-03685-7

38. San Felice, M.C., Cheung, S.S., Lee, O., Williamson, D.P.: The online prize-collecting facility location problem. Electron. Notes Discret. Math. 50, 151–156 (2015)

An Online Variant of Set Cover Inspired by Happy Clients

Christine Markarian[✉]

Department of Engineering and Information Technology, University of Dubai, Dubai, UAE
cmarkarian@ud.ac.ae

Abstract. Over the past decades, the concept of leasing has been widely spread in many industries. Companies have been leasing their resources rather than buying them. Small businesses were now able to join the markets without the need for upfront costs. Companies were now able to get access to the most up-to-date equipments with significantly lower costs. Despite its popularity, leasing was first introduced as a theoretical model in 2005. Following this model, many well-known optimization problems were studied in the leasing setting. This paper is devoted to continuing the algorithmic study on leasing in the context of the well-known *Set Cover* problem (SC). SC is one of the most well-studied NP-hard optimization problems in combinatorics, operations research, and computer science, appearing as sub-problems in many real-world applications. In this paper, we conduct a study from an online algorithmic perspective. That is, unlike the classical offline setting in which the entire input sequence is given to the algorithm all at once, the input sequence is given to the online algorithm in portions over time. In particular, we study an online leasing variant of *Set Cover*, known as the *Online Set Cover Leasing with Happiness Costs* problem (Leasing OSC-HC). We design the first online algorithm for Leasing OSC-HC and analyze its performance in the competitive analysis framework in which the online algorithm is evaluated against the optimal offline solution over all possible instances of a given problem.

Keywords: Online algorithms · Competitive analysis · Combinatorial optimization · Online set cover · Leasing · Happiness costs

1 Introduction

Despite its ever-growing popularity in most markets, leasing was first introduced as a theoretical model in 2005 by Meyerson [21], with the *Parking Permit Problem*, defined as follows. There are L permit types, each characterized by a duration and cost, satisfying the economy of scale. Each day, the algorithm is told whether it is sunny or rainy. If it is sunny, the algorithm needs to provide a valid permit. The goal is to minimize the total permit costs. Following Meyerson's leasing model, many well-known network design problems were studied in the leasing setting [4], including *Online Set Cover* [1], *Online Vertex Cover* [17], *Online Connected Dominating Sets* [18], *Online Steiner Tree* [6], and metric and non-metric *Online Facility Location* and their variants [17, 19, 22, 23]. Unlike the classical setting, in which resources can be used forever once purchased, resources in the leasing setting get expired as soon as their lease duration ends. Many extensions to the original leasing model were later introduced, with the aim to capture more aspects from real-world leasing application scenarios [11, 13, 14, 24].

This paper is devoted to continuing the online algorithmic study on leasing in the context of the well-known *Set Cover* problem (SC). SC is one of the most well-studied classical NP-hard optimization problems in combinatorics, operations research, and computer science, appearing as sub-problems in many real-world applications. [26] presents a survey of applications in various areas such as capital budgeting, cutting stock, scheduling, and vehicle routing. In this paper, we focus on the online setting, in which the so-called *online* algorithm does not know the entire input sequence in advance, but receives it in portions over time. In each step, a portion of the input sequence arrives, and the online algorithm reacts to it, while maintaining the overall optimization objective towards the entire input sequence. Decisions made by the online algorithm are irrevocable and its performance is evaluated using the notion of *competitive analysis*. The latter is a worst-case analysis that compares, over all instances of the problem, the quality of the solution outputted by the online algorithm to that of an optimal offline solution.

Definition 1 (Competitive Analysis). *Let $\mathcal{I}$ be the collection of all instances of a given problem P. We denote by $C(ALG, i)$ the cost of an online algorithm ALG of P on instance $i \in \mathcal{I}$ and by $C(OPT, i)$ the cost of an optimal offline algorithm on instance $i \in \mathcal{I}$. We say ALG has competitive ratio r or is r-competitive if, for all instances $i \in \mathcal{I}$, $C(ALG, i) \leq r \cdot C(OPT, i) + c$ for some constant c independent of i.*

Meyerson [21] assumed a simplified version of the lease structure, referred to as the *interval model* (Theorem 2.2 in [21]), to facilitate the competitive analysis.

- Lease lenghts are powers of two.
- There is no overlap between the leases of the same type.

He showed that by assuming this structure, one only loses a factor of 4 in the competitive ratio. He designed a deterministic and a randomized algorithm, along with matching lower bounds for the *Parking Permit Problem*, with competitive ratios $O(L)$ and $O(\log L)$, respectively, where L is the number of permit or lease types. The same structure was adopted in most leasing problems studied thereafter [1, 13, 22]. To simplify the analysis of our algorithm, we assume in this paper the same lease structure.

The study of the *Set Cover* problem (SC) has led to the emergence of numerous fundamental techniques in the fields of operations research, computer science, and combinatorics [8–10, 25]. The simplest form of the *Set Cover* problem (SC) is defined as follows. We are given a universe of elements, a collection of subsets whose union equals the universe, and a non-negative cost associated with each subset. The *Set Cover* problem (SC) asks to identify a minimum cost sub-collection of the subsets whose union equals the universe.

Consider, for instance, the following client-server application scenario. We are given a collection of clients and servers. Each server is associated with a cost and is able to serve a subset of the clients. We aim to minimize our server costs as much as possible while serving all of our clients. This scenario can be abstracted as the *Set Cover* problem (SC), in which elements represent clients and subsets represent servers. Serving clients is translated to covering elements by choosing a collection of subsets with minimum costs. Many real-world applications contain this client-server structure and hence include SC as a sub-problem, making SC a targeted problem in many areas. Due to its simple yet special covering structure, SC has attracted researchers in both theory and practice. It has appeared in many industrial applications, including airline, manufacturing, service planning, and many others [26]. In theory, SC is known as many variants and has been studied in the *offline* and *online* settings [2,5,7,9,10,12,25]. Unlike in the classical offline setting, the elements in the online setting are revealed to the algorithm over time. In each step, the online algorithm is given an element that needs to be covered. The online algorithm needs to ensure that each element is either covered by the current subsets in the solution or adds a new subset to the solution. The goal of the online algorithm is to eventually build a solution of minimum subset costs, to minimize its competitive ratio. Normally, the online algorithm does not know the universe and the collection of subsets in advance. Nevertheless, some online algorithms in the literature, as in [2], assume this information is given in order to achieve a *deterministic* solution to the problem.

2   Our Contribution

In this paper, we address a variant of SC in the online setting, known as the *Online Set Cover Leasing with Happiness Costs* problem (Leasing OSC-HC). Leasing OSC-HC is a generalization of the *Online Set Cover with Happiness Costs* problem (OSC-HC) which we introduced in [16]. Hence, this paper is an extension of our work in [16]. The results we obtain for Leasing OSC-HC lead to the same competitive ratio achieved for OSC-HC in [16].

The generalization is inspired by real-world optimization scenarios in which resources are leased rather than bought. Assume, for instance, a company that serves its clients through servers it does not own. To be able to use a server, the company needs to lease it. Once the lease period is over, it can't use the server anymore unless the lease period is extended. Each client may require a different set of services and to make clients happy, we would like to serve them through the same server. The company needs to serve all of its clients by keeping them as happy as possible, while minimizing its leasing costs. This is abstracted as the *Online Set Cover Leasing with Happiness Costs* problem (Leasing OSC-HC), defined as follows.

Definition 2 *(Leasing OSC-HC). Given a universe of n elements and a collection of m subsets of the universe. A subset can be leased with L different lease types, each characterized by a lease length and cost. A request consisting of at most k elements arrives in each step. Each element may appear in at most one request. Each request is associated with a happiness cost. A request arriving at time step t is served by either a single subset leased at time t containing all of its elements or by a number of subsets leased at time t that jointly contain all of its elements. In the latter case, the algorithm needs to pay the happiness cost associated with the request. The goal is to serve all requests while minimizing the total subset leasing and happiness costs.*

Notice that for each client that is not served through one provider, we pay a happiness cost. These happiness costs belong to the algorithm's optimization objective in addition to the subset leasing costs. The elements represent the clients and the subsets represent the servers. Each server can be leased for L different durations. A server can be used to serve clients only while there is an active lease for it. The special case in which there is one lease type of infinite length is the *Online Set Cover with Happiness Costs* problem (OSC-HC) [16]. The special case in which the happiness cost of each element is zero and a request is composed of one element is the simplest form of the *Set Cover* problem (SC) in the online setting.

To the best of our knowledge, there is no online algorithm for Leasing OSC-HC in the literature. For the special case, the *Online Set Cover with Happiness Costs* problem (OSC-HC), we have developed an online randomized algorithm [16] with $\mathcal{O}(\log d \log n)$-competitive ratio, where d is the maximum number of subsets an element belongs to and n is the number of elements. The algorithm of [16] uses the commonly known approach of relaxing the problem to its fractional variant and then using multiplicative update and randomized rounding to compute a feasible integral solution.

In this paper, we design the first online algorithm for Leasing OSC-HC. Our algorithm is randomized and uses techniques inspired by those used in [16]. It has an $\mathcal{O}(\log(dL) \log n)$-competitive ratio, where:

- d is the maximum number of subsets an element belongs to
- L is the number of lease types
- n is the number of elements

2.1 Overview

The rest of the paper is structured as follows. In Sect. 3, we present some preliminaries and a literature review. In Sect. 4, we describe our online algorithm for Leasing OSC-HC. In Sect. 5, we show the competitive analysis of our algorithm. We conclude in Sect. 6 with a discussion and some future work.

3 Preliminaries and Literature Review

The principal idea of the algorithm for Leasing OSC-HC is to formulate a given instance of Leasing OSC-HC as a graph problem with connectivity objectives while maintaining the desired competitive ratio. The challenge is to express the given leasing options, the happiness constraints, and their associated prices within the nodes and edges of the graph. The serving requirements form the connectivity objectives. The formulated graph problem is then solved using the classical fractional relaxation and randomized rounding techniques.

Lower Bounds for Leasing OSC-HC. No online deterministic algorithm for Leasing OSC-HC can achieve a ratio smaller than $\Omega(L)$, following the lower bound for the *Parking Permit Problem* [21].

No online randomized algorithm for Leasing OSC-HC can achieve a ratio smaller than $\Omega(\log L)$, following the lower bound for the *Parking Permit Problem* [21].

Moreover, no online deterministic algorithm for Leasing OSC-HC can achieve a ratio smaller than $\Omega(\frac{\log m \log n}{\log\log m + \log\log n})$, following the lower bound for the *Online Set Cover* problem (OSC) [2]. A stricter bound of $\Omega(\log m \log n)$ holds for polynomial-time randomized algorithms for OSC, due to [12], assuming $BPP \neq NP$.

Literature Review. The online variant of SC, known as the *Online Set Cover* problem (OSC), was introduced in [2]. The authors presented an online deterministic algorithm, with $O(\log n \log m)$-competitive ratio. They also showed that no online deterministic algorithm for OSC can achieve a competitive ratio better than than $\Omega(\frac{\log m \log n}{\log\log m + \log\log n})$, where n is the number of elements and m is the number of subsets.

The online leasing variant of OSC in which subsets are leased rather than bought was studied in [1]. The authors presented an online randomized algorithm with $O(\log dL \log n)$-competitive ratio, where d is the maximum number of subsets an element belongs to, L is the number of lease types, and n is the number of elements. A deterministic online algorithm was later proposed in [18], with $\mathcal{O}(\log l_{max} \log(mL + m\frac{l_{max}}{l_{min}}))$-competitive ratio, where l_{max} is the longest lease length, m is the number of subsets, L is the number of lease types, and l_{min} is the shortest lease length.

Another related problem in which requests are formed as a group of elements but subsets are capacitated yielding to packing constraints was studied in [5].

4   Online Algorithm

In this section, we first present a graph representation of a given instance I of Leasing OSC-HC and then describe the online algorithm that solves the corresponding graph problem instance I' and generates a feasible solution for I from I'.

The graph we construct will be directed and have non-negative weights on its edges. The elements, subsets, and requests of instance I will be represented as nodes. The relationships between these will be represented as directed edges. There will be some additional nodes to represent the conditions associated with the happiness costs and the options associated with leasing. The leasing options will be represented as edges, each of weight equal to the corresponding lease cost. Happiness costs will appear as weights on the edges. The solution to the graph problem instance will contain nodes and edges. The algorithm will then output a feasible solution for I by purchasing the subsets associated with the nodes in the constructed solution and paying the happiness costs associated with the edges in the constructed solution.

Instance Transformation. The algorithm is initially given the universe of n elements and the collection of m subsets. But it does not know which elements will eventually show up and in which order and group. It is also given the leasing options with their characteristics including the durations and prices. Before the adversary reveals the first request to the algorithm, the following is constructed.

1. Each element j of instance I is represented by a node, referred to as *element node of j*.

2. Each subset i of instance I is represented by two nodes, referred to as *subset node of i* and *twin subset node of i*
3. There are L directed edges from each subset node to its corresponding twin subset node, representing each of the L available lease types. The weight of each such edge is equal to the lease cost of the corresponding lease type.
4. There is a directed edge from a twin subset node to an element node if the corresponding element belongs to the corresponding subset. The weights of these edges are set to 0.

As soon as the adversary reveals a new request, a *request node* representing the request and a so-called *happiness node* are formed. There is a directed edge, of weight 0, from the request node to each subset node if the corresponding subset contains all the elements of the corresponding request. There is a directed edge from the request node to the happiness node, of weight equal to the happiness cost associated with the request. There is a directed edge, of weight 0, from the happiness node to each subset node if the corresponding subset contains at least one element of the corresponding request but does not contain all of the request's elements.

Figure 1 shows an illustration of an instance comprising **three** subsets, **five** elements, **five** lease types, and a request containing **two** elements.

Definition 3 (*Directed Graph Connectivity Problem for Leasing OSC-HC*). *Given a directed graph G and a non-negative weight for each edge, formed from an instance of Leasing OSC-HC. As soon as a request is given, find a directed path from the corresponding request node to each element node corresponding to the elements of the request.*

The algorithm constructs a solution for I derived from a solution for I' by purchasing each subset lease that corresponds to an edge in the solution for I'. Moreover, for each request, a feasible solution for I' may or may not contain the corresponding happiness node. The algorithm pays the happiness cost associated with the request if the happiness node is in the solution for I'.

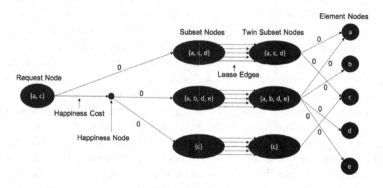

Fig. 1. Leasing OSC-HC instance comprising **three** subsets, **five** elements, **five** lease types, and a request containing **two** elements. (from [16]).

Algorithm Description. Each edge in the graph instance I' will be associated with a *value*, initially set to 0, and non-decreasing throughout the execution of the algorithm. The algorithm will use the notions of *maximum flow* and *minimum cut*. The *maximum flow* from one node to another is the smallest total *values* of edges which if removed disconnect the two nodes. These edges form a *minimum cut*. The online algorithm is randomized and its randomization process is based on generating, before any request arrives, a random number r chosen as the minimum among $2\lceil\log n\rceil$ independent random variables distributed uniformly in the interval $[0, 1]$, where n is the total number of elements. Let w_e denote the weight of edge e and v_e its value.

Given a request $r = \{e_1, e_2, ..., e_s\}$ of s elements. Let $i = 1$.

While $i \leq s$:

1. If the so-far constructed solution contains a directed path from the request node corresponding to r to the element node corresponding to e_i:
   - Increment i by 1 if $i < s$
   - Exit the loop and wait for a new request if $i = s$
2. While the maximum flow from the request node to the element node is less than 1: Construct a minimum cut $\mathcal{K}$ from the request node corresponding to r to the element node corresponding to e_i and increase the value v_e of each edge $e \in \mathcal{K}$ based on the equation: $v_e \leftarrow v_e(1 + \frac{1}{w_e}) + \frac{1}{|\mathcal{K}| \cdot w_e}$
3. Add edge e to the solution if its value $v_e \geq r$.
4. If the so-far constructed solution does not contain a directed path from the request node to the element node, add to the solution the edges of a smallest-weight directed path from the request node to the element node.
5. Purchase the subset leases and pay the happiness costs corresponding to the edges in the so-far constructed solution.
6. Increment i by 1.

Feasible Solution. After constructing the nodes and edges of the graph associated with a given request, the algorithm divides it into parts, each associated with an element in the request. As per the graph formed, a request node will be connected to an element node through a directed path containing a subset node and its twin subset node. These two represent a subset containing the element in the original instance. The lease edges represent what the algorithm pays in terms of subset leases. If the solution path does not contain the intermediary node, then the edge associated with a happiness cost is not in this path as per the graph construction. In this case, the algorithm does not pay a happiness cost. Note that, at some point in a given time step, if the algorithm decides to purchase a subset that contains all the elements of the request, then all the remaining elements of the request are covered and the step ends. On the other hand, even if the algorithm pays the happiness cost at some point in a given time step, it may eventually decide to purchase a subset that contains all the elements of the request. In such a case, the algorithm, in practice, does not have to pay for the happiness cost, since its decisions are revocable within a time step. However, as we will see in the next section, this does not affect our competitive analysis of the algorithm.

5   Competitive Analysis

Notice that the algorithm adds edges to the solution in Steps 3 and 4. Hence, we will analyze the total cost of the edges in these two steps. We denote by Opt the cost of an optimal offline solution.

Edges Added in Step 3. Let E' be the collection of edges added in Step 3 and $C_{E'}$ by the total weight of these edges. The algorithm adds an edge to the solution if its corresponding value is above r, the number generated before the arrival of any request. We fix any edge e and $i : 1 \leq i \leq 2\lceil \log n \rceil$. We let $X_{e,i}$ be the indicator variable of the event that e is added by the algorithm in Step 3. We can now express $C_{E'}$ as follows.

$$C_{E'} = \sum_{e \in E'} \sum_{i=1}^{2\lceil \log n \rceil} w_e \cdot Exp\left[X_{e,i}\right] \tag{1}$$

$$= 2\lceil \log n \rceil \sum_{e \in E'} w_e v_e \tag{2}$$

Notice that each minimum cut the algorithm constructs must contain an edge from the optimal offline solution. This is because of the definition of minimum cut and the feasibility of the optimal solution. The next Lemma upper bounds the number of times the algorithm constructs a minimum cut in total, the total edge value increases associated with each minimum cut, and the size of the largest minimum cut constructed.

Lemma 1. *The total number of times the algorithm constructs a minimum cut in total is at most $\mathcal{O}(Opt \cdot \log |\mathcal{K}|)$, where $|\mathcal{K}|$ is the size of the largest minimum cut. The total edge value increases associated with each minimum cut is at most 2. The size of any minimum cut constructed does not exceed dL, where d is the maximum number of subsets an element belongs to and L is the number of lease types.*

Proof. Since each minimum cut the algorithm constructs must contain at least one edge from the optimal solution, it suffices to observe the value increases of the optimal edges. We fix any edge in the optimal solution. The value corresponding to this edge becomes 1 after $\mathcal{O}(w_e \log |\mathcal{K}|)$ increases as per the equation in Step 2 of the algorithm. At this point, the edge does not appear again in any future minimum cut. Therefore, the total number of times the algorithm constructs a minimum cut in total is $\mathcal{O}(Opt \cdot \log |\mathcal{K}|)$.

To upper bound the total edge value increases associated with each minimum cut, let us fix any minimum cut $\mathcal{K}$ constructed by the algorithm. Edge e in $\mathcal{K}$ is associated with an increase of $w_e \cdot \left(\frac{v_e}{w_e} + \frac{1}{|\mathcal{K}| \cdot w_e} \right)$. Before the increase is made, the maximum flow is less than 1 as per the algorithm. This means that $\sum_{e \in \mathcal{K}} v_e < 1$. The same holds true for all the edges in the cut. Thus, we have that $\sum_{e \in \mathcal{K}} w_e \cdot \left(\frac{v_e}{w_e} + \frac{1}{|\mathcal{K}| \cdot w_e} \right) < 2$.

The size of the largest minimum cut constructed depends on the maximum number of directed paths from any request node to any element node. Since each element belongs to at most d subsets and there are L directed edges between the subset nodes, the size of the largest minimum cut constructed would be at most dL.

We can thus conclude that $\sum_{e \in E'} w_e v_e \leq \mathcal{O}(Opt \cdot \log dL)$. Therefore,

$$C_{E'} \leq \mathcal{O}(Opt \cdot \log n \cdot \log dL) \tag{3}$$

Edges Added in Step 4. Let E'' be the collection of edges added in Step 4 and $C_{E''}$ be the total weight of these edges. The algorithm adds an edge to the solution in Step 4 if no directed path has been added in Step 3 associated with the element at hand. Let us fix an element in a given request. We need to study the probability that no directed path has been added from the corresponding request node to the corresponding element node. This depends on the randomization process or the way the number r is generated. The *flow* of a given path is defined as the minimum value among the edge values of the path. In Step 3, the algorithm ensures that the sum of flows of all paths to the element node is at least 1. Thus, the probability that there is no directed path to the element node purchased in Step 3 is:

$$\prod_{e \in \mathcal{K}} (1 - v_e) \leq e^{-\sum_{e \in \mathcal{K}} v_e} \leq \frac{1}{e}$$

We now compute this for all i: $1 \leq i \leq 2\lceil \log n \rceil$. The probability that there is no directed path to the element node would be at most $\frac{1}{n^2}$. In the case where there is no directed path to the element node purchased in Step 3, the algorithm purchases a smallest-weight path to the element node. This path has weight at most Opt, since it is a smallest-weight. Since we have n elements in total, each arriving once, $C_{E''}$ would have a negligible cost of at most $n \cdot \frac{Opt}{n^2}$. Therefore, we conclude the following theorem.

Theorem 1. *There is an online $\mathcal{O}(\log(dL) \log n)$-competitive randomized algorithm for the Online Set Cover Leasing with Happiness Costs problem (Leasing OSC-HC), where d is the maximum number of subsets an element belongs to, L is the number of lease types, and n is the number of elements.*

The following result is for the special case of the problem in which there is only one lease type of infinite length ($L = 1$). The same competitive ratio was achieved in our work in [16].

Corollary 1 [16]. *There is an online $\mathcal{O}(\log d \log n)$-competitive randomized algorithm for the Online Set Cover with Happiness Costs problem (OSC-HC), where d is the maximum number of subsets an element belongs to and n is the number of elements.*

6   Discussion

Our proposed framework takes into consideration the happiness of clients addressing only one aspect in which clients are happy when served with one provider. It would be interesting to explore other perspectives of happiness and incorporate them into the current framework.

Many other optimization problems have a structure fitting as well into this framework. Examples include the *Online Facility Location with Service Installation Costs* problem, in which the distances between clients and the facilities they are served by are minimized [15,20]. Hence, it would be worth investigating them.

Considering other adverserial models for the input sequence that would probably be less restrictive for the algorithm is always worth the investigation. Given that both leasing and Set Cover problems appear as sub-problems in many real-world applications, these investigations could play a vital role in closing the gap between theory and practice.

Elements in our problem arrive once. That is, if the same element needs to appear again, it is represented as a separate element and this seems to be required to maintain the desired competitive ratio. Other covering problems have handled this aspect of repetition [3] and so it would be interesting to cover it here as well.

Implementing the proposed algorithm on a simulated or real environment is an interesting next step. This would allow us to understand the difficulty of the problem as well as the performance of the algorithm and its effectiveness in practical applications.

References

1. Abshoff, S., Kling, P., Markarian, C., Meyerauf der Heide, F., Pietrzyk, P.: Towards the price of leasing online. J. Comb. Optim. **32**(4), 1197–1216 (2016)
2. Alon, N., Awerbuch, B., Azar, Y., Buchbinder, N., Naor, J.S.: The online set cover problem. SIAM J. Comput. **39**(2), 361–370 (2009)
3. Alon, N., Azar, Y., Gutner, S.: Admission control to minimize rejections and online set cover with repetitions. In: Proceedings of the Seventeenth Annual ACM Symposium on Parallelism in Algorithms and Architectures, pp. 238–244 (2005)
4. Anthony, B.M., Gupta, A.: Infrastructure leasing problems. In: Fischetti, M., Williamson, D.P. (eds.) IPCO 2007. LNCS, vol. 4513, pp. 424–438. Springer, Heidelberg (2007). https://doi.org/10.1007/978-3-540-72792-7_32
5. Bhawalkar, K., Gollapudi, S., Panigrahi, D.: Online set cover with set requests. In: Klaus J., Rolim, J.D.P., Devanur, N.R., Moore, C. (eds.) Approximation, Randomization, and Combinatorial Optimization. Algorithms and Techniques (APPROX/RANDOM 2014), vol. 28 of Leibniz International Proceedings in Informatics (LIPIcs), Dagstuhl, Germany, pp. 64–79. Schloss Dagstuhl-Leibniz-Zentrum fuer Informatik (2014)
6. Bienkowski, M., Kraska, A., Schmidt, P.: A deterministic algorithm for online steiner tree leasing. In: WADS 2017. LNCS, vol. 10389, pp. 169–180. Springer, Cham (2017). https://doi.org/10.1007/978-3-319-62127-2_15
7. Buchbinder, N., Naor, J.: Online primal-dual algorithms for covering and packing. Math. Oper. Res. **34**(2), 270–286 (2009)
8. Caprara, A., Toth, P., Fischetti, M.: Algorithms for the set covering problem. Ann. Oper. Res. **98**, 353–371 (2000)
9. Feige, U.: A threshold of ln n for approximating set cover. J. ACM (JACM) **45**(4), 634–652 (1998)
10. Feige, U., Lovász, L., Tetali, P.: Approximating min sum set cover. Algorithmica **40**(4), 219–234 (2004)
11. Feldkord, B., Markarian, C., Meyer Auf der Heide, F.: Price fluctuation in online leasing. In: Gao, X., Du, H., Han, M. (eds.) COCOA 2017. LNCS, vol. 10628, pp. 17–31. Springer, Cham (2017). https://doi.org/10.1007/978-3-319-71147-8_2
12. Korman, S.: On the use of randomization in the online set cover problem. Weizmann Inst. Sci. **2** (2004)

13. Li, S., Markarian, C., auf der Heide, F.M.: Towards flexible demands in online leasing problems. Algorithmica **80**(5), 1556–1574 (2018)
14. Markarian, C.: Leasing with uncertainty. In: Kliewer, N., Ehmke, J.F., Borndörfer, R. (eds.) Operations Research Proceedings 2017. ORP, pp. 429–434. Springer, Cham (2018). https://doi.org/10.1007/978-3-319-89920-6_57
15. Markarian, C.: Online non-metric facility location with service installation costs. In: Filipe, J., Smialek, M., Brodsky, A., Hammoudi, S. (eds.) Proceedings of the 23rd International Conference on Enterprise Information Systems, ICEIS 2021, Online Streaming, 26–28 April 2021, vol. 1, pp. 737–743. SCITEPRESS (2021)
16. Markarian, C.: Online set cover with happiness costs. In: Panetto, H., Macchi, M., Madani, K. (eds.) Proceedings of the 2nd International Conference on Innovative Intelligent Industrial Production and Logistics, IN4PL 2021, 25–27 October 2021, pp. 40–45. SCITEPRESS (2021)
17. Markarian, C., auf der Heide, F.M.: Online algorithms for leasing vertex cover and leasing non-metric facility location. In: Parlier, G.H., Liberatore, F., Demange, M. (eds.) Proceedings of the 8th International Conference on Operations Research and Enterprise Systems, ICORES 2019, Prague, Czech Republic, 19–21 February 2019, pp. 315–321. SciTePress (2019)
18. Markarian, C., Kassar, A.-N.: Online deterministic algorithms for connected dominating set & set cover leasing problems. In: ICORES, pp. 121–128 (2020)
19. Markarian, C., Khallouf, P.: Online facility service leasing inspired by the covid-19 pandemic. In: 18th International Conference on Informatics in Control, Automation and Robotics, ICINCO 2021, pp. 195–202 (2021)
20. Markarian, C., Khallouf, P.: Online facility service leasing inspired by the COVID-19 pandemic. In: Gusikhin, O., Nijmeijer, H., Madani, K. (eds.) Proceedings of the 18th International Conference on Informatics in Control, Automation and Robotics, ICINCO 2021, Online Streaming, 6–8 July 2021, pp. 195–202. SCITEPRESS (2021)
21. Meyerson, A.: The parking permit problem. In: 46th Annual IEEE Symposium on Foundations of Computer Science (FOCS 2005), pp. 274–282. IEEE (2005)
22. Nagarajan, C., Williamson, D.P.: Offline and online facility leasing. Disc. Optim. **10**(4), 361–370 (2013)
23. de Lima, M.S., San Felice, M.C., Lee, O.: Connected facility leasing problems. In: ICTCS/CILC, pp. 162–173 (2017)
24. de Lima, M.S., San Felice, M.C., Lee, O.: On generalizations of the parking permit problem and network leasing problems. Electron. Notes Disc. Math. **62**, 225–230 (2017)
25. Slavík, P.: A tight analysis of the greedy algorithm for set cover. J. Algor. **25**(2), 237–254 (1997)
26. Vemuganti, R.R.: Applications of Set Covering, Set Packing and Set Partitioning Models: A Survey, pp. 573–746. Springer, Boston (1998). https://doi.org/10.1007/978-1-4613-0303-9_9

General Architecture Framework and General Modelling Framework: Interoperability of Enterprise Architecture

Qing Li$^{(\boxtimes)}$ [ID], Zhixiong Fang, and Bohang Liang

Department of Automation, Tsinghua University, Beijing, China
liqing@tsinghua.edu.cn

Abstract. With the gradual unification of theories, methods and tools of software engineering, systems engineering and enterprise engineering, as an engineering tool for understanding, designing, developing, implementing and integrating complex software systems, enterprise systems and system of systems, architecture, methodology and system modeling techniques have been widely studied and applied in engineering, as well as forming a series of generalized architecture frameworks, such as Zachman framework, CIM-OSA, GIM/IMPACS, PERA, GERAM, FEAF, DoDAF, TOGAF, UAF, etc. These frameworks support the cognition, description, analysis and design activities of complex systems. On the basis of these generalized architecture frameworks, the architecture of industrial systems such as Reference Architecture Model Industry 4.0 (RAMI4.0), the Industrial Internet of Things Reference Architecture, and Smart Manufacturing Ecosystem has also been established and applied. On the other hand, along with the in-depth research and extensive application of model-based system engineering (MBSE), the framework methodology and design tools such as Harmony, Magic Grid are also changing the traditional pattern of industrial design. In order to solve the problem of adaptation, integration and interoperability of different architecture frameworks as well as their methods and tools in engineering applications, it is necessary to develop a general architecture and modeling framework to support systems, software and enterprises engineering based on different architectures, methods and tools to achieve internal and external integration and interoperability. In this paper, we first propose a general architecture framework (GAF) and its related general modeling framework (GMF). GAF provides MBSE tools and methods for system analysis, design and development. GMF provides a set of models and methods to describe different views of systems. In order to illustrate the common characteristics of GAF and GMF, this paper also discusses the interoperability between GAF, GMF and mainstream architectures and modeling frameworks in detail.

Keywords: Architecture · Modelling · Interoperability · Integration

A. Smirnov et al. (Eds.): IN4PL 2020/IN4PL 2021, CCIS 1855, pp. 135–158, 2023.
https://doi.org/10.1007/978-3-031-37228-5_9

1   Introduction

Architecture, methodology and modelling methods are effective ways to analyze systems, software and enterprises (SSE). In the past forty years, experts from different professional domains committed themselves in the study of architecture, and produced a set of significant works, including Zachman Framework, CIM-OSA (Computer Integrated Manufacturing Open System Architecture), PERA (Purdue Enterprise Reference Architecture), ARIS (Architecture of Integrated Information System), GERAM (Generalized Enterprise Reference Architecture and Methodology), FEAF (Federal Enterprise Architecture Framework), DoDAF (Department of Defense Architecture Framework), TOGAF (The Open Group Architecture Framework), UAF (Unified Architecture Framework), GEAF (Gartner's Enterprise Architecture Framework), ESA-AF (European Space Agency-Architectural Framework), and so forth. These architecture frameworks have great international influence and have a wide range of applications in many fields. Many of them have some extended version when applied in different field. Such as TEAF (Treasury Enterprise Architecture Framework, based on Zachman Framework). Based on DoDAF, many organizations develop their own extended defense-based architecture framework: MODAF (British Ministry of Defence Architecture Framework, developed by The UK Ministry of Defense), NAF (NATO defense standard), AGATE (the France DGA Architecture Framework).

In some specific fields, there are many proprietary frameworks, such as RASDS (Reference Architecture for Space Data System) in the space industry (CCSDS, 2016), AUTOSAR (Automotive Open System Architecture) in the automotive industry.

In the meanwhile, international standards such as ISO 15704 (ISO, 2005), 19439 (ISO, 2006), 19440 (ISO, 2007), and 42010 were published to underpin the identification of requirements for models, the establishment of modelling framework and the formation of modelling methodology respectively. ISO 42010 proposed a standardized system description method centered on architecture description, architecture framework, architecture description language (ISO, 2011).

In additional to systems, software, enterprises (SSE) architecture, modelling methods and languages have undergone rapid evolutions in order to satisfy the demanding analysis requirements for complex systems. Modelling languages such as IDEF (Integration Definition methods) series modelling languages (including IDEF0, IDEF1x, IDEF3, IDEF5, et. al.), UML (Unified Modelling Language, which includes multiple views and diagrams), DFD (Data Flow Diagram), ERD (Entity Relationship Diagram), EPC (Event Process Chain), BPMN (Business Process Modelling Notation), UPDM (Unified Profile for DoDAF/MODAF,) BPEL (Business Process Execution Language), Gellish (Generic Engineering Language, a textual modelling language), SoaML (Service-oriented architecture Modeling Language), ESL (Energy Systems Language), AADL (Avionics Architecture Description Language), EAST-ADL (designed for complement AUTOSAR), Petri net and the newly developed ArchiMate and SysML are gaining increasing popularity in the field of system modelling. Among them, UML has a wide range of influence in the field of information system development and software engineering. As an extension of UML, SysML is widely used in systems engineering. In ISO/IEC 19514:2017, SysML v1.4 was published as an International Standard (ISO, 2017).

The complex systems, software, enterprises design and development process is now evolving while modern industry is trying to free itself from tedious paperwork. Modeling is an effective way to solve the design and research problems of complex management and technology integration systems. At present, industrial design and development is facing an important pattern-change, which is that Model Based Systems Engineering (MBSE) is replacing Traditional/Text-based Systems Engineering (TSE). The International Council on Systems Engineering (INCOSE) proposed MBSE in "Systems Engineering Vision 2020" (INCOSE, 2007). It aims at enabling the modeling method to support the whole process of system design, including requirements validation, design, analysis, verification and validation, starting from conceptual design and covering the whole life cycle of product design (Friedenthal et al. 2007; Haskins, 2011). NASA, Boeing, Lockheed Martin, and Airbus are all actively practicing and promoting MBSE. At the same time, MBSE has entered petrochemical, construction, healthcare, smart city and other industries and fields. In 2014, INCOSE published "Systems Engineering Vision 2025" (INCOSE, 2014). In this report, INCOSE stated that in the future, the application of MBSE will expand from tradition fields to engineering, natural and social fields.

More and more system development projects include different architecture, methodologies and modelling methods. How to integrate these architecture, methodologies and modelling methods becomes a big challenge.

This paper presents a General Architecture Framework (GAF) and a relative General Modelling Framework (GMF). GAF provides tools and methodology of MBSE to systems design and development. GMF involves a set of models and methods to describes different aspects of a system. The paper also discusses the mapping and integration relationship between GAF, GMF with mainstream architecture and modelling frameworks.

The paper is structured as follows. In Sect. 2, the General Architecture Framework is proposed, including the corresponding General Modelling Framework. Section 3 discusses the mapping relationship between GAF and other mainstream architecture frameworks. In Sect. 4, the General Modelling Framework is compared with other modelling architecture frameworks. Finally, Sect. 5 puts forward the conclusions.

2   General Architecture Framework (GAF) and General Modelling Framework (GMF)

GAF and GMF are common methods obtained by comparing and summarizing various enterprise architecture and modeling frameworks. GMF provides modelling views based on GAF.

2.1   General Architecture Framework (GAF)

The General Architecture Framework (GAF) is a system, software, enterprise (SSE) architecture framework raised by Li (2007). As shown in the top of Fig. 1 (Li, 2021), GAF has three axes: View, Lifecycle and Realization.

View: This dimension is consistent with ISO 42010. It integrates the concerns of system stakeholders (including owners, managers, designers, operators and users), and provides the perspective of analysis, design, implementation and evaluation of the system for them. It defines the modeling field and object for system modeling. As shown in the left bottom of Fig. 1, it focuses on three types of system structure, which will be discussed in Sect. 2.2.

Lifecycle: The lifecycle of GAF is based on the project management lifecycle, with an additional segment named operation and maintenance. The project lifecycle just starts from project definition and ends up with implementation. There is a difference because architecture can greatly help an integrated system in tracking, modification and optimization when the system is running. And the modelling methods of architecture are equally important for system operation.

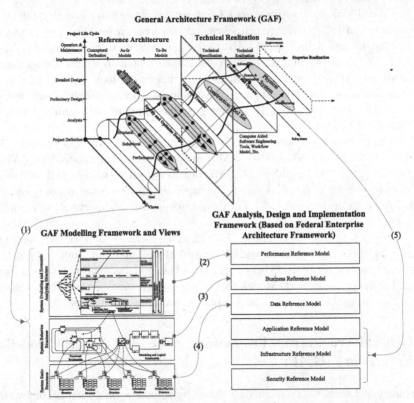

Fig. 1. General architecture framework and general modelling framework (Li, 2021).

Realization: This axis reflects how to use architecture methodology and modelling method instead of a large number of words to describe all aspects of the system and accomplish system analysis, design, operation and maintenance. Firstly, build the As-Is models of the system after Conceptual Definition phase. In this phase, the views provided by the first axis as well as other enterprise modeling methods show how to analyze the current system. Based on these views, modeling tools and modeling languages are used to build the As-Is model of the system. The As-Is models describe the structure of the system, the way it works and how it performs. Through the analysis of the As-Is model, the deficiencies and problems of the system are clarified, which point the direction of the transformation and optimization of the system. Secondly, get the To-Be models. Now problems and contradictions of the current system have been discovered through the analysis of the As-Is models, they should be solved step by step according to their importance and urgency. Based on the requirements of the different stakeholders, the To-Be models should be developed to describe what the tentative system will be by modifying or redesigning the As-Is models. The To-Be models provide a solution on the principle and abstract layer to meet the requirement, which is also called preliminary design. Thirdly, conduct detailed design. In this stage, constructing tools can help translating the requirement embodied by various models into design specification in three concrete domains (or called subsystems). The new real system can be built. What should be emphasized is that the mapping relationship between the design specification and the description of models (or views) is "multi-to-multi". Fortunately, many tools or tool sets have been developed to manage this mapping relationship.

From this architecture, we can know that the identification and construction of the system are gradually evolving and that the second and third axes correspond to each other. This feature is reflected in the form of ladders in the figure. Architecture framework users do different things with different methods in different stage, and what are done in the last stage will affect what to do and how to do in the next stage.

In the project definition stage, GAF users should treat the system as a whole, build its conceptual model and then develop its goal view. The goal view describes which stakeholders the system has, what demands and needs they have, what services the system should provide them, and what performance indicators these services should meet. It is important to determine the strategic goals of the system, because they provide evaluation criteria for system analysis so that it is clear whether the existing system is good or not.

In the analysis stage, GAF users should focus on the structural, behavioral and performance views of the system. If the project is for system transformation, GAF users should use reference models to construct As-Is models of the current system, and find out problems according to requirements in the goal view developed in the previous stage. If the project is to build a new system, GAF users should use reference models to translate goals to specific requirements including structural, behavioral and performance requirements.

In the preliminary design stage, GAF users should also use reference models to describe what the new system will be, and how it meets requirements in the previous stage.

In detailed design stage, GAF users should deliver all models and documents to system designers and designers will transform them into technical guidance of building the system through the construction tool set as a reference for specific design and implementation specifications.

In implementation stage, the system should be built or transformed under the guidance of technical specifications, which include three domains: information (cyber), human & organization (social) and manufacturing (physical).

In operation & maintenance stage, the system built in the previous stage should be improved and optimized. Since the system description is the guidance for system construction, it can certainly be used as the reference object for system operation to modify and optimize the actual system.

2.2   General Modelling Framework (GMF)

As shown in the left bottom part of Fig. 1, the General Modelling Framework (GMF) is divided into three layers: performance and evaluation structure layer, system behavioral/dynamic structure layer and system static structure layer. Each layer represents an aspect of the enterprise. The specific contents are as follows:

System static structure layer: models at which define the static structure of the enterprise, including organizational structure, resource structure, data/information structure, product/service structure and functional structure, define the existence of the enterprise and answer the question of what the system is. The organizational structure describes the decomposition of the enterprise organization, the responsibilities and authorities of the individuals and organizational units, personnel and positions related to organization operation. The resource structure describes the resource set and their configuration for enterprise operation, including physical resource, soft resource related to competition, and human resource etc. Therefore, the major description of human resource and organization view mainly has the same derivation and comparability. The data/information structure describes information of entities and correlation of these information structures in the process of enterprise operation. Besides, it describes the source of data generation, the way of data collection and storage, the specific meaning of data, and the way of data use etc. The product/service structure describes representative products, services and relative configurations. The functional structure describes the functional components provided by the enterprise's information system, production system and personnel organization. Various static structures have mutual correlation. For instance, functional units can be associated with relative organizational units, resource units, information units and product units, reflecting the necessary conditions for this function. Organizational units can also be associated with resource, information, function and product units, reflecting the basic conditions for operating organizational units. In fact, structured units at every aspect of architecture can all be used as the focus to associate with other units which reflects that views are the embodiment of a certain aspect of the enterprise system.

System behavioral/dynamic structure layer: models at which describe the logic, sequence and relevant characteristics of the whole system, combine the elements defined by the static structure layer to define the model of enterprise operation mechanism. System logical relations describe the input and output of system activities and the flow relationship of data, information, personnel, materials, etc. between various activities. System sequence relationship describes the sequence and trigger conditions of system activities.

System performance structure layer: models at which define the target of the system, the related performance indicators and measurement methods. System evaluating structure describes the decomposition relationship and calculation method of performance indicators at different levels of the system. The evaluating structure defines four levels of performance: goal, indicators, factors and elements. The goal reflects the success of the enterprise and is the symbol of measuring the competitiveness of the enterprise. Indicators are the specific embodiment of the strategic objectives and competitiveness of enterprises, including time, cost, quality, service, environment and feasibility. The weight proportion of these indicators is determined by AHP, ANP, decision supporting methods and other evaluation methods. Factors are the embodiment of indicators in different fields. For example, cost indicators can be broken down into software development cost, hardware development cost, design cost, deployment cost, and so on. The weight proportion of these factors is determined by weighted sum, geometrical methods, vector space and other integrating methods. Elements are the basic units used to calculate factors. Factors can be calculated by mathematical or physical formulas according to the internal relationship with elements. In the process of target decomposition and system implementation, the evaluating structure is used from top to bottom to provide guidance and standards for system design, implementation and operation. In the process of system analysis and system monitoring and control, the evaluating structure is used from bottom to top to verify whether the system operation meets the requirements.

In fact, various structures are interrelated. Therefore, the structured units in all aspects of the architecture can be used as the focus associated with other units, reflecting that the view is the embodiment of a certain aspect of the enterprise system. For example, if there is no description of the production process, the product structure cannot reflect the panorama of the product; without the constraints of the internal operation mechanism of the organization, the organizational structure cannot well reflect the operation of the enterprise; the resource structure only reflects the existence and quantity, and what really affects the operation of SSE is the dynamic resource allocation and utilization.

The models of system static and behavioral layer describe the system structure and operation mechanism constrained by system objectives, which constitute the basis of performance analysis. The system performance structure layer is based on the system structure and behavioral layer to provide modelling form for the performance aspect of SSE, learns from the existing model content and establishes analysis methods to inform decision makers. Under the guidance of SSE strategy and performance evaluation mechanism, a network description with structural components is formed according to the interrelated (input, output, control, mechanism) or sequential logical relationship. Because performance evaluation is very important for decision-makers and stakeholders in the early stage of SSE project, performance-related modelling has become one of the key parts in the field of enterprise modelling. For example, ISO 22400 was developed for automation systems and integration - key performance indicators (KPIs) for manufacturing operations management (ISO, 2014); ISO/IEC 42030 was developed for Systems and Software Engineering – Architecture Evaluation. Evaluation modelling and analysis can point out the optimization direction of enterprise development (ISO, 2005). In ISO 15704 - 2005, AHP/ANP (Analytical Hierarchy/Network Process) method and Activity Based Costing (ABC) are proposed to facilitate the decision-making process on the multiple criteria's aspect of system integration justification.

2.3 GAF Implementation

The right bottom part of Fig. 1 is GAF analysis, design and implementation framework based on Federal Enterprise Architecture Framework (FEAF) 2.0, which has an integrated mapping relationship with GAF and GMF.

Performance reference model, business reference model and data reference model are the analysis and design framework. The performance reference model corresponds to the system evaluating and economic analyzing structure in GMF. This provides an evaluation system for the performance analysis of the system, including the evaluation indicators from top to bottom, the weight proportion of each evaluation factor at the same level and the calculation method of evaluation factors at different levels. In addition, business is the object of performance analysis, and data is the basis of performance analysis. Different levels of evaluation indicators correspond to different levels of business processes. In addition to analysis, the performance reference model also provides performance requirements for system design. These performance requirements penetrate into business activities at all levels from top to bottom. The data required by performance analysis and business activities constitute the data reference model as the basis of data design.

Application reference model, infrastructure reference model and security reference model are the implementation framework. According to the business design, data design and corresponding performance requirements, the implementation or transformation of the system is mainly carried out from the two aspects of application and infrastructure. Application is the integration and implementation of system business, including workflow system, software system and production process system. And infrastructure provides public service support for the system, including energy supply, transportation, security, data management and human resources. However, when the system changes, it often brings new risks. The security reference model needs to describe the risk factors existing in the new system, including the evaluation and analysis results, control measures and technical solutions, as well as the emergency plan when the accident occurs, and the accident accountability system matching the management system.

When we start a project, the first thing we should do is to analyze the performance of the system. Based on the performance analysis of existing system and required system, we can design a business model that meets the requirements by transforming, deleting and innovating the existing business processes. And then we should describe various business processes' functional and logical relationship. In order to support the proper operation of the business, we need to another model to explain what kinds of functional components are needed, what kinds of team, organization and people will participate in, what resources and information will be used and what products or services are produced in various business processes. After analysis and design, it's time to implement the design scheme. During in the process of implementation, we need construction tools like CAD/CAE to transfer designed system to physical system.

This part points out SSE modelling can be combined with its technical architecture.

3 Interoperability of Enterprise Architecture Frameworks Through GAF

Computer Integrated Manufacturing Open System Architecture (CIM-OSA), FEAF, and Generalized Enterprise Reference Architecture and Methodology (GERAM), and Zachman Framework are four mainstream Architecture Frameworks. They or some of their contents can be mapped to GAF, and there is also a mapping relationship in these mainstream Architecture Frameworks.

3.1 Relationships Between Mainstream Architecture Frameworks

Although different architecture framework has its own concepts, principles and features, architecture frameworks share some common ideas with each other, as shown in Fig. 2.

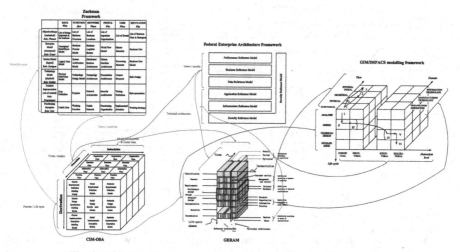

Fig. 2. Relationships between mainstream architecture frameworks.

The instantiation, generation and derivation dimensions in CIM-OSA can be mapped to the instantiation, views and life-cycle phases dimensions in GERAM. The top three layers and the bottom three layers of FEAF 2.0 are mapped to views in the first six phases of the life-cycle dimension and machine & human views in GERAM respectively. And the top three layers of FEAF 2.0 can be mapped to the generation dimension of CIM-OSA. The horizontal and vertical dimensions of Zachman architecture can be mapped to the generation and derivation dimensions of CIM-OSA. The Life-cycle phases dimension and the Instantiation dimension of GERAM can be mapped to the Life cycle dimension and the Abstraction level dimension of GIM/IMPACS respectively. The customer service, management and control, software and hardware views in the requirement and design phase of GERAM can be mapped to the functional, decisional, informational and physical views of GIM/IMPACS. And the organization, human, resource, machine and information views in the implementation and decommission phase of GERAM can be mapped to the organization description, manufacturing technology and information technology domains of GIM/IMPACS.

Through GAF, the relationships among different architecture frameworks will be clearer.

3.2 GAF and Zachman Framework

The Zachman Framework was proposed by John Zachman (1987) for the first time and has been expanded for many times. One (John F. Sowa and John Zachman, 1992) of those expanded frameworks is shown in the right of Fig. 3. It has only two dimensions, but may be the first popular framework and is the basis of many other popular enterprise architecture frameworks.

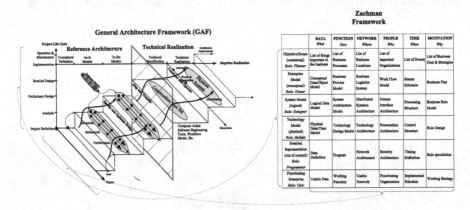

Fig. 3. Relationship between GAF and Zachman Framework.

The horizontal dimension of Zachman architecture puts forward six problems about business operation to enterprises. What are the business objects, data and information? How does the business work? Where does the business operate? Who are running the business? When is the business process executed? Why chooses this solution? These six questions provide six views of enterprise modeling and analysis, including data, function, network, people, time and motivation.

The vertical dimension of Zachman framework refers to six system stakeholders in different stages of business life cycle, and they view the system from different perspectives. The planner focuses on the overall objectives of the system, including external requirements and driving factors. At this stage, the business plan and key problems to be solved should be determined. The owner focuses on business concepts and models. At this stage, business requirements and resources required for business plan execution should be determined. The designer focuses on system logic. At this stage, models of six views are developed to determine how to meet business requirements. The builder focuses on technical realization. At this stage, information about how to implement business plan what tools, technologies, materials and constraints will be used should be determined. The programmer focuses on the implementation of s single module. At this stage, detailed representation of products, services or hardware should be determined. The user focuses on the functioning enterprise and evaluation. At this stage, information guidance on functional systems and how they work in an it or business environment should be determined to help users.

The horizontal and vertical dimensions of Zachman Framework can be mapped to GAF's View axis and Life Cycle axis.

Data, network and people view of Zachman Framework are parts of GAF's structural views. They both describe the static structure configuration of the system or enterprise, including personnel organization, environment, data and information, and the structural relationship between them. Function and time views correspond to behavioral views of GAF. They describe the functional hierarchy of the system business activity process, the input and output and logical relationship between functional modules, and the time sequence of activity execution. Motivation view corresponds to performance view. They describe the goals and strategies of the system business, how to achieve them through planning, and how to evaluate and verify the achievement of goals and plans.

Planner, owner, designer, builder, programmer, and user are different system stakeholders in the life cycle. At the project definition stage, the planner is the main stakeholder of the project. The planner is responsible for defining system objectives and major issues. And the owner needs to analyze the deficiencies and problems of the system according to the planning needs, describe the conceptual model of the system, and clarify what products or services the system will provide in what form. Then the designer and builder are responsible for the preliminary and specific design of the system, including the business architecture and technical architecture of the system, and the business logic and physical logic of the system. At the implementation stage, the programmer is responsible for the specific development of the project, transforming the design scheme into operable and usable system objects. At the operation & maintenance stage, the user operates and uses the system according to rules and strategies designed by previous stakeholders.

3.3 GAF and CIM-OSA

CIM-OSA is developed by the consortium AMICE (1993) from ESPRIT supported by several European countries. The target of this project was to elaborate the open system architecture for CIM (Computer Integration Manufacturing) and to define a set of concepts and rules to facilitate the building of future CIM systems. The two main results of the project were the Modeling Framework, and the Integrating Infrastructure.

As shown in the right of Fig. 4, CIM-OSA is represented as a cube with three axes:

The first axis is called instantiation. This axis describes the process of enterprise modeling from general to specific. It includes three levels of models: generic building blocks, partial models and particular models. These three levels of models correspond to different ranges and numbers of enterprise objects. For example, generic building blocks may be used for every enterprise, partial models may be used for enterprises in specific domain and particular model may be customized for a specific enterprise.

The second axis is called derivation, providing the modeling description in different phases of the development lifecycle. It includes three steps: requirements definition, design specification and implementation description. The requirement definition model is established in the early stage of the project life cycle, which describes the requirements of the system through models such as use case diagrams and requirements diagrams. The design specification describes the functional structure and activity sequence of the system through the models. The implementation instructions describe the specifications followed to convert the design prototype into a physical prototype, such as the process sequence when manufacturing products.

The third one is called generation. It provides four views to model different aspects of the global system, including function, information, resource and organization. Function view is a hierarchical and structured description of enterprise functions and their behaviors and structures. It is based on the goal of the enterprise and reflects the external constraints and input-output relationship. The information view describes the information used or produced by the enterprise in the operation process and its associated enterprise objects, which are identified in the function view. Resource view is a description of the organizational form of resources required for enterprise operation, including energy, human resources, materials and assets. The organizational view describes the organizational structure of the enterprise and the responsibilities of individuals and groups. The four views have some overlapping.

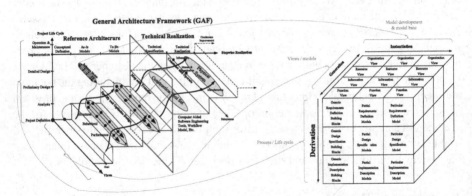

Fig. 4. Relationship between GAF and CIM-OSA.

The instantiation dimension in CIM-OSA corresponds to the reference model in GAF. They reflect the gradual development process of model construction and the process of transforming general model into professional domain knowledge model.

The derivation dimension of CIM-OSA corresponds to the project life cycle dimension of GAF. The requirements definition models are established in the project definition and analysis stages. The design specification models are established in the preliminary design and detailed design stages. The implementation description models play a role in the implementation phase of the project. However, the derivation dimension does not take into account the long-term maintenance after the system is running.

The generation dimension of CIM-OSA corresponds to the views dimension of GAF. They all provide the perspective of system decomposition and analysis. The function view describes part of the dynamic and static structure of the system at the same time. It is both a structural view and a behavioral view in GAF. Information, resource and organization views are the system structure views. The generation dimension lacks a performance view, so CIM-OSA lacks a quantitative analysis method for the system.

CIM-OSA and GAF show the same idea that the integrated enterprise should be modelling in different views and the process of system definition and construction is gradual and evolutionary.

3.4   GAF and FEAF 2.0

FEAF is an enterprise architecture proposed by the U.S. Office of Management and Budget. The first version was published in 1999 and it (CIOC, 2001) believes that the business drivers and design drivers will promote the transformation of the enterprise from the existing architecture to the target architecture. In such circumstance, we should carry out transformation of business architecture, data architecture, application architecture and technology architecture under the guidance of the enterprise strategic directions, vision and principles.

FEAF 2.0 was released in 2013 and is very different from the first version. It is used to reduce differences in cooperation and communication between enterprises, governments and other institutions. FEAF 2.0 (OMB, 2013) provides six general reference models as shown in Fig. 5. Through the unified definition and classification of the contents involved in these six models, it provides the basis for the reuse of models and the exchange of information between enterprises. There is a progressive relationship between these reference models.

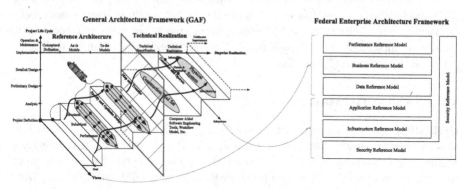

Fig. 5. Relationship between GAF and FEAF 2.0.

The performance reference model focuses on cross agency and intra agency goals and sets performance indicators for them. The performance reference model links strategic investment plans with performance indicators. This helps show the effect of investment and provides direction for enterprise performance improvement. The business reference model provides a classification method based on business functions rather than an organizational structure view to describe the structure of the enterprise. The data reference model defines the standard for describing, classifying, and sharing data. It helps enterprises find data, understand the meaning of data, access data and conduct performance analysis through data. Data analysis can be used as the basis for performance improvement, business improvement and safety evaluation. The data reference model also puts forward technical requirements for the development of applications and the establishment of infrastructure. The application reference model describes software components that do not aim at specific businesses but provide basic management functions such as the creation, use, storage and sharing of data and information. It provides a standard for the sharing and reuse of applications between different institutions and reduces the development cost. The infrastructure reference model classifies the IT infrastructure of application component deployment, including deployment platform, network communication and physical entities. Unified infrastructure standards provide the basis for the transfer and redeployment of applications. The security reference model considers security factors in other five reference models.

Performance reference model, business reference model and data reference model are views and models used for system analysis and design. They correspond to the performance, behavioral and structural views of GAF. The performance reference model and the performance & evaluating structure are similar and they both establish a standard performance metrics framework and give calculation and evaluating methods. However, the content of the performance reference model is more specific. Both the business reference model and the behavior view describe the logic and timing relationship of the activity process of the system and the enterprise, as well as the close relationship between the activity and the goal. The data reference model is similar to the information view in the structural model. However, the data reference model emphasizes the connection between data and business and application, while information view pays more attention to the connection between information and entity objects. Application reference model, infrastructure reference model and security reference model are views and models used for system implementation and operation. They correspond to the technical realization part of the stepwise realization dimension of GAF.

3.5 GAF and GIM/IMPACS

GIM/IMPACS is a combination of two studies. The GRAI method was proposed by Guy Doumeingts in the 1980s. And it has then been extended into GRAI Integrated Methodology (GIM) by GRAI Laboratory (1992) and was combined with the research results from another ESPRIT project called IMPACS to form GIM/IMPACS. The GRAI method is a tool used to help system decision-making in manufacturing system. Then, the system structure analysis tool IDEF0 is selected for functional and physical modeling. Merise was chosen for the information model. GIM has established a good and clear structured method for implementing CIM modeling analysis and development program.

The initial idea was to consider that the enterprise could be modeled using a global functional view and three subsystems: the physical, information, and decision subsystems. Later, as shown in Fig. 6, a cubic structure was proposed to show this architecture.

There are four views on the left side of the architecture: functional, physical, decisional and informational views. The four views show a user-oriented approach for business analysis and design. There are three domains on the right side: manufacturing, organization and information domains. The three domains show a technology-oriented approach for technical design and implementation.

The life cycle and abstraction level are applied to the vertical and horizontal axes of the architecture to describe the different stages and progressive relationships of the system development process. The life cycle dimension has four phases: analysis, design, technical design and development. The abstraction level dimension has three levels: conceptual level, structural level and realizational level.

It is easy to find that the life cycle and the abstraction layer correspond to each other, which is the same as GAF. In the system analysis stage, the conceptual model of the system is built to show the whole system. At the same time, the design requirements are determined through the analysis of the relationship between the input and output of the conceptual model. In the system design stage, it is necessary to build a structural model to represent the internal structure of the system. So far, we have been using models to represent the functional, physical, decisional and informational views of the system, which describes to the user how his requirements are translated into the system structure. Then came the technology-oriented approach. In the technical design stage, it is necessary to consider the existing technical capacity constraints and carry out the system structure design based on the technical scheme which can meet the design requirements.

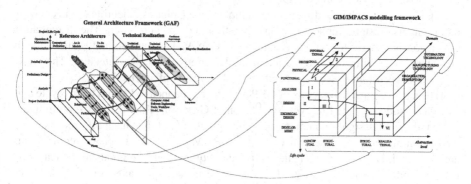

Fig. 6. Relationship between GAF and GIM/IMPACS.

As shown in Fig. 6, the View dimension and the Life cycle dimension can be mapped to the Views axis and the Project Life Cycle axis of GAF. The Abstraction level dimension and the Domain dimension can be mapped to Reference Models and Subsystems, which are parts of the Stepwise Realization axis of GAF.

The functional view describes the services provided by the system behavior and the levels and dependencies between these activities. The physical, decisional and informational views describe the static structure of the system. The decisional view. The decisional view is also related to the performance structure, because the performance indicators are the data basis to support the decision making. The Life cycle dimension of GIM/IMPACS lacks the operation and maintenance phase after system development.

The three steps of the Abstraction level dimension show the process of reference model from whole to detail, from concept to implementation. The organization description, manufacturing technology and information technology correspond to the three subsystems (information, human & organization, and manufacturing subsystems), which are the technical realization of the physical system.

3.6 GAF and GERAM

GERAM was published by IFAC and IFIP in the 1990s (P. Bernus, and L. Nemes, 1994). It is included in the ISO 15704 that try to form a generalized enterprise reference architecture and methodology to realize interoperate between different architecture. GERAM is not a completely innovative reference architecture, but a summary of existing enterprise engineering knowledge, which can be applied to all types of enterprises. GERAM was developed on the basis of enterprise architecture frameworks such as CIM-OSA, PERA (Purdue Enterprise Reference Framework) and GIM (GRAI Integrated Methodology). GERAM defines relevant concepts, models, methods and tools for integrated enterprise, which may be part of an enterprise or a single enterprise or a group of enterprises.

As shown in the Fig. 7, this reference architecture also includes three dimensions: life-cycle phases, views and instantiation.

The life-cycle phases dimension includes seven phases: identification, concept, requirements, design, implementation, operation and decommission. The instantiation dimension is exactly the same as that in CIM-OSA. The generic and partial models are reference architecture and particular models are particular architecture. The views dimension has different views depending on the present lifecycle phase.

The key concepts and factors of GERAM can be mapped to GAF. The lifecycle axis of GAF is similar to the life-cycle dimension of GERAM. They both have preliminary design, detailed design, implementation and operation, but they have different views at the beginning and end of the project cycle. GERAM believes concept and requirements are identified. However, GAF believes that the requirements are obtained by analyzing the conceptual model and the As-Is model. The instantiation axis corresponds to the reference models in GAF. The views axis corresponds to the one in GAF. They all believe that different views should be used at different stages, but they don't have the same views. In the requirements analysis and preliminary design phase, GAF establishes models for performance, behavior and structure views but GERAM establishes customer service, management and control views. In the detailed design and technical specification phase, GAF focuses on project implementation management tools, such as software engineering tools and workflow models, but GERAM focuses on the specific physical manifestation after the system is implemented, software or hardware. In the implementation phase, GAF focuses on the structure of physical system, including information subsystem, human & organization subsystem, and manufacturing subsystem. But GERAM focuses on how to implement the designed system, including resource, organization, information and function views.

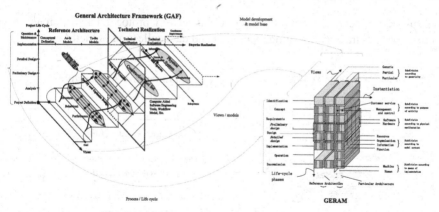

Fig. 7. Relationship between GAF and GERAM.

4 Interoperability of Modelling Frameworks Through GMF

There are plenty of SSE modelling languages and methods. In any SSE projects, multiple modelling methods will be included in. GMF can be used to organize related modelling methods sets and relative models.

4.1 GMF and FEAF 2.0

FEAF 2.0 is widely used in the field of government administration and enterprise informatization. This reference architecture has been described previously. In fact, FEAF 2.0 is not a modeling language. It does not provide unified graphical symbols and semantics, which is different from UML, SysML, and ArchiMate. FEAF 2.0 is similar to GMF in conceptual abstraction level. They only provide views and classification methods, without defining how these views should be modeled. Therefore, when FEAF 2.0 and GMF are used, the appropriate modeling language should be selected according to the view to describe the model.

As shown in Fig. 8 (Li, 2021), the bottom three layers of FEAF 2.0 are related to technical realization, they are mapped to SSE realization of GAF.

The application reference model includes three areas: systems, application components and interfaces. It identifies and classifies twelve types of systems, thirteen types of software components and five types of interfaces. These systems and software components can be further refined according to the functions provided. These systems cover the security, human, legal, economic and customer aspects of enterprises or institutions. These application components include data analysis, visualization, security control and knowledge mining. These interfaces include information exchange, application call and file transfer.

The infrastructure reference model includes three domains: platform, network and facility. Platform refers to hardware, operating system, communication hardware, peripherals and virtualization, where servers and applications are deployed and information is transmitted. Network area focuses on the classification of network space scope, network transmission content, network infrastructure and network protocol. Facility area focuses on the type, geographical location, operation and data collection of facilities.

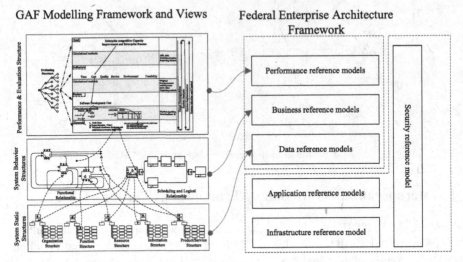

Fig. 8. Relationship between GMF and FEAF 2.0 (Li, 2021).

The security reference model includes three areas: purpose, risk and control. Purpose area focuses security related laws and standards, as well as the risk situation and external threats faced by the institution. Risk area focuses on risk assessment and corresponding measures. Control area focuses on the specific implementation of risk control measures and the evaluation of the implementation effect.

The other three layers: Performance reference models, Business reference models, Data reference models, are related to business.

The initial FEAF just had four layers. In order to describe strategic goals of business and evaluate its performance, it added Performance reference models. Performance reference models are the external manifestation of the enterprise. The performance reference model is divided into three areas: goals, measurement area and measurement category. They have hierarchical relationships. The measurement category is the refinement of the measurement area, and they are all used to calculate and evaluate goals. The business reference model is divided into three areas: mission sectors, business functions and service. Mission sectors includes ten business areas of enterprise architecture. The ten business areas provide 40 business functions and 228 business services. The data reference model includes 4 domains, 22 subjects and 144 topics.

The performance reference model, business reference model and data reference model are related to enterprise performance, behavior and structure, which is mapped with Performance & Evaluation Structure, System Behavior Structure and System Static Structure of GMF.

Thus, models in the analysis and design stage of FEAF 2.0 can be mapped to GMF directly. They have the same hierarchical structure.

4.2 GMF and UML

UML has a wide range of influence in the field of system development and software engineering. It is a general visual modelling language for intuitive, clarified, componentized and documented software system products. This is benefited from its various diagrams which help to describe system excessively. UML was developed by Rational Software, then adopted as a standard by OMG, and then became an ISO standard.

UML provides a unified, standard and visual modeling language for object-oriented software design, which consists of two parts: UML semantics and UML representation. UML models are composed of things, relationships and diagrams. Things are the most basic elements in UML and the abstract representation of system components. Relationships tie things together. Diagrams are visual representations of things and relationships.

The diagrams describe the system from different perspectives, and there are correlations between these diagrams. UML has evolved and has many versions. The types of diagrams in different versions are also different. The latest version is version 2.5 but the version 2.4 is showed here. As shown in Fig. 9 (Li, 2021), UML model framework contains many diagrams. UML divided them into two parts: Structure Diagram and Behavior Diagram. The structure diagram provides the basis for the behavior diagram.

Structure Diagram includes Class Diagram, Object Diagram, Package Diagram, Composite Structure Diagram, Component Diagram, Deployment Diagram and Profile Diagram.

The Behavior Diagram includes UseCase Diagram, Activity Diagram, State Machine Diagram and Interaction Diagram.

The structure diagram and behavior diagram of UML can be mapped to system static structure and system behavior structure of GMF. However, they have different concerns because they are at different levels of abstraction. Diagrams can be used to construct views in GMF. For example, the Class Diagram can be used to describe the organizational structure of the enterprise. The Object Diagram can be used to describe the relationship between specific departments, offices or employees at a certain time in the enterprise. They are about organization structure of the system static structure. The Deployment Diagram can be used to describe the hardware used by the enterprise. It is about the function and resource structure. The Activity Diagram and the Sequence Diagram can be used to describe the workflow of the enterprise. The Timing Diagram is used to describe the project schedule. They are about functional relationship scheduling and logical relationship of the system dynamic structure.

Another difference between GMF and UML is that UML only describes user requirements and system functions through the UseCase Diagram, but it lacks the mathematical relationship description of system performance. However, GMF provides such an evaluating structure of system, and it is linked to system behavior.

GAF Modelling Framework and Views   UML2.4 Framework

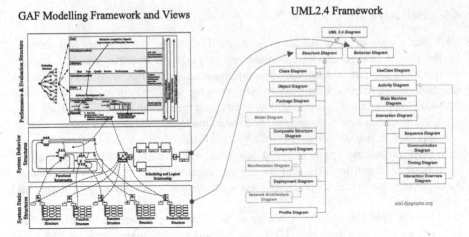

Fig. 9. Relationship between GMF and UML (Li, 2021).

4.3 GMF and SysML

UML is mainly used for software system engineering, and SysML is used for system engineering. SysML is developed by INCOSE and OMG on the basis of UML (L. Delligatti, 2013).

SysML is a general graphical modeling language that supports the analysis, specification, design, verification and validation of complex systems. These systems may include hardware, software, personnel, procedures, facilities, and other artificial and natural system elements. SysML can help to realize the specification definition and architecture design of the system, and define the specifications of components. These components can be designed using other domain languages, such as UML for software design, VHDL for electrical design, and 3D geometric modeling for mechanical design. SysML contributes to the application of MBSE methodology and creates a cohesive and consistent system model.

SysML reuses part of the UML meta model to a certain extent. At the same time, it extends UML for system engineering, adds elements describing the system such as requirements, blocks and constraints, and related graphics support, and finally ensures that it supports the architectural framework standards such as DoDAF/C4ISR.

As shown in Fig. 10 (Li, 2021), the diagrams of SysML can be divided into three parts: Behavior Diagram, Requirement Diagram and Structure Diagram. It is clear that the State Machine Diagram, the Sequence Diagram, the Use Case Diagram and the Package Diagram are the same as UML.

The Activity Diagram, the Block Definition Diagram and Internal Block Diagram are modified from ones of UML. They abandon the terms with software characteristics such as class and object, and instead use blocks to represent things.

There are two new diagrams: Requirement Diagram and Parametric Diagram. The addition of them is an important development from UML to SysML.

Requirement refers to the capability or condition that the system must meet. The Parametric Diagram defines a set of system attributes and the parameter relationships among them. The parameter relationship is used to represent the dependency relationship between the attributes in the structural model of the system. Parametric model is an analysis model, which combines behavior model and structure model with engineering analysis model, such as performance model and reliability model, and can be used to support trade-off analysis and evaluate various alternative solutions.

GAF Modelling Framework and Views

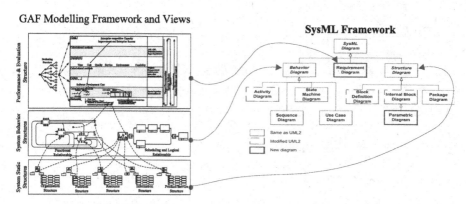

Fig. 10. Relationship between GMF and SysML (Li, 2021).

The Behavior Diagram, the Requirement Diagram and the Structure Diagram can be mapped to the system static structure, system behavior structure and performance & evaluation structure. The Package Diagram, the Block Definition Diagram and the Internal Block Diagram can be used to describe the organization, function, resource, information and product views of systems. The Parametric Diagram can help describe the quantitative relationships in these views. The Use Case Diagram can be used to describe functional relationship between activities. And the Activity Diagram, the State Machine Diagram and the Sequence Diagram can be used to describe the scheduling and logical relationship between activities. The Requirement Diagram can be used to describe system goals and strategies. The Parametric Diagram can help refine requirements during the development process and then be used for function analysis and design synthesis.

4.4 GMF and ArchiMate

ArchiMate is also consistent with GMF. ArchiMate is an enterprise architecture modelling specification supporting TOGAF. It is an enterprise architecture description language and a visual business analysis model language. In February 2009, the Open Group published the ArchiMate v1.0 standard as an official technical standard (The Open Group, 2009).

As shown in Fig. 11 (Li, 2021), the core of ArchiMate 1.0 has only three layers: Technology layer, Application layer and Business layer. Because it was originally developed as a more general alternative to BPMN. However, such a rough modeling language framework was enough to meet the needs of most organizations at that time. The Technology layer provides the hardware and infrastructure services to support the Application layer. The Application layer provides the software and information services to support the Business layer. The Business layer describes the business process and logic of the organization. These three layers can be related to FEAF 2.0 business layer, application layer and infrastructure layer, which can be mapped to GAF and GMF.

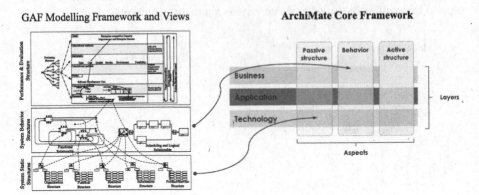

Fig. 11. Relationship between GMF and ArchiMate (Li, 2021).

ArchiMate 1.0 includes three aspects: Passive structure, Behavior and Active structure. They describe structure elements and behavior elements of ArchiMate modeling conceptual elements. The former represents various structured entities such as participants, application components and data. The latter is used to describe various behaviors that can be performed by structured elements, such as business activities, application functions, services, etc. In addition, according to the relationship with the behavior elements, the structure elements can be further divided into active structure elements and passive structure elements. The former represents the structure elements that initiate actions (such as participants, application components, etc.), while the latter is used to describe the various objectives of the behavior elements (such as business data, information data, etc.).

Archimate 2.0 extends motivation aspect (which is the part of why in Zachman), implementation & migration layer, and closely connects the architecture with the macro planning process and implementation process of the organization.

In June 2020, the Open Group released version 3.1 of ArchiMate (The Open Group, 2020). In addition to core layers, the newest ArchiMate added Strategy layer and Physical layer.

The Passive structure and the Active structure can be mapped to the System Static Structure, and the Behavior structure can be mapped to the System Behavior Structure. The Strategy layer and Motivation aspect realize the modelling of stakeholders and analyze the driving factors of innovation. They are mapped to the Performance & Evaluation Structure of GMF. The Physical Layer can be mapped to the System Static Structure of GMF.

4.5 GMF and Other Modelling Frameworks

There are many other modeling languages that can be organized by GMF.

IDEF0 describes system functions by decomposing functions and classifying the relationships between functions (e.g. by input, output, control and mechanism). DFD shows how information enters and leaves the system, what changes the information, and where it is stored. They can be used to describe the Functional Relationship of system activities.

IDEF1 is used to describe important information in the process of enterprise operation. IDEF1X is an extended version of IDEF1 in the IDEF series of methods. It is a method that adds some rules on the basis of the principle of E-R (entity relation) method to enrich the semantics. ERD is the visual representation of different entities in the system and how they are related to each other. ERD are widely used in designing relational databases. ERD, IDEF1 and IDEF1X can be used to describe the Information View in The System Static Structure of GMF.

IDEF3 supports structured description of system user views. BPMN is a common and standard language for process modeling, which is used to draw business process diagrams so as to better understand business processes and relationships among departments. BPMN and IDEF3 can be used to describe the Time Sequence and Logical Relationship in the System Behavior Structure of GMF.

These modeling languages provide tools for describing system structure of GMF. It is necessary to use the best and appropriate modeling language for specific business scenarios and enterprise objects.

5 Conclusions

This paper presents the general architecture framework (GAF) and relative general modelling framework (GMF). GAF includes following features:

GAF includes three dimensions: Views, Project Life Cycle, and Stepwise Realization. The Project Life Cycle dimension and the Stepwise Realization dimension show how to design, develop and realize reference architecture and models at different stages of the project. The Views dimension has three layers and seven views. They are shown in GMF in detail, which presents a new consideration to the organization of enterprise model views.

And the paper also introduces five mainstream architecture, which are Zachman Framework, CIM-OSA, FEAF 2.0, GIM/IMPACS, and GERAM. Relationships between GAF and them are shown, and relationships between GMF and SSE modelling methods sets are also demonstrated. Therefore, GAF can be used to organize model-based SSE engineering projects and GMF can be used to manage modelling tasks and relative models.

Acknowledgements. This research is supported by the science and technology innovation 2030 - "new generation artificial intelligence" major project (2018AAA0101605), the National Natural Science Foundation of China (No.61771281, No.61174168), the special project for industrial transformation and upgrading of MIIT 2018 (ZB182505), and independent research program of Tsinghua University (2018Z05JZY015).

References

AMICE. CIMOSA: Open System Architecture for CIM version 2 (1993)

CCSDS/ASRC. Consultative committee for space data systems (2016)

CIOC. Chief Information Officer Council. A Practical Guide to Federal Enterprise Architecture (2001)

Friedenthal, S., Griego, R., Sampson, M.: INCOSE model based systems engineering (MBSE) initiative. In: INCOSE 2007 Symposium (2007)

Haskins, C.: 4.6. 1 a historical perspective of MBSE with a view to the future. In: INCOSE International Symposium (2011)

INCOSE. INCOSE systems engineering vision 2020 (2007)

INCOSE. INCOSE systems engineering vision 2025 (2014)

ISO JTC1. Information technology: object management group systems modeling language (OMG SysML) (2017)

ISO JTC1 SC7. ISO 42010:2011 Systems and software engineering: architecture description (2011)

ISO TC 184 SC5. ISO 15704:2000/Amd 1:2005. Industrial automation systems - requirements for enterprise-reference architectures and methodologies (2005)

ISO TC 184 SC5. ISO 19439:2006. Enterprise integration - framework for enterprise modelling (2006)

ISO TC 184 SC5. ISO 19440:2007. Enterprise integration - constructs for enterprise modelling (2007)

ISO TC184 SC5. ISO 22400-2:2014. Automation systems and integration - Key performance indicators (KPIs) for manufacturing operations management - Part 2: Definitions and descriptions (2014)

Delligatti, L.: SysML Distilled: A Brief Guide to the Systems Modeling Language. Addison-Wesley Professional, Illustrated Edition (2013)

Li, Q., Liang, B., Fang, Z.: Mapping and integration of architecture and modelling frameworks. In: Proceedings of the 2nd International Conference on Innovative Intelligent Industrial Production and Logistics (IN4PL 2021), pp. 216–226 (2021)

OMB. The U.S. Office of Management and Budget. Federal Enterprise Architecture Framework version 2 (2013)

GRAI Laboratory: GIM Method, (Lecture Notes) (1992)

Li, Q., Chen, Y.: Modelling and Analysis of Enterprise and Information Systems - From Requirements to Realization. Springer and High Education Press (2007)

Bernus, P., Nemes, L.: A framework to define a generic enterprise reference architecture and methodology. In: Proceedings of the International Conference on Automation, Robotics and Computer Vision (ICARCV 1994), Singapore, 10–12 November 1994 (1994)

The Open Group. ArchiMate 1.0 Specification (2009)

The Open Group. ArchiMate 3.1 Specification (2020)

Sowa, J.F., Zachman, J.: Extending and formalizing the framework for information systems architecture. IBM Syst. J. **31**(3), 590–616 (1992)

Author Index

A. Smirnov et al. (Eds.): IN4PL 2020/IN4PL 2021, CCIS 1855, p. 159, 2023.
https://doi.org/10.1007/978-3-031-37228-5

Printed in the United States
by Baker & Taylor Publisher Services